From New Jerusalem to New Labour

From New Jerusalem to New Labour

British Prime Ministers from Attlee to Blair

Edited By

Vernon Bogdanor
Professor of Government, University of Oxford, UK

palgrave
macmillan

First published 2010 by
PALGRAVE MACMILLAN

Palgrave Macmillan in the UK is an imprint of Macmillan Publishers Limited,
registered in England, company number 785998, of Houndmills, Basingstoke,
Hampshire RG21 6XS.

Palgrave Macmillan in the US is a division of St Martin's Press LLC,
175 Fifth Avenue, New York, NY 10010.

Palgrave Macmillan is the global academic imprint of the above companies
and has companies and representatives throughout the world.

Palgrave® and Macmillan® are registered trademarks in the United States,
the United Kingdom, Europe and other countries.

ISBN 978–0–230–57455–7 hardback

This book is printed on paper suitable for recycling and made from fully
managed and sustained forest sources. Logging, pulping and manufacturing
processes are expected to conform to the environmental regulations of the
country of origin.

A catalogue record for this book is available from the British Library.

A catalog record for this book is available from the Library of Congress.

10 9 8 7 6 5 4 3 2 1
19 18 17 16 15 14 13 12 11 10

Printed and bound in Great Britain by
CPI Antony Rowe Ltd, Chippenham and Eastbourne

For Gresham College

Contents

Preface

These chapters, with the exception of the chapter by Philip Ziegler on Heath, were first delivered as lectures at Gresham College, London, in 2006 and 2007. All the prime ministers, except for Attlee, Churchill and Eden, were known to those who lectured about them. D.R. Thorpe is the biographer of Macmillan, whose biography he is currently completing, and of Sir Alec Douglas-Home. Philip Ziegler is the official biographer of Wilson and of Heath, whose biography he in turn is completing. Kenneth Morgan was the official biographer of Callaghan. Anthony Giddens was an adviser to Tony Blair and remains a close friend. The essays benefit, therefore, from the personal touch – knowledge and reminiscences which only these authors can provide.

Gresham College, where all but one of these essays were first delivered as lectures, is named after Sir Thomas Gresham, Lord Mayor of London in 1537/38. It is one of the best kept secrets in London. For over 400 years, it has appointed professors in various subjects to give free public lectures in the City of London, and to reinterpret the 'new learning' of Sir Thomas Gresham's day in contemporary terms. Details of the College can be found on its website, www.gresham. ac.uk. There is a short history of the College, obtainable from the College, published in 1997 to celebrate its 400th anniversary in 1997, written by the Bishop of London, the Rt Revd and Rt Hon. Richard Chartres, and David Vermont, a past Chairman of Gresham College Council.

The editor and contributors would like to thank Barbara Anderson, the Academic Registrar at Gresham College, for the skill and efficiency with which she arranged these lectures. The editor would like to thank Anthony Teasdale and Geoffrey Warner for their helpful comments on Chapters 2 and 11; but they are not to be implicated in its arguments or conclusions. The editor would also like to thank Pat Spight for skilful secretarial help which went far beyond the call of duty.

Notes on Contributors

Paul Addison taught History at the University of Edinburgh from 1967 until his retirement in 2005. He was Director of the Centre for Second World War Studies (now the Centre for the Study of the Two World Wars) from 1996 to 2005, and is currently an Honorary Fellow of the Centre. He is an Honorary Professor of History at the University of Worcester and a former Visiting Fellow of All Souls. His publications include *The Road to 1945: British Politics and the Second World War* (1975), *Churchill on the Home Front* (1992) and *Churchill: The Unexpected Hero* (2005).

Vernon Bogdanor is Professor of Government at Oxford University and a former Gresham Professor of Law. His books include *The People and the Party System: The Referendum and Electoral Reform in British Politics* (1981), *Multi-Party Politics and the Constitution* (1983), *Power and the People: A Guide to Constitutional Reform* (1997), *Devolution in the United Kingdom* (1999) and *The New British Constitution* (2009). He is editor of, amongst other books, *The British Constitution in the 20th Century* (2003) and *Joined-Up Government* (2005). He is a frequent contributor to TV, radio and the press.

David Carlton is Professorial Research Fellow at the Global Policy Institute of London Metropolitan University, having recently retired from the University of Warwick, where he served in the Department of Politics and International Studies for 17 years. His best-known works are *MacDonald versus Henderson* (1970), *Anthony Eden: A Biography* (1981), *Britain and the Suez Crisis* (1988), *Churchill and the Soviet Union* (2000) and *The West's Road to 9/11* (2005).

Anthony Giddens was Director of the London School of Economics from 1997 to 2003, and is now an emeritus professor there. He was formerly a Fellow of King's College, Cambridge. His many books include *The Constitution of Society* (1984), *Beyond Left and Right* (1994), *The Third Way* (1998) and *Europe in the Global Age* (2006). His most recent major work is *The Politics of Climate Change* (2009). His books have been translated into more than 40 languages. He was the BBC Reith Lecturer in 1999. In 2004 he was made a life peer and sits on the Labour benches in the House of Lords.

Keith Middlemas is emeritus Professor of Contemporary History at Sussex University. Before that he was a clerk in the House of Commons for nine years. His many books include *Politics in Industrial Society* (1979) and a trilogy, *Power, Competition and the State* (1986–91). He has also analysed how the European Union works in his book *Orchestrating Europe* (1995).

Kenneth O. Morgan was Fellow in Modern History and Politics at The Queen's College, Oxford, from 1966 to 1989, and Vice-Chancellor of the University of Wales, Aberystwyth, from 1989 to 1995. His many books include *Wales in British Politics* (1963), *The Age of Lloyd George* (1971), *Consensus and Disunity* (1979), *Rebirth of a Nation, Wales 1880 – 1980* (1981), (ed.) *Oxford Illustrated History of Britain* (new edn, 2009), *Labour in Power 1945 – 1951* (1984), *Labour People* (1987), *The People's Peace: Britain since 1945* (new edn, 2001) and biographies of *Lloyd George* (1974), *Keir Hardie* (1975), *Lord Addison* (with Jane Morgan, 1980), *James Callaghan* (1997) and *Michael Foot* (2007). He is a Druid of the Welsh Gorsedd of Bards, and was created a life peer in 2000. He sits on the Labour benches in the House of Lords.

D.R. Thorpe is a Senior Member of Brasenose College, Oxford, a former Archives Fellow at Churchill College, Cambridge, and an Alistair Horne Fellow at St Antony's College, Oxford. His first book, *The Uncrowned Prime Ministers* (1980), was a study of Sir Austen Chamberlain, Lord Curzon and R.A. Butler, and he has subsequently written biographies of *Selwyn Lloyd* (1989), *Sir Alec Douglas-Home* (1996) and *Anthony Eden* (2003). His biography of *Harold Macmillan* will be published in 2010.

Philip Ziegler was a member of the Foreign Service from 1952 to 1967, and then joined the publishing firm William Collins, where he worked from 1967 to 1980. Since then, he has been a full-time writer. His principal publications are *Duchess of Dino* (1962), *Addington* (1965), *The Black Death* (1968), *William IV* (1971), *Melbourne* (1976), *Diana Cooper* (1981), *Mountbatten* (1985), *The Sixth Great Power: Barings 1762–1929* (1988), *King Edward VIII* (1990), *Harold Wilson* (1993), *Osbert Sitwell* (1998), *Soldiers, Fighting Men's Lives* (2001), *Rupert Hart-Davis:Man of Letters* (2004) and *Legacy: The Rhodes Trusts and the Rhodes Scholarships* (2008).

Introduction

Vernon Bogdanor

'I think it's a damned bore,' Lord Melbourne cried, upon being informed, in 1834, that he was to be called to the Palace to form a government; he was, he said, 'in many minds what to do'. But his secretary, 'a vulgar, familiar, impudent fellow', to quote Greville, from whom the story has come down to us, persuaded him to accept. 'Why damn it, such a position never was occupied by any Greek or Roman, and if it only lasts two months, it is well worth while to have been Prime Minister of England [sic].' 'By God, that's true,' Melbourne replied – 'I'll go!'[1] None of Melbourne's twentieth-century successors, except possibly Sir Alec Douglas-Home, would have shared his doubts. Most of them sought, with greater or less determination, to reach what Disraeli called the top of the greasy pole. Today, every newly elected MP has a prime minister's baton in his knapsack.

Whether they enjoyed the job once they got there is another matter. Lord Rosebery, prime minister from 1894 to 1895, declared that there were 'two supreme pleasures in life. One is ideal, the other is real. The ideal is when a man receives the Seals of Office from his Sovereign. The real is when he hands them back'.[2] Harold Macmillan said that power was like a Dead Sea fruit: 'When you achieve it there's nothing there.'[3] John Major once asked Roy Jenkins whether he ever regretted not having been prime minister. Jenkins is said to have retorted by asking Major whether he regretted having been prime minister. Major's response is not recorded.

The title 'Prime Minister' was for long a mere courtesy title. It seems first to have been used satirically by Jonathan Swift during the reign of Queen

---

[1] David Cecil (1954) *Lord M*, Reprint Society (1955), p. 224; Greville diaries, 4 September 1834.

[2] Robert Rhodes James (1963) *Rosebery*, Weidenfeld and Nicolson, p. 384.

[3] Anthony Sampson (1967) *Macmillan: A Study in Ambiguity*, Allen Lane The Penguin Press, p. 169.

Anne. Walpole, often regarded as the first prime minister, vehemently denied that he held any special role over and above that of the king's other advisers. The term 'prime minister' was not used in an official document until 1878, when the preamble to the Treaty of Berlin stated that the Earl of Beaconsfield, the ennobled Disraeli, had attended as 'First Lord of the Treasury and Prime Minister of her Britannic Majesty'. The title was not used in any other official communication until, in December 1905, it finally received royal recognition when a warrant of Edward VII addressed to the Earl Marshal, declared that the prime minister had precedence after the Archbishop of York. The first man to be officially appointed prime minister was, therefore, the now largely forgotten Liberal, Sir Henry Campbell-Bannerman, in 1905. The office did not achieve statutory recognition until the Ministers of the Crown Act of 1937, and even then it was mentioned only incidentally. The office of prime minister, like the British constitution, evolved through a series of accidents. No one created the prime ministership; and, by contrast with, for example, the presidency in the United States and France, there is no document setting forth the powers and duties of the head of the government.

From New Jerusalem to New Labour considers the 11 post-war prime ministers from Attlee to Blair. The jury is, of course, still out on Gordon Brown. The essays, based on lectures first delivered at Gresham College, seeks to evaluate the aims of the 11, what they sought to achieve. If few prime ministers could match Lord Melbourne for insouciance, the reason is not that they were abnormally self-seeking, but that they had abnormally strong convictions, even if for some, such as, for example, Harold Wilson, it was merely the conviction that the country would be much better governed when their own party was in power. Most prime ministers, however, have sought not merely to be in the driver's seat but to steer the coach in a particular direction. Whereas history in pre-modern times is written largely in terms of kings and queens – the reign of Henry VIII or Charles I – the political history of Britain since 1945 can be written in large part in terms of the ideals held by these 11 prime ministers and by their success or failure in achieving them. The premiership of Margaret Thatcher has the same sort of unity as the reign of Queen Elizabeth I.

But first it is worth asking: what factors brought the 11 to Downing Street? Until Gordon Brown, the only prime minister who seemed a foreordained occupant of No. 10 was Anthony Eden. Perhaps that was the reason why he was unsuccessful. He had been compelled to wait in the wings for far too long. He had been trained, Harold Macmillan unkindly but presciently remarked, to win the Derby in 1938. Unfortunately, he was not let out of the starting stalls until 1955.[4] And, despite his seemingly endless disputes with Churchill on the

---

[4] D.R. Thorpe (2003) *Eden*, Chatto, p. 430.

date of the great man's retirement, he never really had to fight to win the right to the keys of Downing Street. Every other post-war prime minister has had to fight hard and often tenaciously to achieve the office. Some, indeed, got there quite unexpectedly.

Napoleon always used to ask of his generals – has he got luck? Without it, other qualities – ability, integrity, vision – were quite useless. The first four post-war prime ministers – Attlee, Churchill, Eden, and Macmillan – were all products of luck in the sense that, without the Second World War, none of them would have entered Downing Street. Had Neville Chamberlain's policy of appeasement proved successful, a general election would have been held in 1940, an election which the Conservatives would almost certainly have won. Attlee, widely seen as a stopgap leader of the Labour Party, would probably then have been replaced by the more experienced Herbert Morrison. In any case, Attlee would not have been considered for the Labour leadership had he not been one of the few ministers to survive Labour's electoral wipe-out in 1931.

Churchill, Eden, and Macmillan had all been opponents of appeasement, and could not have expected high office in a Conservative government. In any case, Churchill was already 65 in 1940, a figure of the past, not the future. Eden had resigned in 1938 in protest against Chamberlain's attempt to appease Mussolini, and would have found it difficult to work his way back into the upper reaches of the Conservative Party. Macmillan was an eccentric back-bencher with no significant following. It would have been hard to find anyone in the 1930s who would have predicted that he would one day be his party's leader.

The next two prime ministers – Alec Douglas-Home and Harold Wilson – were similarly lucky. Home was the beneficiary of the sudden illness which brought Macmillan down. Amidst the chaos and confusion of the 1963 party conference, he seemed, for the moment at least, the wise statesman who could rescue the party. Wilson, like Blair in 1994, was the beneficiary of the sudden death of his predecessor – Hugh Gaitskell in 1963, John Smith in 1994. Both Gaitskell and Smith would almost certainly have become prime minister had they lived. Under Gaitskell's leadership, Wilson's chances of advancement seemed limited. He was widely distrusted by the Gaitskellites for having stood against the leader in 1960 after Gaitskell had been defeated at the party conference on the issue of unilateral nuclear disarmament. He was also widely distrusted amongst back-benchers. But, faced with a vacancy for the leadership itself, MPs felt unable to entrust its responsibilities to the unstable and alcoholic George Brown. Wilson was chosen faute de mieux. A few years earlier, there would have been other alternatives, such as Alfred Robens, who had left politics in 1960; a few years later, the field would have widened, since younger men such as Crosland, Healey and Jenkins would have had a chance to establish themselves. Margaret

Thatcher and Major were even more products of luck. Six months before they became party leader, hardly anyone could have been found who would have predicted their rise. In 1974, Margaret Thatcher seemed little more than a not particularly successful former Education Secretary. It was the unwillingness of any other front-ranking Conservative to challenge Edward Heath, discredited by two general election defeats, that gave the first female prime minister her chance. Had Heath resigned immediately after losing the October 1974 general election, she would probably not have been in the running. John Major, too, found himself in the right place at the right time when Margaret Thatcher was defenestrated by her party in November 1990. When the game of pass the parcel finally stopped, he it was who found himself in possession.

In the nineteenth century, many prime ministers could have made their mark in fields other than politics. Gladstone could have been a classical or theological scholar, Disraeli a novelist, Rosebery a biographer, while Lord Derby spent his leisure translating the Iliad into blank verse, as well as French and German poetry and other classical works. Their post-war successors have been less remarkable. Of the 11 prime ministers, the only ones who might have had outstanding careers outside politics were Churchill, who could have become a professional writer or perhaps a general, and Macmillan, who was also a highly successful publisher. But all of the 11, including Churchill and Macmillan, and including the one seeming amateur amongst them, Sir Alec Douglas-Home, were highly professional politicians. Some of them had what Denis Healey called hinterlands – areas of interest outside politics – Churchill had his painting, Heath his music, while Attlee relaxed by reading the works of the forgotten Victorian novelist George Meredith – but all of them lived primarily for politics.

When Lloyd George entered No. 10 in 1916, he told his loyal supporter, Christopher Addison, that, with the exception of Disraeli, he was the first prime minister 'who had not passed through the Staff College of the old Universities'.[5] He had forgotten Wellington. Of the 11 post-war prime ministers, all but three had been to Oxford. The other three had not been to university at all. They make an incongruous trio – Churchill, Callaghan, and, finally, John Major, who, as assiduous journalists discovered, left his grammar school at the age of 16 with just three O levels. 'Never,' Major used to say to those who inquired about his education, 'has so much been written about so little.'

The first four Conservative prime ministers after the war – Churchill, Eden, Macmillan, and Home – exemplified the patrician style which seemed between the wars to have been superseded by industrial capitalists – Bonar Law, Baldwin, and Chamberlain. More often, in the post-war period, prime ministers have sought to present themselves to the electorate as ordinary men writ large. The

---

5 David Lloyd George (1933) *War Memoirs*, vol. 1, Nicholson and Watson, p. 621.

first prime ministers to attempt this had been Campbell-Bannerman, Bonar Law, and Stanley Baldwin. 'I am just one of yourselves,' declared Baldwin, in what may have been an accurate estimation of his abilities, 'who has been called to special work for the country at this time. I never sought the office.'[6] Both Attlee and John Major might have said the same. A heroic figure such as Churchill, whom Roy Jenkins believed to be the greatest prime minister ever to have occupied 10 Downing Street, would probably never have achieved supreme power except in wartime. Indeed, after the Munich agreement in 1938, less than two years before becoming prime minister, he was facing deselection by his local constituency party in Epping. Most observers thought that his time had passed. After nearly 40 years as an MP, he had a following of just three – his son-in-law Duncan Sandys; Brendan Bracken, the newspaper proprietor; and an eccentric publisher, Harold Macmillan. Churchill's political fortunes were transformed by the very personal intervention of Adolf Hitler, as Harold Macmillan was to remind him in October 1954. 'It took Hitler,' Macmillan insisted, 'to make him P.M. and me an under-secretary. The Tory Party would do neither – '.[7] Luck, then, is as important as ability.

How powerful is the prime minister? Can the Cabinet control a determined prime minister? Have general elections become plebiscites between competing leaders? There is a large political science literature that seeks to answer these questions. The trouble is, however, that they can be answered, if answered at all, only by adopting a much longer historical perspective than political scientists generally allow themselves. The claim that the prime minister has become over-powerful seems to have originated during the administration of Sir Robert Peel from 1841 to 1846. After Peel's resignation in 1846, Gladstone complained to him: 'Your Government has not been carried on by a Cabinet, but by the heads of departments each in communication with you.'[8] Complaints about bilateral relations in Cabinet or 'sofa government' are nothing new. By 1889, when John Morley wrote, in his biography of Walpole, a chapter on the Cabinet – a chapter that had in fact been written by Gladstone – he could declare: 'The flexibility of the cabinet system allows the Prime Minister to take upon himself a power not inferior to that of a dictator, provided always that the House of Commons will stand by him;'[9] while, in 1963, shortly before the end of Harold Macmillan's premiership, Richard Crossman, writing a new introduction to Bagehot, declared: 'The post war

---

[6] Stanley Baldwin, *On England*, p. 19. Speech at Worcester, 7 November 1923, entitled 'Worcester Memories'.

[7] Peter Catterall, ed. (2003) *The Macmillan Diaries: The Cabinet Years, 1950–1957*, Macmillan, p. 361. Entry for 13 October 1954.

[8] John Morley (1903) *Gladstone*, Macmillan (1905), p. 298.

[9] John Morley (1889) *Walpole*, Macmillan, p. 168.

epoch has seen the final transformation of Cabinet Government into Prime Ministerial Government.'[10] In 1965, a book appeared describing the prime minister as an 'elected monarch'.[11] Fears of overweening prime ministerial power are nothing new.

In fact, the thesis of increasing prime ministerial power or the 'presidentialisation' of the role of prime minister is far too simplistic to account for the complex facts of modern political life. The power of the prime minister depends, and always has depended, upon vicissitudes, electoral and personal, and no clear evolutionary trend is discernible. Those who believe that there has been a progressive accretion of prime ministerial power are ahistorical. They overrate the power of a modern prime minister and underrate that of prime ministers of the past. Gladstone and Lloyd George were at least as powerful and dominant over their colleagues as Margaret Thatcher and Tony Blair. Balfour, not normally thought of as a 'strong' prime minister, peremptorily sacked three Free Trade ministers in 1903; Campbell-Bannerman did not bother to tell his Cabinet about staff conversations with France, initiated by his Foreign Secretary, Sir Edward Grey, in 1905, conversations which in effect laid the basis for a mutual security pact; while Churchill committed Britain to the defence of Soviet Russia in 1941 without consulting anyone at all. Attlee, as Peter Hennessy has shown, kept from his Cabinet the announcement that Britain was to become an atomic power. There is no mention of it in the minutes of the crucial Cabinet meeting of 6 May 1948, or in the handwritten record of the Cabinet Secretary. When asked 10 years later why he had hidden this from his Cabinet, Attlee replied, of his colleagues, 'I thought some of them were not fit to be trusted with secrets of this kind.'[12] Harold Macmillan sacked seven Cabinet ministers – one-third of his Cabinet – in 'the night of the long knives' in 1962. Modern prime ministers may envy these precedents. They are not always able to emulate them. Most prime ministers have felt the limitations of their position more than its strengths.

Today, the power of a modern prime minister depends not only, as Morley suggested, on whether the House of Commons will stand by him, but also upon his standing with the electorate. If Margaret Thatcher and Tony Blair seemed powerful prime ministers, it is because, we, the voters, made them such, by giving them, under our peculiar electoral system, landslide majorities. Perhaps our resentment at the power which the prime minister was then able to wield is merely the rage of Caliban looking at himself in the glass. Even so, Margaret Thatcher was eventually pushed out by her colleagues, while Tony Blair was

---

[10] Walter Bagehot (1963) *The English Constitution*, Fontana edition, p. 51.

[11] F.W.G. Benemy (1965) *The Elected Monarch: The Development of the Power of the Prime Minister*, Harrap.

[12] Peter Hennessy (2007) *Britain and the Bomb*, Oxford University Press, p. 69.

forced to accelerate his retirement. Of post-war prime ministers, only Harold Wilson left office voluntarily. Eden and Macmillan resigned on grounds of ill health. The rest sought, in Churchill's graphic words, to stay in the pub till closing time, only to be removed either by the voters or by their colleagues. Caliban has proved a fickle master for post-war prime ministers, but none of them has been able to escape his verdict.

What is clear is that only a strong prime minister can give a government a clear sense of direction. Where a prime minister fails to do so, as most notably perhaps with the Cabinets of Anthony Eden, Harold Wilson, or John Major, government fails and the Cabinet becomes little more than a federation of departments. Cabinet government, if it is to work effectively, presupposes a strong prime minister with clear aims and a determination to achieve them. There is, therefore, no contradiction between a strong prime minister and Cabinet government. The one presupposes the other.

Perhaps the best account of the role of the prime minister was written well before the post-war era, in a book by H.H. Asquith, prime minister from 1908 to 1916, entitled *Fifty Years of Parliament*, published in 1926. Asquith realised that, precisely because the premiership was a product of historical evolution rather than a constitutional document, 'There is not, and cannot be, from the nature of the case, any authoritative definition of the precise relation of the Prime Minister to his colleagues.' 'The office of Prime Minister,' Asquith went on, 'is what its holder chooses and is able to make of it.'[13] It is hoped that this book will cast some light on what the post-war holders of the office have been 'able to make of it'. No doubt, biographies of prime ministers and essays on prime ministers, such as the present collection, tend, inevitably perhaps, to exaggerate the role. But, of course, prime ministers cannot run their governments all on their own, without needing to secure the consent of their colleagues or advice from their officials. Indeed, the success of some prime ministers – Attlee is a fine example – consists less in what they themselves achieved than in their skill at harnessing the energies of a formidable and potentially fractious team of ministers towards common goals.

But to be a great manager is not the same as being a great leader. Many great leaders – Churchill and Roosevelt are obvious examples – have been poor managers. Conversely, some great managers have been poor leaders in the sense that they have been unable to inspire or give a general sense of direction to government. The manager helps an organisation survive; the leader gives it a sense of purpose. Most prime ministers, indeed, have sought power, not primarily for its own sake or for purposes of self-aggrandisement, but because they had large public purposes which they sought to fulfil, and which, so they believed, only they could fulfil. Attlee sought to create a society based on fellowship,

---

[13] The Earl of Oxford and Asquith (1926) *Fifty Years of Parliament*, Cassell, pp. 184–5.

Churchill to restore Britain's authority in the world. Harold Macmillan wanted to readjust Britain's role to her circumstances, while Harold Wilson sought to show the relevance of socialism to a new era of science and technology. Margaret Thatcher saw herself as heroically fighting against her country's decline, while both John Major and Tony Blair sought to humanise her legacy. *New Labour to New Jerusalem* seeks to discover how successful Britain's post-war prime ministers were as leaders – did they achieve the purposes they set themselves, or was Enoch Powell right to say that all political lives, unless cut off in mid-career, end in failure?

1
Clement Attlee, 1945–1951
Paul Addison

When Clement Attlee was elected leader of the Labour Party in 1935, Hugh Dalton commented in his diary: 'a little mouse shall lead them'.[1] It was generally assumed that he was only an interim leader, but the little mouse was still in charge in February 1940, when Beatrice Webb went to hear him speak on the subject of war aims. 'His hour's lecture was pitiable', she wrote in her diary. 'He looked and spoke like an insignificant elderly clerk, without distinction in the voice, manner or substance of his discourse...To realise that this little nonentity is the Parliamentary Leader of the Labour Party...and presumably the future P.M., is humiliating.'[2] By October 1940, when Cecil King of the *Daily Mirror* encountered him for the first time, the little mouse was a member of Churchill's War Cabinet. 'Attlee is a man I should say of very limited intelligence and no personality,' wrote King in his diary. 'If one heard he was getting £6 a week in the service of the East Ham Corporation, one would be surprised he was earning so much.'[3] Such low estimates of Attlee persisted through the war years. Hence the celebrated letter which Harold Laski, as chairman of the party, wrote to Attlee in May 1945, advising him to resign on the grounds that 'the continuance of your leadership is a grave handicap to our hopes of victory in the coming election...Just as Mr Churchill changed Auchinleck for Montgomery before El Alamein, so, I suggest, you owe it to the party to make a comparable change on the eve of this greatest of our battles.'[4] This was the letter to which Attlee famously replied: 'Dear Laski, Thank you for your letter, contents of which have been noted.'

---

[1] Ben Pimlott, ed. (1986) *The Political Diary of Hugh Dalton 1918–1940*, Cape, entry for 26 November 1935.

[2] *The Diary of Beatrice Webb Vol IV: The Wheel of Life* (1985) Harvard University Press, p. 447, entry for 29 February 1940.

[3] Cecil King (1970) *With Malice Toward None: A War Diary*, Sidgwick and Jackson, p. 82, entry for 12 October 1940.

[4] Kenneth Harris (1982) *Attlee*, Weidenfeld and Nicolson, p. 252.

These highly unflattering views of Attlee are very difficult to reconcile with the esteem he currently enjoys as a respected statesman and the greatest of Labour leaders. In a survey carried out in 2004, 139 academics were asked to award a mark out of 10 to all twentieth-century prime ministers. Attlee came first with an average rating of 8.34, Churchill second with 7.88, Lloyd George third with 7.33, Margaret Thatcher fourth with 7.14 and Harold Macmillan fifth with 6.49.[5] How, then, are we to account for the revolution in Attlee's reputation?

In part the answer is bound up with the record of the administration he led. In Labour party tradition it is remembered as a government which, however imperfect, had great achievements to its name. The contrast with the second Labour government, which collapsed in the financial crisis of August 1931, is particularly stark. Whatever the economic difficulties after 1945, and whatever the extent of the government's responsibility for them, the Attlee governments had a clear sense of social purpose and delivered the welfare reforms promised in the party's manifesto. They demonstrated for the first time that Labour could govern effectively, and that parliamentary democracy could work in the interests of organised labour.

In the sixties it became fashionable for young socialists to accuse the Attlee governments of betraying socialism, but an older generation of activists recalled them with pride. In 1945 Betty Harrison was a trades union organiser in the Fire Brigades Union. Looking back on the period in the 1970s, she recalled it as one in which the government embodied and expressed the aspirations of the rank and file: 'We gained shorter hours and better conditions all round; a new Education Act and the Beveridge scheme, a new Health Service, all these things which some of us had worked for years. They may not have been completely satisfactory, at least they were vastly advanced on what had been before. That was when I felt the trades unions and the labour movement had really come into its own.'[6]

The historical significance of the Attlee governments is hard to doubt. They rank with the Thatcher governments of 1979 to 1990 as one of the two groundbreaking administrations that made a fundamental difference to politics and society after 1945. At home the legacy included the nationalisation of the railways, coal, gas, electricity, iron and steel, and the creation of the welfare state. In external affairs, where they were much less in control of events, they redefined Britain's role while refusing to abandon British claims to great power status. They aligned Britain with the United States and against the Soviet Union in the Cold War, sent troops to fight in Korea, and took the decision to manufacture a British atom bomb. Their refusal to participate in the European Coal

---

[5] *The Guardian*, 30 November 2004.
[6] Margaret Morris (1976) *The General Strike*, Penguin, p. 282.

and Steel Community set Britain on the path of a troubled relationship with 'Europe' that has never been fully resolved. By withdrawing from India, Burma and Palestine they signalled the ultimate end of the British Empire, though few at the time anticipated that it would break up as rapidly as it did.

How great was the achievement? In his book *The Lost Victory*, Correlli Barnett argued that under the Attlee governments 'Britain let slip a unique and irrecoverable opportunity to remake herself as an industrial country while her rivals were still crippled by defeat and occupation.'[7] His critique of their imperial pretensions and high levels of military spending was no less scathing than his assault on them for allegedly diverting scarce resources from industrial modernisation to housing and other social programmes. If most historians remain sceptical of the Barnett analysis, it is partly because his analysis of the opportunity cost of welfare reforms is misleading[8] and partly because a polemic based on hindsight and present-day agendas introduces a false yardstick into the past. But historians do not lack critical awareness of the shortcomings of Attlee and his colleagues. The works of historians such as Kenneth Morgan, Peter Hennessy and Alec Cairncross all testify to the feeble grasp of economics possessed by most members of the government, and it has often been argued that the decision to embark on a massive programme of rearmament in 1950 was – as Aneurin Bevan argued in Cabinet at the time – a disastrous mistake. Whatever their weaknesses, however, the Attlee governments exercised political power with a radical sense of purpose, and an almost brutal effectiveness, which have only been matched since then by the governments of Margaret Thatcher.

The comparison with the Thatcher years also highlights one of the more striking differences. At the height of her fortunes Mrs Thatcher's dominance of the political scene was so great that the government looked like a projection of her own will, and the radical Conservatism of the period like an expression of her own values: 'Thatcherism'. The Attlee governments were much closer to a collective model of leadership. As prime minister, Attlee was *primus inter pares* – first among equals – but flanked by a number of major figures, each with his own personal following and independent standing in the party. Biographers and historians have explored the roles played by Herbert Morrison in the nationalisation of industry, Ernest Bevin at the Foreign Office, Aneurin Bevan at the Ministry of Health, Hugh Dalton and Stafford Cripps at the Treasury. In different ways each of them displayed strong leadership qualities and each contributed substantially to the policies and priorities of the government. Attlee, on the other hand, was deficient in many of the attributes normally associated

---

[7] Correlli Barnett (1995) *The Lost Victory*, Macmillan, p. 11.

[8] Jim Tomlinson (1995) 'Welfare and Economy: The Economic Impact of the Welfare State 1945–1951' in *Twentieth Century British History*, pp. 194–219.

with a politician of the front rank and would never have obtained the glittering prize of the premiership but for a substantial helping of good luck. Once in possession of the powers of the prime minister, however, he displayed virtues that compensated for his limitations, and marked him out as a leader of an exceptional type: a dedicated but self-effacing public servant. Attlee's reputation, writes Peter Hennessy, 'has risen steadily since his death in 1967, so much so that he has become a kind of lodestar for the efficient and successful conduct of peacetime Cabinet government and premiership in the postwar years, and not just on the Labour side'.[9]

Attlee's lifespan coincided with the rise of Labour and it seems unlikely that he would ever have been heard of had he not decided, at the age of 25, to join the Independent Labour Party. Although he was a terribly shy young man and must have needed to pluck up all his courage, he took up his position beneath a gas lamp and began to address the passers-by in a street in Stepney.

How and why did Attlee become a socialist? The Attlees were a prosperous upper middle-class family with a comfortable home in Putney. Attlee's parents sent him to prep school, then on to Haileybury, and University College, Oxford, where he read History. His father was an eminent solicitor and it was decided that 'Clem' would follow in his father's footsteps and train for the bar. Indeed he passed his bar exams but after this the plan went wrong. By all accounts the Attlees were a happy family, but they were also Victorian evangelicals who observed the Sabbath strictly, said family prayers with the servants every morning before breakfast, and engaged in philanthropic activities. It is not surprising that one of Attlee's brothers became a clergyman, and his sister a missionary. His brother Tom, to whom he was always close, became a Christian socialist. Attlee, however, lost his religious belief at school and it never came back. Towards the end of his life, when his biographer Kenneth Harris sounded out his views on religion, Attlee summed them up as follows: 'Believe in the ethics of Christianity. Can't believe the mumbo-jumbo.'[10]

Attlee enjoyed life at Oxford, but lacked ambition in the conventional sense. He was bored by the law. What he needed was a mission in life, and he stumbled upon it almost by accident when his brother took him to Haileybury House, a club for working-class boys in Stepney, run by Haileybury School. Within a few weeks he was a regular visitor, and he subsequently took up residence in the East End as the Club manager. Attlee was shocked by the discovery of poverty, but viewed the poor with respect as admirable men and women whose misfortunes were no fault of their own.

---

[9] Peter Hennessy (2001) *The Prime Minister: The Office and its Holders since 1945*, Penguin, p. 150.

[10] Harris, *Attlee*, p. 564.

When Attlee first visited the Haileybury Club his politics were those of a Tory imperialist and disciple of Joseph Chamberlain. Now, as he grappled in his mind with the problems of poverty, his politics began to change. But instead of moving a degree or two to the Left, and becoming a supporter of Liberal welfare reform, Attlee turned to the socialism of the Independent Labour Party, the ILP, a creed as evangelical as the religion in which he had been raised. For Attlee, socialism was an ethical movement grounded in the belief that most people were by nature good, and capable of working together for higher purposes than material self-interest.

Attlee's conversion to socialism grew out of his own background and involved very little break with social convention. He never quarrelled with his family, but went home to Putney at weekends. Although he now preached socialism at the street corner, he continued to practise a more practical but conservative type of social work at his boys' club. The ILP was strongly anti-militarist, but the main activity of the Haileybury club was military training. It was affiliated to a regiment in which Attlee held a commission by virtue of his position in the Club. He revelled in the parade ground exercises and the summer camps. If he was a socialist, he was also a patriot, and saw no contradiction between the two. When war broke out in 1914 Attlee's brother Tom, who had also joined the ILP, opposed the war and was later sent to prison as a conscientious objector. But Clem volunteered immediately, saw active service at Gallipoli, in Mesopotamia, and finally on the Western front, was twice wounded, and was promoted from captain to major in 1917. 'What really interested him,' observes Richard Whiting, 'was developing a fighting unit with an officer group drawn from a wide social mix.'[11]

Underlying Attlee's activities was a great simplicity and integrity of character. Whether as a socialist, social worker or army officer, he exemplified the service ethic, the ideal of the high-minded, hard-working professional class from which he sprang. This is not to imply that he lacked ambition, but he was well aware that he was not a man of ideas, an exciting orator or a larger-than-life character. The path of service to others offered him not only the sense of fellowship he craved, but the most likely prospect of self-advancement.

After his return from the war Attlee decided to embark on a political career, and he was elected in 1922 as the MP for Limehouse. While many Labour MPs were natural back-benchers, Attlee was a professional politician from the start. He loved electioneering, worked hard on speeches and was good in committees. His interest in political theory was minimal, but he paid much attention to the machinery of government. Hungry for office, an appetite sharpened by the need to support a wife and growing family, he was loyal to his party leader, Ramsay MacDonald, who gave him a junior appointment at the War Office in

---

[11] R.C. Whiting, 'Clement Richard Attlee', Oxford Dictionary of National Biography.

1924. During the second Labour government he made Attlee Chancellor of the Duchy of Lancaster and subsequently Postmaster General, both posts outside the Cabinet.

Then came the first of the accidents that propelled Attlee to the top. The collapse of the Labour government was followed in November 1931 by a general election that swept away the majority of Labour MPs, leaving a rump of 46, which included Attlee. As one of the few remaining Labour MPs who had held office, he became one of the party's leading spokesmen in the House of Commons, and acting leader while Lansbury was ill during the first half of 1934. When Lansbury resigned in October 1935, Attlee was elected temporary leader pending the general election which took place the following month. In the new session of Parliament he was re-elected, beating off challenges from Herbert Morrison and Arthur Greenwood, both of whom had campaigned furiously while Attlee puffed quietly on his pipe and relied on his record. Morrison's flaw was a reputation for intrigue, Greenwood's a weakness for drink: Attlee won because he was the most steady and reliable of the candidates.

Having won the leadership, Attlee held on to it. He spoke out firmly against Neville Chamberlain's policy of appeasement and edged the party gradually away from its previous opposition to rearmament. Nevertheless, he was generally regarded as an interim leader. Opinion polls and by-election results indicate that Chamberlain was on course to win a peacetime general election in 1939 or 1940, in which case Attlee's future as party leader would have been called into question. But Hitler's invasion of Poland led to the postponement of the election for the duration of the war, leaving Attlee once again in place.

On the eve of war in September 1939 Attlee was out of action, recovering from an operation, and it was his deputy, Arthur Greenwood, who, urged by the Conservative anti-appeaser Leo Amery, 'spoke for England' and demanded that Chamberlain commit the nation to war. But in May 1940, after the Norway debate, when Chamberlain's majority had fallen from 200 to 41, it was Attlee who told the prime minister that Labour would not serve under him, compelling him to resign and make way for a Coalition government led by Churchill. This was another stroke of luck for Attlee, though it occurred against a background of national disaster. He and other Labour ministers were now in office without having won a general election. As leader of the Labour Party, Attlee was automatically a member of the War Cabinet and remained so throughout the life of the Coalition. As Lord Privy Seal (1940–1942) and later Lord President (1943–1945), he was in charge of important home front committees. As deputy prime minister (1942–1945) he presided over the War Cabinet during Churchill's many absences overseas.

Attlee struggled to find his feet in wartime Whitehall. In the summer of 1940 Churchill made him chairman of the food policy committee. By March 1941 Bridges, the Cabinet Secretary, was advising Churchill that the committee was ineffectual owing to Attlee's inability to resolve disputes between the Ministries of Food and Agriculture. In 1943 he took charge of the Lord President's Committee, at that time the main forum for policy on the home front, but with Attlee in the chair its significance declined and he complained that ministers were no longer attending it. Such episodes, however, are not the whole story. Attlee was notable for the efficiency with which he despatched War Cabinet business when he was deputising for Churchill, a sign of growing self-confidence, and his grip on the leadership of the party was greatly strengthened by the acquisition of a powerful ally, the Minister of Labour, Ernest Bevin. The two men came to trust and admire one another, with Bevin happy to act in the role of loyal bodyguard and supporter. From Attlee's point of view it was even more fortunate that Bevin loathed Morrison, his main rival for the leadership of the party. Immediately after the general election of 1945 a plot by Morrison and his supporters to replace Attlee as party leader was nipped in the bud by Bevin.

Attlee grew in assurance as questions of post-war policy came into view. The publication of the Beveridge Report in December 1942 split the Coalition along party lines and Churchill sought to postpone action on it until the war had been won. Spurred on by a rebellion of their own back-benchers, Labour ministers attempted to break down Churchill's resistance, and several months of argument and manoeuvre ensued before a compromise was reached. Bevin, Dalton and Morrison all took a very firm line, but so did Attlee. He stood up to Churchill and gave him a stern warning:

When I joined the Government, I understood and have repeatedly stated that, whilst this Government was necessarily precluded from carrying out a Party programme, it would be prepared to legislate on matters on which agreement could be reached. I have added that while in my view there will necessarily come a time when a divergence of policy would cause a reversion to normal Party Government, there was a considerable field in which members of different political views could cooperate in order to carry through measures which the course of events and public opinion demanded.... I think that it would be wrong to think that the people of this country are not prepared for considerable changes. The very valuable review of public opinion circulated by the Minister of Information, Brendan Bracken, bears this out. In particular it shows a remarkable consensus of opinion on many points between people of different political parties and different economic and social backgrounds. I have myself been in contact with a number of prominent businessmen and with many people not of my own political views and have found it possible to arrive at a very large measure of agreement...I do not think the people of this country especially the fighting men would forgive us if we failed to take decisions and to implement them, because of some constitutional inhibition. I am not concerned at the moment with the Beveridge Report, and its merits or demerits, but with the general principle.[12]

Attlee understood that a Conservative-dominated Coalition could not be compelled to adopt socialist measures. But he saw in the proposals of the Beveridge Report the opportunity of securing many of the great social advances of which Labour had long dreamed, and a milestone on the road to the New Jerusalem. Once the Churchill veto was overcome, the Coalition's Reconstruction Committee, of which Attlee was a member, made substantial progress in the fields of social security, employment policy, and other measures for the immediate post-war period. 'At the present time,' he wrote to Harold Laski in May 1944, 'I am engaged for a good many hours a day on postwar problems which cover a very wide range from detailed matters of our internal economy to the widest matters of international political and economic import. I discuss these with my colleagues and endeavour naturally to get as much of our policy accepted, and I find on many matters more agreement than you would perhaps expect, but on other matters I may have to accept a compromise.'[13]

By the time Attlee became prime minister he was, therefore, very well briefed on questions of social and economic reconstruction. The same was true of the central question of post-war foreign policy, the future of Germany. In August 1943 a ministerial committee on Armistice Terms and Civil Administration was set up with Attlee in the chair. 'This was the committee,' Trevor Burridge writes, 'that accepted a recommendation by the Chiefs of Staff that Germany should be divided into three main zones of occupation, split among the three Powers, plus a combined Berlin zone: Britain should occupy the north-west of Germany, Russia the east, and the Americans the south... The "Attlee Plan" for Germany represented a triple British insurance policy – against a German resurgence, American withdrawal and Russian intransigence.'[14] Of the three potential threats, however, it was the German danger that weighed most heavily with Attlee as the war in Europe drew to a close.

The electoral appeal of Labour in the 1920s owed much to the charisma of Ramsay MacDonald, while Labour's victories in 1964 and 1966 were to owe much to the public relations skills of Harold Wilson. There is little evidence to suggest that Attlee was a vote-winner in 1945. He campaigned hard during the general election and broadcast what now reads like a masterly rebuttal of Churchill's 'Gestapo' speech. But shortly after Labour's landslide victory only 4 per cent of the public questioned by Gallup named him as the politician they

---

[12] Attlee Papers, 2/2, no date but must be 1943, Churchill College, Cambridge.
[13] Kingsley Martin (1969) *Harold Laski*, p. 151.
[14] Trevor Burridge (1985) *Clement Attlee: A Political Biography*, Cape, p. 172.

would most like to see leading the new government. Eden was named by 31 per cent and Churchill by 20 per cent.

Attlee seems to have become more of an electoral asset as the public got to know him, and his approval ratings as prime minister averaged out at 47 per cent, a respectable enough performance by comparison with other post-war premiers.[15] The premiership, however, made no difference to his modest public persona. In style and appearance he remained indistinguishable from 'the man on the Clapham omnibus'. His parliamentary speeches, cogent and well reasoned as they usually were, tended to lower the temperature of debate, and his occasional broadcasts were equally colourless. 'Attlee is a charming and intelligent man,' wrote Harold Nicolson after hearing him on the radio in November 1947, 'but as a public speaker he is, compared to Winston, like a village fiddler after Paganini.' Attlee himself discouraged all attempts to build him up as a personality. The government's public relations officers, he declared, existed in order to explain its policies: 'Moreover I should be a sad subject for any publicity expert. I have none of the qualities which create publicity.'[16] Here was a prime minister who ignored the headlines in the newspapers and only took *The Times* for the crossword puzzle, which he completed every day, and the announcements of births, marriages and deaths. At press conferences his notoriously brief replies to questions used to baffle reporters. 'Nothing in that,' he would say, or 'You're off beam again' or 'I've never heard that, have you?'[17]

There is a well-known story from the period when Attlee was prime minister and Churchill Leader of the Opposition. After a debate in the House a Conservative MP remarked to Churchill: 'I thought the little fellow got the better of you today.' Churchill replied: 'Feed a grub on royal jelly and it may become a queen.'[18] This may be apocryphal but has a grain of truth. During the war years Attlee had never had a secure power base. Unlike Bevin at the Ministry of Labour or Morrison at the Home Office, he did not have the weight of a major Whitehall department behind him, and his party had only a minority of seats in the House of Commons. Once in possession of the powers of the prime minister, however, he was able to translate his clarity of mind, shrewdness of judgment and firmness of purpose, unspectacular qualities that had been barely been noticed before, into the effective exercise of authority.

Attlee sometimes intervened on matters of policy, but he was seldom the principal policymaker. Having formed his Cabinet, and allotted major roles to

---

[15] Robert J. Whybrow (1989) *Britain speaks out, 1937–87: A Social History as Seen through the Gallup Data* , Macmillan, p. 20. The poll was carried out in August 1945.

[16] Nigel Nicolson, ed. (1971) *Harold Nicolson: Diaries and Letters 1945–62*, Fontana, pp. 105, 151–2, entries for 10 November 1947, 14 January 1949.

[17] James Margach, *Sunday Times* 5 February 1978, p. 33.

[18] Kingsley Martin (1969) *Editor*, Penguin, pp. 22–3.

Bevin, Dalton, Morrison, Cripps and Bevan, he was content to delegate, and allowed his ministers a great deal of scope within their own spheres. As the near verbatim minutes taken by the Cabinet Secretary demonstrate, Attlee was a practitioner of Cabinet government. Almost all major issues were referred to the Cabinet, and, although the discussions were dominated by Attlee's more heavyweight colleagues, other ministers were frequent contributors. The most taciturn of the figures around the table was Attlee himself. Famously laconic, he turned brevity of utterance into a political technique more effective than Churchill's eloquence. By remaining silent while others spoke, interjecting perhaps the occasional question on a point of fact, he was able to weigh up the balance of opinion before stating his own conclusion. Economy of speech was also a key element in the disciplined regime he imposed on the conduct of business. As far as possible, Attlee insisted that it should be conducted on paper, with talk kept to a minimum. Cabinet agendas were usually long and varied and it was Attlee's aim, as Harold Wilson recalled, to get through the agenda as expeditiously as possible: 'He cut short any lengthy explanation by any Minister who had submitted a paper for Cabinet approval, saying: "We have all read it. Anything to add...no? Cabinet agree?...Next business."'[19]

Attlee's clipped phrases and lack of small talk were usually attributed to his innate shyness but also reflected a mind with a sharp cutting edge. There was an asperity in his judgements that reflected a capacity for hard-headed decision-making, coupled with a remarkable inner tranquillity. Attlee did not lie awake at night agonising over the previous day's events or worrying about what would happen next. Nor was he troubled by jealousy and paranoia. 'It seems genuinely not to have worried him,' writes Francis Beckett, 'that he appeared to many people to be in the shadow of other much better and greater men. Clem cared only for what is real. His shyness concealed a great, calm pride. He was so serenely certain of his own worth and judgements that he did not greatly need the approval of others.'[20]

That said, Attlee was more sure of himself in some areas than others. In spite of the sudden ending of Lend-Lease, and the cliff-hanger of the Anglo-American loan negotiations, the first 18 months of the Attlee governments were a period of triumphant advance in domestic affairs. The Labour Party was united in support of the nationalisation programme and the social reforms promised in 1945. For Attlee they were the fulfilment, if only in part, of all that he and his party had worked for. Then came the troubles of 1947: the fuel crisis, divisions in the Cabinet over the nationalisation of steel, and the crisis over convertibility. Steel raised troublesome questions about the purpose of nationalisation to which Attlee had no clear answer. The fuel and convertibility crises

---

[19] *Attlee As I Knew Him* (1983) London Borough of Tower Hamlets, p. 43.
[20] Francis Beckett (2000) *Clem Attlee*, Politico's, p. 179.

demonstrated that he, like his Chancellor of the Exchequer, was out of his depth in economic policy. Attlee was fortunate that a plot to install Bevin in his place was foiled by the refusal of Bevin himself to have anything to do with it. In the end, the government was rescued by Cripps, who gave its economic policies greater coherence and a semblance of planning, but Kenneth Morgan suggests that Attlee never recovered from the battering: 'In major crises – devaluation of the pound in August 1949, even more the disastrous chain of events that led to Bevan and Wilson's resignation from the Cabinet in April 1951 – Attlee remained passive and offered no lead. He exemplified in his own meekly ambitious person the old Roman tag that if you remained silent you were believed to be a philosopher.'[21]

Attlee had a stronger sense of direction in external affairs. Between 1945 and 1948 his government gave independence to India, removed British forces from Greece and Turkey, and withdrew from Palestine. In the final analysis this scaling down of overseas commitments was due to the pressure of events, but much of the impetus came from Attlee. This was especially true of India, where he took personal charge of policy. When negotiations for an all-India constitution broke down, he sacked the Viceroy, Lord Wavell, and sent out Mountbatten in his place with instructions to transfer power as soon as possible even if this meant the acceptance of partition. When he was asked 20 years later why he had imposed a strict time limit he replied: 'Because I knew Indians very well. They talk, talk, talk all the time, and always try and escape responsibility.'[22] By 1945, as he recognised, the ideal of a gradual transfer of power to an orderly and united India was no longer attainable, and British authority was on the brink of collapse. The withdrawal from India was Attlee's personal contribution to the end of empire, the forerunner of the no less hard-headed decision of the Macmillan government to pull out of Africa.

Among his other roles, Attlee took the chair at meetings of the Cabinet's Defence Committee. 'As chairman,' writes Alan Bullock, 'Attlee played a more active role than in Cabinet and from the first meeting in the New Year [1946] showed himself a radical and persistent critic of the Services' plans.'[23] In conjunction with Dalton, the Chancellor of the Exchequer, Attlee argued that the nation could no longer afford the manpower or the money the armed forces were demanding. In March 1946 he circulated a paper calling for a radical reorientation of defence policy away from the Middle East and the Mediterranean, and towards a strategic area extending eastwards from the United States. Britain's main imperial base would move to central Africa, this creating a wide glacis

---

[21] Kenneth Morgan (1987) *Labour People: Hardie to Kinnock*, 1992 ed., Oxford University Press, p. 147.

[22] Clem Attlee (1967) *The Granada Historical Records Interview*, Granada, p. 41.

[23] Alan Bullock (1983) *Ernest Bevin: Foreign Secretary*, Heinemann, p. 240.

between Britain's military forces and the southern flanks of the Soviet Union. This visionary plan was strongly resisted by Bevin and the Chiefs of Staff, who argued that it was essential to hold the line against the Soviet Union in the Middle East. Attlee continued to press his case and the debate ran on until January 1947, when he was forced to climb down in the face of a threat to resign by all three Chiefs of Staff.[24] In the event, Britain retained most of its bases in the Mediterranean and the Middle East for the duration of Attlee's government. If he had prevailed, Britain's balance of payments crisis might have been eased, cuts in social expenditure avoided, and the standard of living improved – but we can be fairly sure that he would still have insisted on the manufacture of a British atom bomb.

When Attlee first took office he decided, presumably on the grounds that the need for secrecy in vital questions of national security overrode the claims of Cabinet government, to withhold discussion of nuclear policy from the full Cabinet and confine it to a secret subcommittee, GEN 75. Initially his intention was to continue the joint Anglo-American nuclear programme which Churchill and Roosevelt had initiated, but in 1946 Congress passed the McMahon Act, forbidding the United States from sharing its nuclear secrets with any other nation. Work on British preparations continued and the formal decision to manufacture a British bomb was taken in January 1947 by another secret Cabinet committee, GEN 163, which Attlee had set up for this sole purpose. Although anxieties about the Soviet Union were one of the key factors in the decision, the other was the argument that without the bomb the British would be entirely dependent for their security upon the United States.

At the time the decision was taken Attlee was still in two minds about the Soviet Union's intentions and not yet a convinced Cold Warrior. By the end of 1947 his views had hardened and henceforth he pursued, in step with Bevin, a calm and resolute anti-Soviet line through the Berlin crisis of 1948–1949 and the negotiations leading up to the creation of NATO. After the outbreak of war in Korea in June 1950, it was Attlee who persuaded the Cabinet to send in British troops, and he eventually agreed, under pressure from the United States, to a huge increase in the defence budget, which proved to be unsustainable. On the home front, well-grounded fears of Soviet espionage promoted Attlee to set up a Cabinet Committee on Subversive Activities, and in March 1948 he announced that Communists would henceforth be removed from Civil Service posts which gave them access to secret information – in practice a mild and ineffective measure that reflected his faith in the integrity of the higher Civil Service.[25]

---

[24] Jim Tomlinson (1991) 'The Attlee Governments and the Balance of Payments, 1945–1951', *Twentieth Century British History*, pp. 53–5; Bullock (1981) *Ernest Bevin*, pp. 240–4.

[25] Peter Hennessy (2002) *The Secret State: Whitehall and the Cold War*, Allen Lane, pp. 77–89.

Few statesmen accomplish all they set out to do, and Attlee was no exception. When he first took office he hoped that peace would be maintained by the cooperation of the great powers within the United Nations. The achievement of his government was to establish collective security and a balance of power in Europe, at the price of dependence on the United States. At home he saw the nationalised industries and the welfare state as the precursors of a new society in which the profit motive would gradually be superseded by the ethics of socialism. The outcome was a half-way house: the makeshift social democracy of the Fifties and Sixties. Historians can point to problems neglected and opportunities missed, but, given the almost constant pressure of events under which they lived, it is striking how much long-term change the Attlee governments achieved in a short time. They left behind them a nation about to enter an unprecedented era of peace and prosperity in which full employment coexisted with the welfare state.

The virtues of Attlee himself shine ever more brightly as time goes by. He appears to have been underestimated before 1945 because so many people expected a leader of the Labour Party to be a prophet, evangelist and orator. After 1945 the realisation dawned that he was deeply interested in the exercise of power, preoccupied by the substance of policy, and a very effective manager of government business. 'I think history will record,' wrote Hugh Gaitskell in May 1950, 'that he was among the more successful British Prime Ministers, as indeed it would have said of Baldwin if he had lived in a quieter period. It is one of the interesting features of our history, and perhaps that of other countries as well, that the qualities needed for success in peacetime are by no means the ones normally associated with greatness.'[26] A similar view was expressed by the *Guardian* when Attlee died in October 1967:

> Lord Attlee was not in the line of the great Prime Ministers any more than was Baldwin, Neville Chamberlain or Eden, but he is identified with such profound political and economic changes as will give him a place in history little below them [i.e. the great prime ministers]. If he had not the touch of genius that belonged to Lloyd George or Churchill, or the intellectual power of Asquith, he had gifts that providentially matched the needs of his day... His modesty was innate; there was no tinge of affectation in it. But beneath the modesty was a steely will and a capacity, as memoirs and auto-biographies have sufficiently testified, for bold, even ruthless action when it was required... He was a wise Prime Minister given to England at a moment when steady wisdom was needed rather than genius.[27]

---

[26] Philip M. Williams, ed. (1983) *The Diary of Hugh Gaitskell 1945–1956*, Cape, p. 189, entry for 26 May 1950.

[27] *The Guardian*, 9 October 1967, p. 3.

If Attlee stands even higher today than he did in 1967, the explanation is straightforward. Although we still have one of the most accountable and least corrupt political systems anywhere in the world, we have had too much spin and too much sleaze. With his straightforward convictions, modesty, integrity and almost complete indifference to public relations, Attlee has grown in historical esteem in direct proportion to the decline in recent years of the reputation of the political class. Even Mrs Thatcher was moved to write of him: 'Of Clement Attlee I was an admirer. He was a serious man and a patriot. Quite contrary to the general tendency of politicians in the 1990s, he was all substance and no show. His was a genuinely radical and reforming government.'[28] If Churchill was the only twentieth-century prime minister to become a national hero, Attlee was the only one to become a secular saint.

---

[28] Margaret Thatcher (1995) *The Path to Power*, HarperCollins, p. 69.

2
Winston Churchill, 1951–1955

Vernon Bogdanor

The fork in the road

In September 1940, Churchill had told Anthony Eden, his Foreign Secretary, that he 'would not make Lloyd George's mistake of carrying on after the war'.[1] He repeated this promise at the final Cabinet of his 'caretaker' government in July 1945, telling Eden: 'Thirty years of my life have been passed in this room. I shall never sit in it again. You will, but I shall not.'[2] Yet Winston Churchill became the only post-war prime minister other than Harold Wilson to enjoy a second innings. Perhaps the history of the Conservative Party would have been happier if Churchill had stuck to his original intention.

Churchill's return to Downing Street in 1951 was, of course, very different from Harold Wilson's. By 1974, few expected much from Wilson. Indeed, by then, some were beginning to question whether Britain was governable at all in the face of trade union militancy. The atmosphere in 1951, by contrast, was one of optimism and self-confidence, given added impetus by the accession in February 1952 of a new queen and the rhetoric of a new Elizabethan age. But, for Churchill himself, it was hard to see how a peacetime premiership could be anything more than an epilogue to his great achievement in war. His reputation was already secure. During the 1930s, so it seemed in 1951, he alone had been right about Hitler when everyone else had been wrong. In 1940, he had saved his country by ensuring that there was no compromise with or surrender to Nazi Germany. Britain, of course, could not have defeated Hitler on her own. She needed the help of the United States and the Soviet Union to do that. But, by ensuring that Hitler did not win his war, Churchill had made the defeat of Nazism possible, so saving Europe from a new Dark Age. What more could

---

[1] Earl of Avon (1965) *The Eden Memoirs: The Reckoning*, Cassell, p. 145.
[2] Avon, *The Reckoning*, p. 551.

he hope to achieve by a peacetime premiership? A second innings could only tarnish his lustre; it could hardly add to it.

Churchill remained in politics after 1945 in part to prove – to himself as much as to others – that he was not an accidental prime minister, a prime minister who had reached Downing Street merely through the vicissitudes of war. He wanted to prove that he could be the genuine choice of the British people in a general election. Yet, it would be unfair to suggest that his motives were entirely self-interested. He still had grand aims, both in the realm of foreign and of domestic policy. Indeed, his aim in foreign policy was the grandest of all, to replace the suspicions of the Cold War with a new and permanent structure of peace. On the home front, his aim was more limited but perhaps easier to achieve. What he wanted was 'a quiet life',[3] some relaxation and lowering of the political temperature after the years of austerity and the headlong reforms of the Attlee government.

Churchill brought to his peacetime premiership a greater wealth of parliamentary and ministerial experience than any other twentieth-century prime minister. Most prime ministers enter Downing Street after having been in the Commons for around 20 to 30 years. Churchill, by contrast, had first been elected a Member of Parliament in 1900, over half a century before, and had become a Cabinet minister for the first time in 1908, at the age of 33. He had held all the major offices of state except that of Foreign Secretary. No one, so it seemed, could surpass the wisdom and experience that he could bring to the task of government.

Yet Churchill's long experience was a doubtful asset. For his formative political years had been spent in the Victorian and Edwardian age, an age when Britain was unquestionably a world power, perhaps, indeed, the leading power in the world. This power depended, in part, upon an empire which, before 1914, covered around one-quarter of the world's surface and around one-fifth of the world's population. It was the largest Empire that the world had ever seen. Admittedly, parts of this empire – Canada, Australia, New Zealand and South Africa – were already self-governing. But self-government was regarded, even by radicals, as suitable primarily for white people, not for native races. Churchill tended to this view himself, and indeed it was natural to one of his generation. At a dinner with American Vice-President, Henry Wallace, in May 1943, Churchill, who 'had had quite a bit of whisky, which, however, did not affect the clarity of his thinking process but did perhaps increase his frankness – said why be apologetic about Anglo-Saxon superiority, that we were superior'.[4] Harold Macmillan noticed, during a discussion

---

[3] Nigel Lawson, 'Robot and the Fork in the Road. How Churchill might have made Thatcher Unnecessary', *Times Literary Supplement*, 21 January 2005, p. 11.

[4] John Morton Blum, ed. (1973) *The Price of Vision: The Diary of Henry A. Wallace, 1942–1946*, Houghton Mifflin, p. 208.

on immigration in January 1955, that 'the P.M. thinks "Keep England White" a good slogan!'[5]

Churchill was never able to grasp the strength of the demand for self-determination in the post-war world, nor the transformation in Britain's world position which decolonisation in Africa and Asia would bring. To have perceived this would have required a mental reorientation of which few Victorians were capable. In the 1930s, Churchill had fought a heroic but doomed rearguard action against Indian self-government. In the 1950s, he was to fight hard against the policy of his Foreign Secretary, Anthony Eden, of withdrawal from Sudan and the Suez Canal Zone. Towards the end of his life, in 1960, after he had retired from politics, Churchill told his private secretary, Anthony Montague Browne, that he disapproved of Harold Macmillan's 'wind of change' speech in South Africa, since 'the pendulum on colonialism had swung too far and too fast'.[6] He remained, to the end of his life, a child of the Victorian age.

In accepting his election as leader of the Conservative Party in October 1940, Churchill declared that he had 'always faithfully served two public causes which I think stand supreme – the maintenance of the enduring greatness of Britain and her Empire, and the historical continuity of our island life'.[7] To continue to serve these causes in 1951 seemed to require, first, an end to the period of upheaval that had marked the Attlee government, and, second, a reassertion of British power.

Churchill appreciated, however, that his electoral mandate in 1951 was an extremely narrow one. The Conservatives had an overall majority of just 17 seats, but had gained fewer votes than Labour in the general election. Labour, indeed, was relieved that it had not been defeated more heavily, and looked forward to an early return to office. For the Conservatives, so Labour believed, would be unable to preserve the gains of the Attlee government, in particular full employment and the welfare state. The Conservative government, there-fore, would prove little more than a brief interlude interrupting the smooth progress of socialist advance. Attlee appears to have believed that he would be back in Downing Street by 1953. Labour, so Harold Macmillan believed, had 'fought the election (very astutely) not on Socialism but on Fear. Fear of unemployment, fear of reduced wages; fear of reduced social benefits; fear of war. – If, before the next election, none of these fears have proved reason-able, we may be able to force the Opposition to fight on Socialism. Then we can win'.[8]

---

[5] Peter Catterall, *The Macmillan Diaries*, p. 382, entry for 20 January 1955.

[6] Anthony Montague Browne (1995) *Long Sunset*, Cassell, p. 307.

[7] Quoted in John Ramsden (1978) *The Age of Balfour and Baldwin, 1902–1940*, Longman, p. 376.

[8] Catterall, *The Macmillan Diaries*, p. 113. Entry for 28 October 1951.

Churchill was well aware that he was on probation. Like Charles II, he was determined not to go on his travels again. This meant that any radical assault on the welfare state, on full employment or on the privileges of the trade unions was immediately ruled out. It also meant that there was no hope of reversing the 'socialism' which, so Churchill believed, had infected British life since 1945. In forming his new administration, Churchill ensured that the strategic posts were filled by men of a 'national' and consensual orientation rather than by the more ideological free marketers and deflationists in the Conservative Party. By March 1952, when Lord Alexander of Tunis joined the Cabinet as Minister of Defence, there were seven peers in a Cabinet of 17. Three of them – Lord Ismay (Commonwealth Relations Secretary), Lord Leathers (Secretary of State for Coordination of Transport, Fuel and Power), and Lord Alexander himself – had tenuous links, if any, with the Conservatives. A fourth, Lord Woolton, had been a non-party member of Churchill's wartime government, and had joined only on becoming chairman of the Conservative Party in 1946. The Minister for Labour and National Service, Sir Walter Monckton, was also a recent recruit to the Party, who, although he had served in a number of posts under Churchill in the war, had by the late 1940s 'become part of the liberal-minded elite, incorporating men of all three parties, who adopted a consensus view of post-war politics'. Churchill said that Monckton was well qualified for the post because he had no political past. Monckton replied, 'I take it you do not expect me to have a political future.'[9]

In appointing Monckton, Churchill said, 'Oh my dear – I have the worst job in the Cabinet for you!'[10] He was chosen for his emollient qualities to avoid trouble with the trade unions. He was instructed to settle rapidly rather than to resist wage claims, whether or not they were justified. The spirit of the Monckton regime is well summed up in an anecdote from Churchill's Chancellor of the Exchequer, R.A. Butler.

> The railway strike of 1953 was one of the most important problems with which Walter had to deal – I said at the time that it was rather important from the point of view of the economy that we should not have wage increases which we could not afford – I was rung up at about midnight by Winston Churchill who said 'Walter and I have settled the railway strike. So you won't be troubled any more'. I said, 'On what terms have you settled it?' and Winston answered me 'Theirs, old cock! We did not like to keep you up'.[11]

---

[9] Entry on Monckton in *Oxford Dictionary of Political Biography*, by Martin Pugh.
[10] Lord Birkenhead (1969) *Walter Monckton: The Life of Viscount Monckton of Brenchley*, Weidenfeld and Nicolson, p. 274.
[11] R.A. Butler (1982) *The Art of Memory: Friends in Perspective*, Hodder and Stoughton, p. 137.

Butler had been made Chancellor in preference to the more aggressive Oliver Lyttelton, who had spoken on Treasury affairs in opposition, but whose combative manner would, so Churchill believed, antagonise the trade unions. But the Treasury under Butler was not as dominant as it had been under his Labour predecessors, Gaitskell and Cripps. While the government was being formed, the economic adviser to the Chancellor, Sir Robert Hall, noted that there were fears in the Treasury. 'The alarms were all about Winston wanting to reduce the Chancellor to a tax-collector.'[12] In the event, Butler was to be 'assisted', not only by Monckton and by Churchill, but also by two of Churchill's wartime cronies, Lord Cherwell, the Paymaster General, who in fact lived in 11 Downing Street, Butler having elected to remain in his house in Smith Square, and Sir Arthur Salter, Minister for Economic Affairs. 'It is no great matter that you are not an economist,' Churchill reassured his Chancellor. 'I wasn't either. And in any case I am going to appoint the best economist since Jesus Christ [Salter] to help you.'[13] It was indeed Cherwell and Salter who, with Anthony Eden, played a key role in persuading the Churchill government to reject the so-called 'Robot' project to float the pound, an attempt to break free from the balance of payments straitjacket which so constrained government economic policy.

The new economic team faced a 'financial position' that Churchill told Lyttelton was 'almost irretrievable: the country has lost its way. In the worst of the war I could always see how to do it. Today's problems are elusive and intangible, and it would be a bold man who could look forward to certain success'.[14] The rearmament programme introduced by the Labour government to meet the needs of the Korean War had posed a huge strain on the economy. The nationalisation by the Iranian government of the oil industry and consequent closure of the refinery at Abadan had reduced income from the sale of oil, forcing greater reliance on oil from the United States, and costing precious dollars. At the same time, American purchases of raw materials from sterling area countries had fallen, and this was adversely affecting the terms of trade. In November 1951, Butler told the Cabinet that Britain faced an external Balance of Payments deficit of alarming proportions – £700 million a year compared with a surplus of around £350 million a year before, due mainly to rising import prices and the stockpiling of imported materials. He introduced an immediate programme of economies, involving cuts in imports and a rise in interest rates. Further economies were to be announced later. It was in this atmosphere of economic crisis that the Robot proposals were produced.

---

[12] Alec Cairncross, ed. (1989) *The Robert Hall Diaries, 1947–1953*, Unwin Hyman, p. 176, 29 October 1951.

[13] R.A. Butler (1971) *The Art of the Possible*, Hamish Hamilton, p. 156.

[14] Oliver Lyttleton (1962) *The Memoirs of Lord Chandos*, Bodley Head, p. 343.

The Robot proposal took its name from the three officials who were instrumental in promoting it – Sir Leslie **Rowan**, head of the Overseas Finance division of the Treasury, Sir George **Bolton**, an Executive Governor of the Bank of England, and Sir R.W.B. Clarke, always known as **Ot**to Clarke, a Second Secretary at the Treasury.[15] But 'Robot' also referred to the fact that it was intended to lead to a self-regulating economy. Robot proposed a floating pound, convertible for non-sterling area residents, with sterling balances held in London being funded or blocked. The consequences would be radical. In place of the system of economic management introduced during the war, requiring the fine-tuning of the economy to preserve the parity of the pound and strengthen the balance of payments, the economy would be regulated primarily by the exchange rate. Individuals would have to adjust their expectations accordingly. Instead of government intervention in the labour market, whether through exhortation or negotiation, the labour market would be left to regulate itself. Excessive wage claims or a continuation of restrictive practices by management would then cause the pound to float downwards, increasing import prices and unemployment. In consequence, so it was argued, there would be greater incentives towards increasing productivity and industrial efficiency. 'There is something to be said, politically,' so it was argued in Cabinet, 'for moving towards the system by which individuals were influenced by the operation of the price mechanism, to make their own adjustments to changing economic circumstances'.[16]

Butler was sympathetic to this proposal, but, after long discussion in three Cabinet meetings in February 1952, it was defeated. The project lingered on for the rest of the year, but it did not come to Cabinet again. It had radical implications both for external and for domestic policy. It would mean Britain breaking away from the Bretton Woods system of managed currencies, established under American leadership in 1944, as well as the recently established European Payments Union, based on exchange rates fixed to the dollar, also under American leadership, and probably the sterling area also. Anthony Eden feared that, if the European Payments Union collapsed, so also would the European Defence Community, an attempt to achieve German rearmament within a European framework.[17]

---

[15] Otto Clarke was the father of the former Home Secretary, Charles Clarke.

[16] Jim Bulpitt and Peter Burnham (1999) 'Operation Robot and the British Political Economy in the Early 1950s: The Politics of Market Strengths', *Contemporary British History*, p. 1. This article gives a brilliant account of the domestic implications of the Robot project.

[17] Lawson, 'Robot and the Fork in the Road', p. 12. In the event, the European Defence Community agreement was signed in Paris in May 1952, but rejected by the French National Assembly in 1954.

The domestic implications of Robot were even more radical. If the pound floated downwards, as was likely in 1952, import prices and the cost of living would increase. That would stimulate wage demands. The consequences were spelt out by Cherwell to Churchill in March: 'If the workers, finding their food dearer, are inclined to demand higher wages, this will have to be stopped by increasing unemployment until their bargaining power is destroyed. This is what comfortable phrases like "letting the rate take the strain" mean, nothing more and nothing less.'[18] In 1952, it was believed that unemployment and poor living conditions between the wars had been the result of an excess of market economics and the failure of the state. Churchill himself felt that he had been a victim of economic liberalism when, as Chancellor, he had been persuaded by his Treasury officials and by the Bank of England, against his better judgement, to return Britain to the gold standard in 1925. Robot, according to Sir Arthur Salter in a memorandum to Butler, would be 'denounced as a "bankers' ramp", as an attempt of the bank and the City to regain the position they held in the days of the gold standard'.[19] It was inconceivable that a Conservative government, led by Churchill, dedicated to the maintenance of social peace, would support so radical a departure from the new consensus. The unemployment and social dislocation which would surely follow would destroy the claim that the Conservatives had learnt from their experiences, that they too were prepared to accept a larger role for the state. The Churchill government danced to the same tune of the inevitability of state intervention that had so charmed the Left.

The refusal to accept Robot was a key turning point in the history of post-war Britain. It was, in Nigel Lawson's words, the fork in the road, which might have made Thatcherism unnecessary. In the short run, it appeared sensible. Later, in 1952, import prices started falling, giving Britain a windfall benefit to the terms of trade. The 1950s seemed to be a period of affluence, and the fears held in 1951 and early 1952 appeared exaggerated. More recently, however, the forebodings which animated the advocates of Robot have been shown to be not without foundation. The British economic problem seemed to be due not to short-term readjustment, but to a long-term failure of productivity and market rigidities fuelled by the corporate consensus which the Churchill government sustained instead of destroying. Writing in the 1980s, Lord Plowden, an opponent of Robot in 1951, declared that there was a 'lack of appreciation of how weak economically this country had become. I do not believe that, at that time, any Minister, shadow Minister, official, journalist, commentator or the general public truly grasped the real extent of our economic difficulties

---

[18] Bulpitt and Burnham, 'Operation Robot', p. 26.
[19] Ibid., p. 3.

and our economic weakness'.[20] From this point of view, Robot was a far-sighted if premature attempt to remedy a condition more serious than it was believed to be. It has been suggested that it was 'a plausible diagnosis of the British disease in the early 1950s and a clever political manoeuvre to confront that disease. In fact, it *was* "too clever by half". In the circumstances of the time its supporters thought it prudent to downplay its real objectives and, as a result, they lost the argument. It was to be some 30 years before the same strategy was again attempted. It was then somewhat inappropriately labelled "Thatcherism".'[21]

The greatness of Britain

In domestic policy, then, Churchill achieved the quiet life which he sought, even if this was at the cost of ignoring deep-seated economic and social problems, problems which were gradually to force themselves to the attention of later governments, both Conservative and Labour. In domestic policy, Churchill went with the tide, with the new consensus created by his wartime administration and by the post-war Labour government. Far from reversing the tide of 'socialism', Churchill legitimised it. In domestic policy, there was less of a transformation between a government of one political colour and another than was to be the case with any change of government until 1997, when the Blair government broadly accepted the social and economic dispensation which had been bequeathed to it by the Conservatives.

In foreign policy, Churchill's task seemed more difficult. To go along with the tide meant acquiescing with a development towards which he felt profound repugnance, the decline of British power. Churchill had been one of the first to appreciate that 'the enduring greatness of Britain and her Empire' was threatened by the rise of the superpowers. At the first wartime summit, in Teheran in 1943, he had said, 'There was I between the Russian bear with arms outstretched and the American buffalo, the poor little English donkey who alone knew the right way home.'[22] This summit, indeed, was more like a two-and-a-half-power conference rather than a three-power conference, so reduced had Britain's influence become. The Attlee government, in Churchill's view, had failed to arrest this decline. Its policy of 'scuttle', of withdrawal from British imperial commitments, had, indeed, accelerated it. Churchill sought, therefore, to reverse the decline of British power.

How he intended to do this was never very clear. But there seemed a precedent. For, in 1940, also, British power had seemed to be in irreversible decline.

---

[20] Edwin Plowden (1989) *An Industrialist at the Treasury: The Post-War Years*, Andre Deutsch, p. 162.

[21] Bulpitt and Burnham, 'Operation Robot', p. 27.

[22] David Dilks, ed. (1971) *The Diaries of Sir Alec Cadogan: 1938–1945*, Cassell, p. 582.

Churchill had overcome decline. He had done so by an act of will, by an obstinate refusal to compromise and surrender even in the face of superior might. By displaying complete confidence that Britain would win the war, by conveying, in both speech and action, a spirit of national self-belief, then surely victory would follow. Churchill, through sheer obstinacy and defiance, succeeded in reversing what seemed to be inevitable defeat. Perhaps the imbalance of power between Britain and the superpowers after the war could be similarly transformed in the more complex, if less dangerous, post-war world. A government which reasserted British strength, which fought against what Churchill had called, in the 1930s, long, drawling tides of drift and surrender, could achieve in peacetime what had been achieved in 1940. If Britain were still to speak and act as if she were a great power, then a great power she would remain. Yet the history of Churchill's peacetime government was to show that Churchill had set himself an impossible aim, that the changes in Britain's global position were not such as could be arrested by an act of will. In 1940, Churchill, as he had been the first to realise, had expressed the deepest wishes of the British people, determined to defeat Hitler, whatever the cost. 'It was,' he said on his 80th birthday in November 1954, 'the nation and the race dwelling all round the globe that had the lion's heart. I had the luck to be called upon to give the roar.' But 'the nation and the race' were by no means committed to preserving British rule over unwilling subjects. Churchill's campaign against Indian self-government had been defeated by the Conservative Party in the 1930s; and, although there were no opinion polls in Britain until 1937, the likelihood is that the majority of the British public were quite indifferent to the preservation of British rule over India. By the 1950s, imperialism appeared, to most of the population, utterly anachronistic. Churchill himself was eventually to recognise that the British people no longer cared – perhaps they never had cared – whether Britain retained the empire. 'I think that I can save the British Empire from anything,' he told Anthony Montague Browne, 'except the British.'[23]

Churchill had a second aim, in addition to the restoration of British power, and that was the preservation of peace between the West and the Soviet Union. This required, in his view, the defusing of international tensions, détente, an end to the Cold War. He believed that the best way of achieving this was through a summit conference, to complete the unfinished business of the 1945 conference at Potsdam. Churchill, indeed, was the first to coin the term 'summit' in an election speech in 1950. He renewed his call, after the death of Stalin in March 1953, when he saw a chink of light in the Soviet monolith of which the West could take advantage. But the call for a summit fell on deaf ears. He was opposed, not only by the Americans, but by his own Cabinet, and by senior diplomats in the Foreign Office. One wonders, however, whether

---

[23] Anthony Montague Browne, *Long Sunset*, p. 41.

they were able to suppress the thought that they had opposed him once before when he had been right and they had been wrong.

We now know that Churchill's intuition served him as well as it had done in the 1930s. There was, indeed, a window of opportunity between Stalin's death in March 1953 and the spring of 1955. During that period, both Malenkov and Beria, the effective leaders of the Soviet Union immediately after the death of Stalin, and also Molotov, the Soviet foreign minister, were prepared to withdraw Soviet troops from East Germany in return for a neutral Germany. The main opponent of this policy was Khrushchev, and with his rise to power from 1955 it came to be removed from the agenda.[24] The withdrawal of Soviet troops from East Germany might well have begun a process of disengagement in Central Europe. But disengagement was the policy, not of the Right in Western Europe, but of the Left, though not of the Attlee government which had opposed it. It was the policy of the SPD in Germany and the Bevanites in Britain. The Left, however, might well have been correct in its belief that even a limited détente, which was all that was possible in the 1950s, would have had beneficial consequences for the internal politics of the Soviet Union, and might well have stimulated some relaxation of the dictatorship. There are indications that Churchill shared this view. But he faced the insuperable difficulty that the policy of disengagement was utterly rejected both by the government of the Federal Republic and also by the United States, as well as by the vast majority of Conservatives, including every single member of his Cabinet. After his retirement, his successor, Anthony Eden, who had been hotly opposed to a summit while Churchill was Prime Minister, reversed his position. But it was too late. By 1955, Malenkov, accused of 'softness', had been displaced by a tough new leader, Nikita Khrushchev. The Geneva summit of that year proved barren of achievement, and 'the spirit of Geneva' proved evanescent. The lines dividing Europe were being frozen, and it would, as the Federal German Chancellor Konrad Adenauer foresaw, take the collapse of communism in the Soviet Union to unfreeze them.

It seemed, then, that an act of will would not be sufficient to secure the restoration of British power. In 1940, Britain had stood alone, and Churchill had enjoyed sufficient authority to ensure that his wishes were carried out. But these were highly exceptional circumstances, and neither of these conditions held in 1951. The global balance of power had changed overwhelmingly to Britain's disadvantage, so that it was difficult, if not impossible, for her to achieve a summit without the support of the United States; while, at home,

---

[24] See, based on Soviet archival and secondary sources, Geoffrey Roberts (2008) 'A Chance for Peace? The Soviet Campaign to End the Cold War, 1953–1955', Cold War International History Project, Woodrow Wilson International Center for Scholars. I am indebted to Geoffrey Warner for this reference.

Churchill was no longer in command of his Cabinet. Indeed, most of his ministers felt that his retirement had been delayed for far too long. They were quite unwilling to allow him the unilateral leaps of policy that had characterised his wartime administration.

But even if these restraints had not been present, an act of will was no longer enough. Britain's diplomatic position was such that crucial choices had to be made. Yet they were, sadly, choices that Churchill's peacetime administration was unable and ill-equipped to make.

Three alternative strategies were open to Britain. The first was to opt out of power politics entirely and become another Switzerland or Norway. That was an option which no leading politicians were prepared to adopt, and which the British public, still intoxicated by the rhetoric of the 'finest hour', would not have allowed them to make. The second was to accept the realities of power politics and settle for the role of a junior partner to the United States, Greece to America's Rome, as Harold Macmillan, condescendingly, put it. The Suez expedition, which occurred just 18 months after Churchill left No. 10, was to provide stark evidence of the weakness of Britain's position when she tried to take an initiative independent of that of the United States. The third alternative, and the only one which gave Britain a chance to play an independent role, was to play a part, and it would almost certainly have been a leading part, in the European movement, whose strength most British politicians greatly underestimated. Britain, had she made the choice, could have played the part that Gaullist France was to play in the 1960s.

In opposition, Churchill had given hints, and sometimes more than hints, that he favoured this third alternative. At Zurich in 1946, he had spoken of 'a remedy which, if it were generally and spontaneously adopted, would, as if by a miracle transform the whole scene and would in a few years make all of Europe, or the greater part of it, as free and happy as Switzerland is today'. That remedy 'can be given in a single word; Unite!' 'We must,' Churchill insisted, 'build a kind of United States of Europe.'[25] In June 1947, introducing what became known as the Marshall Plan, General Marshall, the United States Secretary of State, said that it had been Churchill's call for a United Europe in his Zurich speech that had influenced his belief that the European countries could organise their own economic recovery with financial help from America. But, even earlier, with great prescience, a few days after Alamein in 1942, the first British victory of the war, he wrote to his foreign secretary, Anthony Eden, saying: 'I must admit that thoughts rest primarily in Europe – the revival of the glory of Europe, the parent continent of the modern nations and of civilisation.' He then went on to say: 'Hard as it is to say now, I look forward to a United States

---

[25] Robert Rhodes James, ed. (1974) *Churchill: Complete Speeches 1897–1963*, vol. 7, Chelsea House, p. 7380.

of Europe in which the barriers between the nations will be greatly minimized and unrestricted travel will be possible.'[26] Churchill was the prophet of reconciliation in Europe.

In his Zurich speech, Churchill had said that Britain must be among 'the friends and sponsors of the new Europe'. But, in 1952, he declared that the European Defence Community with its idea of a European Army was meant 'for them and not for us'.[27] It is sometimes suggested, therefore, that Churchill, even in opposition, had thought Britain was not herself a part of the European family, and that is how his position is usually interpreted.

In fact, however, he often went much further, suggesting that Britain should become part of a supranational Europe. At London's Albert Hall, in May 1947, for example, just a few months after his Zurich speech, Churchill spoke of 'the idea of a United Europe in which our country will play a decisive part', and he argued that Britain and France should be the 'founder-partners in this movement'. 'If Europe united is to be a living force,' he concluded, 'Britain will have to play her full part as a member of the European family.'[28] In a speech in the Kingsway Hall, over two years later, in November 1949, he said:

'The French Foreign Minister, M. Schuman, declared in the French Parliament this week that "Without Britain there can be no Europe." This is entirely true. But our friends on the Continent need have no misgivings. Britain is an integral part of Europe, and we mean to play our part in the revival of her prosperity and greatness.' 'No time must be lost,' he continued, 'in discussing the question with the Dominions and seeking to convince them that their interests as well as ours lie in a United Europe.'[29]

Speaking in the House of Commons in June 1950, Churchill declared that: 'The Conservative and Liberal parties say, without hesitation, that we are prepared to consider, and if convinced to accept, the abrogation of national sovereignty provided that we are satisfied with the conditions and the safeguards. – The Conservative and Liberal parties declare that national sovereignty is not inviolable, and that it may be resolutely diminished for the sake of all the men in all the lands finding their way home together.' He cited the French saying, 'Les absents sont toujours tort.'[30]

Yet, in office, as Prime Minister from 1951 to 1955, Churchill did nothing to link Britain with the European movement; and, in particular, he followed the

---

[26] Quoted in Harold Macmillan (1969) *Tides of Fortune, 1945–1955*, Macmillan, p. 701.

[27] Michael Charlton (1983) *The Price of Victory*, BBC Books, p. 137.

[28] Rhodes James, *Churchill: Complete Speeches*, pp. 7484–5, 7487.

[29] Ibid., p. 7900.

[30] Ibid., vol. 8, pp. 8026, 8022.

previous Labour government in refusing to join the European Coal and Steel Community, forerunner of the European Community, so that, by the end of his premiership in 1955, Britain was in the position which it was so long to occupy, of being outside the mainstream of European development.

In 1940, Churchill had pressed for Anglo-French union, the complete merging of the two countries into one, in a desperate but unavailing attempt to keep France in the war – a proposal that was to be revived by French premier, Guy Mollet, during the time of Suez. If it had been right at a moment of supreme crisis such as 1940 for Britain to take the risk of merging sovereignty, it was clear, surely, that Britain's security was inextricably linked with that of the Continent. And, in 1954, the Churchill government was to accept the logic of this, agreeing to the permanent stationing of British troops and of a tactical air force on the Continent. But Churchill was unwilling to accept the obvious corollary of British participation in the political or economic future of Europe.

In a lecture delivered in 1954, Sir Oliver Franks, a former Ambassador to the United States, declared that he would surprise his audience by saying that 10 August 1952 was the most important date in the post-war history of Western Europe. That was because 'It was the day on which the Schuman Plan became a reality.'[31] The inauguration of the Schuman Plan was a key moment. For it proved to the Continental countries that they could integrate without Britain. The leadership position which Britain had held, until then, the deference and respect which every European country had paid to Britain, began, from that time, to lessen. Britain would no longer be in a position to shape the future of Europe. Britain has still never quite caught up, never quite been able to overcome the strategic mistakes made in 1950 and 1951, mistakes for which Churchill's government was as much responsible as its predecessor, Attlee's Labour government. Britain's failure to join the Coal and Steel Community cost her the leadership of Europe, which she had enjoyed from the end of the war. And it made it much less likely that Britain would participate in the next stage, the second stage of European integration, the Treaty of Rome creating the European Economic Community, signed in 1957. Indeed, perhaps the roots of de Gaulle's veto of Britain's applications, in 1963 and 1967, lie in Britain's refusal to join the Coal and Steel Community, and what it showed about Britain's attitude of detachment from the continent. De Gaulle's veto was, in a sense, a response to British faint-heartedness in 1951. So it was that Britain became, for many years, an outsider, a supplicant, objecting to the visions of others while having no real vision of her own.

---

[31] Oliver Franks (1955) *Britain and the Tide of World Affairs: The BBC Reith Lectures 1954*, Oxford University Press, pp. 23–4.

How do we explain this discrepancy between Churchill's attitude towards Europe in opposition and his attitude in office? The answer reveals much about British assumptions during the immediate post-war era.

One reason lies in Churchill's attachment to the white Commonwealth, which he always preferred to call the Empire. He never appreciated the significance of the transformation of the African and Asian Empire, a relationship based on dominance, to the Commonwealth, a relationship based on equals. He assumed that the newly independent members of the Commonwealth would continue to follow the lead of Britain in world affairs. That would enable Britain to remain at the centre of a power bloc, so that she could remain a great power, one of the Big Three. When Harold Macmillan sought – unsuccessfully as it turned out – to enter the European Community in 1961, Churchill, quite uncharacteristically, could not make up his mind. He wrote to the chair of his constituency party:

> For many years I have believed that measures to promote European unity were essential to the well-being of the West. In a speech at Zurich I urged the creation of the European Family, and I am sometimes given credit for stimulating the ideals of European unity which led to the formation of the economic and the other two communities. – We might well play a great part in these great developments to the profit not only of ourselves, but of our European friends. But we have another role which we cannot abdicate: that of leader of the British Commonwealth. In my conception of a unified Europe, I never contemplated the diminution of the Commonwealth. The application for membership is the sole way in which, so to speak, a reconnaissance can be carried out to find out for certain whether terms for British membership of the Community could be agreed which would meet our special needs as well as those of the Commonwealth – To sum up my views, I would say this: I think that the Government are right to apply to join the EEC, not because I am yet convinced that we shall be able to join, but because there appears to be no other way by which we can find out exactly whether the conditions of membership are acceptable.[32]

By 1961, Churchill, it is clear, had come to believe that the Commonwealth was a fundamental obstacle, although the French had been able, as founder members of the European Community, to secure perfectly good safeguards for their own colonies. Even so, he wrote to the Belgian statesman, Paul-Henri Spaak, after de Gaulle's veto in 1963, that 'The future of Europe if Britain were to be excluded is bleak indeed.' But he did not send the letter.[33]

---

[32] Montague Browne, *Long Sunset*, pp. 273–4.
[33] Ibid., p. 273.

The Commonwealth, then, was one reason for Churchill's hesitancy over Europe. But there is an even more fundamental factor. It was his view of Britain's relationship with the United States, the so-called 'special relationship', something that, with an American mother, he was bound to feel with great intensity. In the nineteenth century, Bismarck had said that the key to the twentieth century would be that the Americans spoke English. The years of Churchill's active political life – from 1900 to 1955 – were also the years when, at least, in Britain's eyes, the special relationship was at its closest. Churchill believed, with some reason, that a strong alliance between Britain and the United States could have prevented both world wars, just as, in the post-war world, it was proving instrumental in preventing a third world war with the Soviet Union. But Churchill went even further than this. For he hoped for some sort of political union, ill-defined admittedly, between the Commonwealth and the United States. He sought a union of the English-speaking peoples. In 1958, he concluded the fourth and final volume of his book, *A History of the English-Speaking Peoples*, with the words:

> The future is unknowable, but the past should give us hope. Nor should we seek to define precisely **the exact terms of ultimate union.** [My emphasis][34]

Of course, Britain alone could not hope to match the power and wealth of the United States, but, as Churchill had said in his November 1949 speech, 'Britain cannot be thought of as a single state in isolation. She is the founder and centre of a world-wide Empire and Commonwealth.'[35] Yet the Commonwealth, whatever its value, could never be a power bloc as the Empire seemed to have been. It could constrain British policy, as it was later to do over Rhodesia; it could not strengthen it. Britain, therefore, could no longer remain an imperial power. This meant that she could no longer remain a global power. That was a conclusion that Churchill was unwilling to accept. In this he was perhaps at one with the British people, as he had been in 1940.

Union with the United States was, of course, quite unrealistic. The Americans never took it seriously. In 1953, after Churchill's visit to the United States for talks with his old wartime comrade, Eisenhower, the president-elect, wrote in his diary that Churchill 'had developed an almost childlike faith that all of the answers are to be found merely in British-American partnership', adding that 'Winston is trying to relive the days of World War II.'[36] In 1954, the Secretary of State, John Foster Dulles, after talks with Churchill, told Eisenhower: 'The Prime

---

[34] Winston Churchill (1962) *A History of the English-Speaking Peoples*, vol. 4, Cassell, p. 304.

[35] Rhodes James, *Churchill: Complete Speeches*, vol. 7, p. 7900.

[36] Robert H. Ferrell, ed. (1981) *The Eisenhower Diaries*, Norton, p. 233.

Minister followed his usual line. He said only the English-speaking peoples counted, that together they could rule the world.'[37] The Suez crisis, in October 1956, just 18 months after Churchill's retirement as prime minister, showed that the special relationship with the United States, to the extent that it existed, was one of superior to subordinate. It could never be a relationship of equals.

The Left, oddly enough, did not put forward any realistic global strategy in opposition to that of the Churchill administration. Indeed, the more it seemed that the Empire–Commonwealth was no longer a power bloc, the more the Left came to embrace it. Both Attlee and Gaitskell were opposed to a British orientation towards the Continent primarily because of the claims of the Commonwealth. The Bevanites, and later the Campaign for Nuclear Disarmament, hoped that Britain could remain a global power through the force of moral example. It was a form of imperialism without tears. The years of Churchill's peacetime premiership were years of illusion in which almost all British political participated. Instead of giving a lead, they comforted not only the British people, but also perhaps themselves with fond illusions.

Churchill understood that the war had undermined Britain's international position. But he saw it as essentially a temporary phenomenon, something that could be transformed through an act of will. He did not appreciate that the war had **permanently** undermined Britain's international position so that she would never be a great power again. Britain could never return to her pre-war role, and, indeed, many of her problems arose from trying to do so. Churchill could not fully appreciate that the era of empire, even though it had so strongly coloured Britain's sense of national identity for so long, was an aberrant period in her long history. Britain's imperial experience, important as it was, was nevertheless a deviation, while her link to the Continent was a fundamental axiom of her existence.

Churchill, as we have seen, saw as the central purpose of his political career 'the maintenance of the enduring greatness of Britain and her Empire'. Yet the central theme of his political career, which lasted from 1900 to 1955, was the **decline** of British power. Perhaps this decline was inevitable, perhaps no one could have arrested it, but it was decline all the same. And Churchill recognised it. He told a political colleague, Lord Boothby, towards the end of his life:

> Historians are apt to judge war ministers less by the victories achieved under their direction than by the political results which flowed from them. Judged by that standard, I am not sure that I shall be held to have done very well.[38]

[37] Peter Boyle, 'The "Special Relationship" with Washington' in John W. Young (1988) *The Foreign Policy of Churchill's Peacetime Administration, 1951–1955*, Leicester University Press, p. 33.
[38] Lord Boothby (1978) *Boothby: Recollections of a Rebel*, Hutchinson, pp. 183–4.

In retirement, he told his private secretary, Anthony Montague Browne, that he was a failure. When Browne demurred, perhaps thinking perhaps that the old man was gaga, Churchill said: 'I have worked very hard all my life, and I have achieved a great deal – in the end to achieve NOTHING' – the last word, according to Browne, 'falling with sombre emphasis'.[39]

Churchill is often said to have been too senile to have been an effective peace-time prime minister. Roy Jenkins declares him 'gloriously unfit for office' in 1951.[40] In December 1951, the French president, Vincent Auriol, recorded in his diary that he had found 'a man whose is hearing is poor and who often repeats himself'. Massigli, the French Ambassador, reported to the Quai d'Orsay in June 1954 that 'he is still active only in appearance;' and in September 1954 he reported that 'At the moment, there is no British government.'[41] In May 1953, shortly before the stroke which nearly killed Churchill, Herbert Blankenhorn, an aide to Adenauer, the German Chancellor, wrote in his diary:

> Churchill sometimes gives an uninformed, absent-minded impression and when he wakes from his dreams and poses questions they are often off the point. The old man sits heavily in his chair, his left eye waters, and if he tries to give a connected opinion – such as on the British desire for peace – he seems, as often with old men, on the edge of tears. It is hardly credible that this man, despite his physical condition, should lead the British Empire. The Chancellor sometimes gets a poor impression from his interlocutor's mistakes and makes notes of his concern on a piece of paper which he pushes over to me.

Sir Ivone Kirkpatrick, Permanent Under-Secretary at the Foreign Office, reassured Adenauer that the Foreign Office kept a constant eye on the Prime Minister.[42]

There can be little doubt that Churchill was ill-equipped to carry out the normal day-to-day business of the premiership. Cabinet meetings began with long rambling monologues and reminiscences of wartime glories. The detailed interventions based on practical knowledge which had served Britain so well during the war were no longer possible. Churchill was unable to provide executive or administrative leadership. He could act neither as chairman of the board nor as micro-manager of the administration. If the premiership were primarily an executive or administrative position, then Churchill was certainly not fit for office.

---

[39] Montague Browne, *Long Sunset*, pp. 302–3.
[40] Roy Jenkins (2001) *Churchill*, Palgrave Macmillan, p. 845.
[41] Maurice Vaïsse, 'Churchill and France, 1951–55' in R.A.C. Parker (1995) *Winston Churchill: Studies in Statesmanship*, Brassey's, paperback ed. 2002, p. 164.
[42] Hans-Peter Schwarz, 'Churchill and Adenauer' in Parker, *Winston Churchill*, p. 174.

Political leadership, however, does not consist solely or even mainly in executive or administrative action, but in teaching, in creating an atmosphere that can inspire the nation. That was what Churchill had done during the war. Attlee was once asked what Churchill had done to win the war. 'He talked about it,' Attlee had replied laconically. In 1940, Churchill had detected the underlying attitude of the British people, that they did not want to give in to Hitler. In 1951, too, he had detected the underlying attitude of the British people. They wanted a period of peace and quiet; they yearned for consolidation after the reforms and upheavals of the Attlee years. 'We meet together here,' Churchill told the newly elected House of Commons in 1951, 'with an apparent gulf between us as great as I have known in fifty years of House of Commons life. What the nation needs is several years of quiet, steady administration, if only to allow socialist legislation to reach its full fruition.'[43] That was what Churchill offered.

The most vital role of the prime minister is to give a sense of direction to the government and to the country, and, in these terms, Churchill in his domestic policy did not fail. That, perhaps, is ironic, since Churchill knew less about economics than he did about foreign policy and defence, and was perhaps less interested in domestic matters than in the grand themes of foreign affairs.

But, in foreign policy, the area of Churchill's greatest expertise, Churchill led Britain in the wrong direction – towards the reassertion of imperial glory, towards a junior position vis-à-vis the United States, and away from Europe. In this his position was little different from that of the Attlee government, indeed from every British government until the premiership of Edward Heath in 1970. Admittedly, even if Churchill had retired in 1945, it is difficult to imagine any of senior colleagues following a very different policy. Indeed, his successor, Anthony Eden, was perhaps the least sympathetic of any member of the Churchill cabinet towards European integration – though Eden would not have fought a rearguard action to preserve untenable imperial positions. So Churchill's decision to continue in politics after the war made less alteration to the history of post-war Britain than might at first sight appear. During his peacetime premiership, Churchill reflected the spirit of his times. He did not, as he had in the 1930s, challenge it.

There was much less difference between the Churchill and Attlee governments than was generally thought at the time. In retrospect, Churchill's role can be seen to be to have legitimised the Attlee settlement by making it the property of the nation as a whole rather than of just that part of the nation which voted Labour. One's judgment on his peacetime premiership, therefore, depends on one's judgment of the effectiveness of that settlement. During the 1950s, it was largely unquestioned. Later, and particularly during

---

[43] House of Commons Debates, 5th series, vol. 495, col. 68, 6 November 1951.

the era of Margaret Thatcher, it came to be argued that Attlee had led Britain in precisely the opposite direction from that in which it ought to have gone. Nationalisation, economic management on broadly Keynesian lines, 'free' public services, a powerful role for the trade unions and, above all, statism seemed to have been the cause of the British disease, not the cure. Margaret Thatcher, of course, approved of the distancing from Europe of the Attlee and Churchill governments, but by the end of the 1960s both Labour and Conservative governments had tacitly admitted this to be a mistake, since both now sought to join the European Community. Britain, from being a leader in Europe, had become a supplicant.

The post-war settlement, it might be suggested, had become, by 1951, so popular and well-entrenched – in particular the belief that Britain as a great power had no need of Europe – that it would have been electorally suicidal for any government to challenge it. Yet, Churchill was in a different position from other prime ministers. His prestige was such that he, and perhaps he alone, could have persuaded the British people to come to terms with their changed role in the world. He, and perhaps he alone, could have persuaded the British people to take the lead in building a new European power bloc. He, and he alone, could have been the British de Gaulle. But would he have wanted to do so? By 1951, probably not. Perhaps he was simply too old. But, whatever the reason, the Churchillian myth, having been essential for survival in 1940, was now a hindrance to Britain's understanding of her position in the world. In the late 1960s, the historian A.J.P. Taylor said presciently that Churchill was 'best described by words which were written about Bismarck in old age: "He was no beginning, but an end, a grandiose final chord – a fulfiller – not a prophet".'[44]

Every hero, Emerson once declared, becomes a bore at last. Sadly, not even Churchill was able to remain exempt from that rule.

---

[44] A.J.P. Taylor (1969) 'Churchill: The Statesman', reprinted in Taylor (2008) *From the Boer War to the Cold War: Essays in Twentieth-Century Europe*, Faber, p. 443.

3
Anthony Eden, 1955–1957
David Carlton

Introduction

There is surely no doubt that Anthony Eden's brief premiership, which lasted from April 1955 until January 1957, will always be remembered primarily for his extraordinary handling of the rising tensions in the Middle East, culminating in the British invasion of and retreat from Egypt invariably known as 'the Suez Affair'. And in this brief account reflections on this theme will necessarily predominate. But it is perhaps appropriate to devote at least some attention to aspects of his premiership that are now scarcely ever the subject of comment among political pundits or even among professional historians. Yet had the international scene during 1955–1957 been less turbulent – as was the case, for example, during the similarly brief Premiership of James Callaghan from 1976 to 1979 – reflections on Eden's domestic record would, *faute de mieux*, be more widely disseminated.

The domestic record

A first point that is rarely made, but surely should be, is that Eden was the only prime minister in modern times who, succeeding to the post rather than elected to it as a result of a vote of the populace, volunteered to seek a mandate from that populace almost immediately after moving into No. 10. Many other prime ministers have, of course, had the experience of kissing hands without previously winning a general election. And when they have done so they are invariably urged to 'go to the country' by political opponents and by media pundits who tend to pontificate about the lack of authority a new incumbent suffers and even on occasion to rant about an outright 'constitutional outrage'. But only Eden has ever followed such counsels before even receiving them. Some successor prime ministers have, of course, had the effrontery to serve for as long as legally permissible. For example, in October 1963, Alec

Douglas-Home succeeded a supposedly sick Harold Macmillan four years into a Parliament, but brazenly served on until the last possible date one year later. And in the late 1970s Callaghan, after being chosen to succeed Harold Wilson by a Parliamentary Labour Party that even lacked a secure majority in the House of Commons, struggled through miserable years of crisis until he was humiliatingly brought down by a vote of no confidence on the floor of the House. He was then decisively defeated by the voters. Gordon Brown, similarly, refused to face the electorate when he succeeded Tony Blair in 2007. Neville Chamberlain, by contrast, never faced the electorate at all. He succeeded Stanley Baldwin in May 1937 and, three years later, handed on the baton to Winston Churchill even though he had just won a vote of confidence on the floor of the House, albeit on a majority reduced from the normal 200 to 81. Eden, on the other hand, showed unusual courage in 1955. After moving into No. 10 on 6 April he waited only nine days before announcing that a general election would be held on 26 May. He succeeded in turning an overall Conservative majority of 17 into one of 60. But, had he lost, his premiership would have lasted for less than two months. This would have been a record nobody else has come close to matching since the introduction of universal suffrage in 1928. Even the visibly tempted Gordon Brown would have had a five-month premiership had he chosen, as at one point seemed likely, to go to the country in November 2007. Here, then, was a remarkable demonstration of courageous risk-taking on Eden's part – perhaps made all the less explicable when we recall that he was held by many contemporaries to be unusually vain about his reputation. But neither should we forget that he had been awarded the Military Cross during the First World War. Thus, committing an act of reckless valour was nothing new to him. And some would no doubt say that he acted in much the same way when tormented beyond endurance by his Egyptian and American enemies in 1956.

On the other hand, courageous decisiveness was far from apparent in Eden's approach to domestic politics more generally, not only during his premiership but throughout his long ministerial career. On the contrary, he seems to have been determined to avoid putting at risk the reputation he had built up, ever since becoming a front-bencher in the House of Commons in 1931, of being an undogmatic one-nation Conservative apparently ready to accept every reform except perhaps the next. His own family background lay with the landed gentry, but he avoided close association with the stridently reactionary 'Colonel Blimps' and 'Sir Tufton Buftons' on the Conservative benches. Instead, he was happy to have as patrons Austen Chamberlain and Baldwin, both of whom were reformists from middle-class families with close ties to West Midlands industry rather than to the traditional shires. And, during the almost 15 years that the patrician Churchill was Conservative leader, Eden took care to position himself slightly to the left of his chief on domestic questions. Nor was this a mere political calculation. Indeed, during the Second World War Eden had privately fantasised about working in the post-war world with moderate Labour and Liberal figures, on the assumption that the die-hard Conservatives were finished and that the principal opposition to a centre grouping would come from the Communists.[1]

Thus it was Churchill, not Eden, who had doubts about implementing the Beveridge Report, and who in 1945 recklessly compared alleged Labour liking for regimentation with that of the Gestapo. But, of course, both men had broadly accepted Labour's creation of the post-war welfare state, its commitment to maintaining full employment and its approach to managing the economy along lines that later came to be called corporatist. So when Eden finally succeeded Churchill in No. 10, constantly offering platitudes about favouring a property-owning democracy, he was more than willing to preside over 'business as usual' and, incidentally, to retain in post most of the members of his predecessor's Cabinet.

Though a liberal by reputation, Eden was also to be quite unadventurous in pushing for any advances in directions that would have appealed, say, to most readers of *The Manchester Guardian*. A decade later, by contrast, Roy Jenkins, as Home Secretary in Wilson's Labour Government, facilitated the passing of a variety of measures that produced, for good or ill, a social transformation – easier divorce; homosexual law reform; abortion law reform; the ending of theatre censorship; and the abolition of capital punishment. Perhaps, if Eden had served a full term, the 1950s, rather than the 1960s, would have been the 'liberal hour'. For Eden, who was certainly no puritan, gave few signs during the 1950s or later, other than possibly on capital punishment, of being basically out of sympathy with Jenkins. After all, he himself had been divorced in 1950 and remarried in 1953, with the Church Times piously editorialising that he could not have continued as Foreign Secretary had these events occurred a generation earlier and that 'the world is rejecting the law of Christ in this as in so much else'. His latest biographer, D.R. Thorpe, asserts, moreover, that 'he personally had little time for organised religion'.[2] And in his social life generally he was known to be quite relaxed in rather Bohemian company; he was an avid reader of 'advanced' French novels, considered Henry Fielding's *Tom Jones* to be an outstanding work of English fiction, and enjoyed watching stage plays containing 'broad' humour, for example John Gay's *Polly*, a play that had at one time been banned by the Lord Chamberlain. Yet Eden's retention throughout his

---

[1] See David Carlton (1981) *Anthony Eden: A Biography*, Allen Lane, p. 185; and David Dutton (1997) *Anthony Eden: A Life and Reputation*, Arnold, pp. 251–2.

[2] *Church Times* quoted in Carlton, *Anthony Eden*, p. 318; and D.R. Thorpe (2004) *Eden: The Life and Times of Anthony Eden, First Earl of Avon, 1897–1977*, Chatto and Windus, p. 446.

premiership of Gwilym Lloyd George, not known for reforming zeal, as Home Secretary suggests that he had little interest in legislating for social change and would not have developed a different attitude even had he served a full term. A preference for 'letting sleeping dogs lie' was equally apparent when Lloyd George did propose a reform, even if it was not seen as a progressive or a liberal one, namely curbing the growing influx of Commonwealth immigrants. Eden moved decisively to block this suggestion, which would have dented his reputation for being vaguely progressive. Peter Thorneycroft, the President of the Board of Trade, recalled: '... the failure to act was a collective Cabinet responsibility...but...Eden would have been the dominant influence and he was never anxious for controversial domestic legislation'.[3]

Similar diffidence or even timidity may be discerned over most matters relating to the management of the economy during his premiership. He had certainly played a major part at a seminal juncture during Churchill's last premiership by blocking Treasury efforts, supported by R.A. Butler, to move sterling towards convertibility – the 'Robot' plan of 1952 – though his approach does not appear to have been based on any strong grasp of international economics but rather on a political instinct that such a policy departure would have disturbed the post-war national consensus by 'sacrificing the controlled economy and full employment'.[4] And as Prime Minister he similarly did little or nothing to encourage any radical rethinking on how to tackle the country's poor economic growth record, lack of investment or the restrictive practices that stymied efforts to increase productivity. It is noteworthy that he retained Churchill's Minister of Labour, Sir Walter Monckton. The latter was known to favour close and above all non-provocative relations with the leading trade unionists of the day, who were moderate men opposed to shop floor militancy, but who also vetoed any significant overhaul of the laws governing industrial relations. As Monckton wrote in a 'defeatist' Cabinet Paper, from which Eden did not dissent: 'Unless we carry with us the responsible elements, who are at present in a majority, we run the risk of uniting the whole movement against us.'[5] In the light of the industrial strife that prevailed during the era from Wilson to Thatcher, it is of course all too easy to argue that Eden's policy of benign neglect at a time when major unions were in non-Marxist hands lacked vision and was thus not greatly to his credit. On the other hand, such verdicts may savour of hindsight. For had Eden been more proactive in stimulating the Ministry of Labour into

---

[3] Quoted in Richard Lamb, (1987) *The Failure of the Eden Government*, Sidgwick and Jackson, p. 23.
[4] Evelyn Shuckburgh (1986) *Descent to Suez: Diaries 1951–56*, Weidenfeld and Nicolson, p. 37.
[5] Lamb, *Failure of the Eden Government*, p. 26.

promoting radical reforming policies he might now stand accused of 'stirring up a hornet's nest'.

During 1955–1957 the Treasury, too, showed few signs of wishing to confront the problems underlying the country's sclerotic economic performance. But perhaps this was only to be expected when Eden himself had no seriously innovative ideas to offer, notwithstanding his inclination to offer unwelcome advice on points of relatively trivial detail. For example, when facing a worsening economic situation in the summer of 1955, his principal concern appears to have been with putting the right kind of 'spin', as we would now call it, on whatever was done. Tellingly, he wrote in his diary on 26 August: 'We must not appear like the hard-faced men of 1918.'[6] Again, when he saw fit to switch Chancellors almost half-way through his short tenure it was not done to effect a major change of economic course but rather to enable him to place a pliable subaltern at the Foreign Office. At the end of 1955, Macmillan replaced Butler by moving from the Foreign Office to the Exchequer, thereby enabling Selwyn Lloyd to become Foreign Secretary. It was perhaps appropriate, therefore, that during the Suez Crisis Eden appears to have been taken by surprise when a fatal run on sterling developed. Of course, as is invariably stressed, a well-briefed Macmillan had earlier neglected fully to inform Eden about the pound's vulnerability – about which the former was clearly warned in September 1956 by Sir Edward Bridges, the Permanent Under-Secretary to the Treasury. On the other hand, as is less often stressed, Eden took no adequate steps to find out for himself whether the country was at all prepared to face a turbulent period in the international financial arena.[7]

This points us towards the most likely explanation for Eden's lacklustre performance as a prime minister on the domestic front, where the people or at least the *Daily Telegraph* famously waited in vain for the smack of firm government.[8] It is that he lacked detailed knowledge about, and had little passion for, anything that was not focused on foreign policy – and even then only on

---

[6] Dutton, *Anthony Eden*, p. 278.

[7] It is not without interest, however, that on 28 December 1956, following the Suez ceasefire, Eden, still Prime Minister, wrote to Macmillan and suggested that 'we should ask the Governor [of the Bank of England] whether there is any means of reducing our vulnerability to the "confidence factor". He continued: 'This inevitably springs from our position as bankers for the Sterling Area. As such we no doubt derive benefits. But do these offset the damage our reserves suffer when sterling is under pressure?' (Dutton, *Anthony Eden*, p. 275). This shows that Eden was by no means an economic neophyte, as some historians assume. But it does not show him to have been deeply and continuously interested in the management of the British economy. For otherwise would he not have had discussions on the Sterling Area with Macmillan during the preceding months without needing at this late stage of his premiership to have to think of asking the Bank Governor for guidance?

[8] Carlton, *Anthony Eden*, p. 389.

foreign policy as traditionally understood. To some extent he was not to blame for this. For during his entire career on the Government and Opposition front benches stretching almost continuously from 1931 to 1955 he had never held any domestic portfolio. He had been a junior minister at the Foreign Office; three times Foreign Secretary; Dominions Secretary; Secretary of State for War; and Shadow Foreign Secretary. On the other hand, during almost 15 years as an heir apparent under Churchill's leadership he never once appears to have pressed to be given an opportunity to handle a domestic brief. And in 1952 Eden showed no enthusiasm when those close to Churchill suggested that he might like to leave the Foreign Office to become the Government's Home Affairs supremo.[9] So it seems fair to conclude that his lack of experience was in large part of his own making.

The corollary to this undoubted weakness on Eden's part is that nobody ever first came to the premiership with so much experience in the world of diplomacy – though it is a moot point whether this did him or his country much good. At all events, it is to this theme that the remainder of this essay must be devoted.

International affairs

Introduction

In 1977 *The Times* wrote of Eden: 'He was the last prime minister to believe that Britain was a great power and the first to confront a crisis which proved she was not.' This was a verdict I endorsed in a book about the Suez Crisis published in 1988.[10] But perhaps I did so too readily. At all events, 30 years after Eden's death, it may be that a new perspective is beginning to emerge. For, as Churchill generously and presciently said of Neville Chamberlain at the time of his death in November 1940: 'In one phase men seem to have been right, in another they seem to have been wrong. Then again, a few years later, when the perspective of time has lengthened, all stands in a different setting. There is another proportion. There is another scale of values.'[11]

So I do not want here to attempt to retell in any detail the familiar story of the Suez Crisis, but rather to reflect on whether *The Times*'s verdict on Eden can today be seriously challenged. Three possible revisionist approaches will be considered. First, was Eden really the last prime minister to believe that Britain was a great power? Secondly, was he actually the first to confront a

---

[9] Dutton, *Anthony Eden*, pp. 266–7.

[10] David Carlton (1988) *Britain and the Suez Crisis*, Blackwell, p. 11.

[11] Martin Gilbert (1983) *Finest Hour: Winston S. Churchill, 1939–1941*, Heinemann, p. 283.

crisis which proved that she was not? Finally, is it possible that Eden himself was a far greater realist than has usually been recognised and that his approach to the seminal Suez Crisis, in which Britain, France and Israel colluded to attack Egypt in 1956, was based neither on hubris nor mental and physical illness? In short, did he see himself as engaged on an almost desperate bid to avoid both a national and a personal humiliation and on a bold quest to steer his country away from excessive subordination to Washington and towards a new and surprisingly modest strategic alignment in the world?

Did any prime ministers after Eden suffer from delusions of national grandeur?

At least three recent prime ministers appear to some extent to have done so. Wilson was one. For it was he who asserted that Britain's frontiers lay on the Himalayas just before being driven by domestic party pressure to promise to withdraw all British forces from 'East of Suez', including those based in even friendly sheikhdoms in the Persian Gulf.[12] Wilson, too, most economists now agree, clung too long to delusions about the importance of the Sterling Area, with dire consequences for British growth and in terms of national humiliation when the pound was finally forcibly devalued in November 1967. Immediately afterwards the Wilson government's application to join the European Economic Community – which had, predictably, been handled with far too little humility – produced a contemptuous veto from France's President Charles de Gaulle.

Another recent prime minister to behave at times as Eden is supposed to have done was Margaret Thatcher. It was not for nothing that she was widely criticised for practicing 'megaphone diplomacy'. There was, for example, her public failure to prevent the reunification of Germany when Paris and Bonn had signalled a clear intention to bring it about and when even Washington was acquiescent; there was also her personal crusade, in the face of opposition from the Europeans and the Commonwealth, to have no dealings with the African National Congress, which she initially publicly branded as 'a typical terrorist organisation', but that ended with her having to receive Nelson Mandela in Downing Street.[13]

Finally, we can now see that Blair is unlikely to go down in 'history' as a suitably modest leader of a country which, after all, possesses only 1 per cent of the world's population and is merely a regional power with fundamental assets quite similar to those of, say, Italy. For, in Blair's own words, he sees Britain as a

---

[12] Philip Ziegler (1993) *Wilson: The Authorised Life of Lord Wilson of Rievaulx*, Weidenfeld and Nicolson, p. 211.

[13] Geoffrey Howe (1994) *Conflict of Loyalty*, Macmillan, p. 499.

'pivotal player' in the world[14] a claim presumably mainly based on its leadership of the ramshackle Commonwealth and its possession of a UN Security Council veto, notwithstanding the fact that, ironically, this was last exercised to the displeasure of Washington half a century ago by Eden. And Blair, of course, greatly overestimates – as incidentally do many of his critics – Britain's role in toppling Saddam Hussein. The administration of George W. Bush was unalterably determined from quite early in 2002 to do this – and alone if necessary. But its members, with the exception of Donald Rumsfeld, were simply too polite to tell the British that their participation or lack of it would make no essential difference.

Mention of the British relationship with Washington does, however, prompt the reflection that Eden's clashes with the Eisenhower administration are what decisively distinguish him from Wilson, Thatcher and Blair. And in one view, by daring to confront Washington, Eden is thus clearly confirmed as the last prime minister to believe his country to be a truly great power. On the other hand, during the Suez Crisis France was also 'Edenite' in its lack of deferential respect for Washington, and, indeed, rather more so at times. And, of course, under de Gaulle and his numerous successors as President of the Fifth Republic, France has since stuck steadily to such an approach. Yet it has broadly accepted, ever since the loss of Indochina in 1954, that it is a regional rather than a truly global power. So maybe to be an 'Edenite' in London in 1956 was merely to be a British proto-Gaullist rather than to be a peddler of more unrealistic pretensions such as some would associate with Wilson, Thatcher and Blair. In short, perhaps Eden was not the last British prime minister to believe that Britain was a great power but rather the only one so far, with the possible exception of Edward Heath, who incidentally served as Eden's Chief Whip during the Suez Crisis, to realise that she had the resources to be little more than a regional power?

Were prime ministers before Eden driven to recognise that Britain might no longer be a great power?

A case can certainly be made for this proposition. Let us confine our analysis to Eden's three immediate predecessors, with all of whom he served in office. Let us begin with Chamberlain. He began his premiership in May 1937, with Eden as his Foreign Secretary. In private, at least, Chamberlain was keenly aware of the limits set to British power. In January 1938, for example, he wrote to a correspondent:

We are a very rich and a very vulnerable Empire, and there are plenty of poor adventurers not very far away who look on us with hungry eyes...we

---

[14] Peter Mangold, `British Foreign Policy: Pivotal Power', *The World Today*, March 2002, pp. 25–6.

are in no position to enter lightheartedly upon war with such a formidable power as Germany, much less if Germany were aided by Italian attacks on our Mediterranean possessions and communications.[15]

And at a meeting of the Committee of Imperial Defence in July 1938 he said:

The ideal, no doubt, was to be prepared to fight Germany or Italy or Japan, either separately or in combination. That, however, was a counsel of perfection which it was impossible to follow. There were limits to our resources, both physical and financial, and it was vain to contemplate fighting single-handed the three strongest Powers in combination. He did not leave out of account that we should probably have allies in such a war, notably France, but France at the present time was not in a very strong position to give us much help....[16]

It was, of course, Eden who failed to see the point and who accordingly resigned, perhaps capriciously, as a protest against Chamberlain's policy of appeasement – not, it should be noted, appeasement of the Germans but rather of the Italians, whom the Prime Minister wanted to detach from their axis with Berlin. So perhaps this evidence tends to fit in with the now traditional view that Eden in 1956 was, as usual, blind to power realities. But perhaps by 1956 he had learnt some lessons from his earlier experiences.

Another of Eden's predecessors was Clement Attlee. And he too was no jingoist, having a keen grasp of the limits of British power during his post-war premiership. He did not, for example, share Foreign Secretary Ernest Bevin's view that the country's 'economic Dunkirk', when it was forced to accept severe American conditions for a massive dollar loan in 1945, would quickly be forgotten, and that the British would soon be back on a level playing field with the Americans and the Russians. And Attlee easily crushed the aspirations of Bevin's successor, Herbert Morrison, to invade Iran after the nationalisation of the British-owned Anglo-Iranian Oil Company's refineries. He spoke words in Cabinet in September 1951, in his succinct way, that most now think Eden should have spoken in 1956: use of force was inexpedient 'in view of the attitude of the United States Government'.[17] Eden, then Shadow Foreign Secretary, while not being explicitly an advocate of war, contrived to imply that he favoured a more robust approach to Iran than that of the Labour Government.

As for Churchill, he too was by no means consistently reckless in playing his country's hand during his two spells in No. 10, from 1940 to 1945 and

---

[15] Keith Feiling (1946) *The Life of Neville Chamberlain*, Macmillan, pp. 323–4.
[16] Carlton, *Anthony Eden*, p. 106.
[17] Carlton, *Britain and the Suez Crisis*, p. 9.

from 1951 to 1955. One example from each term will have to suffice. Urged in 1944 by the Polish Government-in-Exile to confront the Soviet Union over Stalin's brutal plans for their country's future, Churchill's response showed beyond doubt that he could see how little real power Britain would have in the post-war world:

> Britain would always do her best against tyranny in whatever form it showed itself. But Britain, though better situated, was not much bigger than Poland…. It was no good expecting us to do more than we could…. His heart bled for them, but the brutal facts could not be overlooked. He could no more stop the Russian advance than stop the tide coming in.[18]

And he was similarly realistic in recognising that the Soviets must have a free hand in Romania if there was to be any hope of Britain getting a free hand to secure Greece from the threat of a Communist takeover. True to form, however, Eden, then in his second spell as Foreign Secretary, seemed less aware of the limitations of British power. At all events, Churchill felt driven to send to Eden in January 1945 a minute that must rank among the most inhumane that any British prime minister has ever written. Dismayed by the protests to the Soviets being made by British diplomats in Bucharest about the transportation of thousands of Romanian citizens to the Soviet Union for slave labour purposes, Churchill rebuked Eden for not bearing in mind 'what we promised about leaving Roumania's fate to a large extent in Russian hands'. He added: 'I cannot myself consider that it is wrong of the Russians to take Roumanians of any origin they like to work in the Russian coal-fields in view of all that has passed.'[19] Again, in 1954 Churchill was arguably extremely realistic, other than perhaps in a short-run context, in urging on Eden, then in his third spell at the Foreign Office, a policy over Indochina that would not unduly antagonise Eisenhower and his formidable Secretary of State, John Foster Dulles. But Eden prevailed over his Prime Minister, whose health was failing, and in the short run also over Eisenhower and Dulles. Hence Indochina was partitioned at the Geneva Conference. But of course Eden, and Britain, paid a price two years later when the Americans were never more than lukewarm in their support for proposed countermeasures against Egypt after it had nationalised the Suez Canal Company.

This seems to show, then, that all three prime ministers prior to Eden, rather contrary to *The Times*'s judgement, had faced crises that had taught them

---

[18] Martin Gilbert (1986) *Road to Victory: Winston S. Churchill, 1941–1945*, Heinemann, pp. 682–4.

[19] David Carlton (2000) *Churchill and the Soviet Union*, Manchester University Press, p. 120.

that Britain's great power status was at least considerably less than popularly assumed. But the question we must now address is where Eden stood during his own premiership and especially during the Suez Crisis. Did he simply carry on with the approach that had led him to differ so frequently from his predecessors, preferring at times with almost bovine bravado not to countenance policies based on recognition of national decline and blithely disregarding many of the perils that his country increasingly faced? Or did he belatedly see the error of his previous ways? In short, was Suez the time when he finally recognised the need for Britain to become a mere regional power aligned with France at whatever cost to her supposed global role and to the 'Special Relationship' with the United States that Churchill in particular had seen as the only vehicle for preserving it?

Eden and Suez: towards a new perspective?

Arguably the most important point about Eden as a prime minister is that, possibly for the first time in his political life, he became deeply pessimistic on a sustained basis about his country's future prospects. It was central to this pessimism that he had gradually lost all confidence in the United States as a long-term provider of security for any states outside its own hemisphere. Another premiss that guided him was the belief that at the heart of the threat to Britain's interests was not the Soviet Union and World Communism, but, rather, anti-Western Third World dictators, and especially those in the Greater Middle East who had a potential to halt the vital flow of oil to Western Europe. This was, of course, well before the opening up of North Sea energy resources. As he confided to Nikita Khrushchev and Nikolai Bulganin on their state visit to Britain just months before Egypt's seizure of the Suez Canal Company:

> When we discussed the Middle East in London, I told the Russians that the uninterrupted supply of oil was literally vital to our economy. They showed an understanding of our interest and appeared to be willing to meet it. I said I thought I must be absolutely blunt about the oil, because we would fight for it.[20]

As for the 'Special Relationship', Eden believed that it was simply not 'fit for purpose' as a cure for Britain's security woes. For to him Moscow and Peking were the capitals of traditional Great Powers with interests much like any other, whereas he judged the United States to be mistakenly obsessed with the global ideological menace of Communism supposedly driven by fanatical regimes in both these capitals. The corollary, in Eden's view, was that American policymaking was fatally warped and caused the Americans to be insufficiently

---

[20] Anthony Eden (1960) *Full Circle: The Memoirs of Sir Anthony Eden*, Cassell, p. 358.

sophisticated or even knowledgeable to be able effectively to play the leading role in areas of great complexity outside their own hemisphere. And this,
Eden thought, was particularly true of the Middle East, where, for example, he
deplored the largely negative US attitude towards the Baghdad Pact. His judgements on these matters led to his resignation in 1957 and the medium-term
ruin of his reputation. And even by the time of his death two decades later he
was not widely seen to have been vindicated. For the United States, which had
taken over Western leadership from the British in the Middle East, had not
been shown to have performed there in a wholly disastrous fashion; oil, apart
from a brief interruption in 1973, had continued to flow to Western Europe;
and the 'Special Relationship' in general was alive and well under Callaghan
and Jimmy Carter. After a further three decades, however, the state of the
Greater Middle East and the consequent vulnerability of Britain, and indeed
most of Europe, to energy cut-offs may mean that Eden's assumptions may
now deserve a more sympathetic scrutiny.

It is, of course, one thing to be prescient about developments a decade or
so into the future and something quite different, and maybe not particularly
useful from any practical point of view, to achieve a kind of vindication after
half a century or more. Consider Eden's first premiss in 1956, namely that the
Soviet Union and World Communism were not at the heart of the threat to
Britain. Some would argue that events between 1985 and 1991 make his case.
And consider his second premiss, namely that Third World dictators with their
potential to control oil supplies constituted a central threat to British interests.
This is likewise looking quite impressive more than half a century later. But
for decades after Eden's resignation most British leaders and opinion-formers
continued to be mainly obsessed with Soviet ambitions rather than with 'mad
mullahs'. And if we recall, for example, the repeated Berlin Crises, the suppres-
sion of the 'Prague Spring' and, above all, the Cuban Missile Crisis it is not
difficult to understand their reasoning. With hindsight, of course, we can now
see that the Soviets gradually lost their way under the corrupt Leonid Brezhnev
and his gerontocratic successors; and maybe even concede that the Americans
were so overzealous in trying to undermine Soviet control over Afghanistan
that they unwittingly unleashed forces that led to 9/11 and today's chaotic
Middle East. But Eden did not live to see many of these events and did not
forecast them in any detail. The most that can be said, then, is that the decline
and collapse of the Soviet Union as a crusader for Communism and the rise of
a Third World 'Axis of Evil' would have surprised him much less than most of
his contemporaries.

Again, Eden would probably have drawn some wry satisfaction from the
troubles that the administration of George W. Bush has faced, and he would
have welcomed signs that the Anglo-American 'Special Relationship' could
soon become a good deal cooler than at any time since the Suez Crisis. But

it has been a long wait for vindication – and, of course, it may once again be postponed. All the same, we may expect future historians and biographers to be more acutely aware than hitherto about the extent to which Eden in office during the 1950s became irrevocably disillusioned with the Americans – and not only on account of the Suez Crisis. For example, he wrote as early as 1954 to one British diplomat: 'The Americans may think the time past when they need to consider the feelings or difficulties of their allies. It is the conviction that this tendency becomes more pronounced every week that is creating difficulties for anyone in this country who wants to maintain close Anglo-American relations.'[21] And another British diplomat noted in his diary at the time of the Geneva Conference of the same year: '[Eden's] conviction is that all the Americans want is to replace the French and run Indo-China themselves. "They want to replace us in Egypt too. They want to run the world." '[22] Furthermore, in his memoirs Eden went so far as to write of 'an apparent disinclination by the United States Government to take second place even in an area [Egypt] where primary responsibility was not theirs' and of the 'withholding of wholehearted support which their partner in N.A.T.O. had the right to expect'.[23] But if Eden had ceased to believe in the 'Special Relationship' as the basis for preserving British security in general and its energy security in particular, what did he believe was the alternative?

Some may assume that Eden had become by the time of the Suez Crisis, perhaps under the influence of illness, a crude 'Colonel Blimp' believing only in go-it-alone gunboat diplomacy long after the power basis required to underpin such an approach had disappeared. True, Eden back in 1925 had undoubtedly been something of an unreconstructed imperialist, as is illustrated by this extract from what he had to say to the Commons about the possibility of Britain terminating its mandate status in Iraq:

> ... no words, however strong, could exaggerate the harm which we should do to our reputation not only in Iraq, but throughout the East, if we were now to scuttle, like flying curs, at the sight of our own shadow. Hon. Members know that if we pursued a course like that, our name would be a jibe in the mouth of every tavern-lounger from Marrakesh to Singapore. It might take centuries to recover.
>
> I am not myself enamoured of Western forms of government in Eastern lands. With us democracy, whatever its merits or demerits may be, is at least a plant of natural growth. In the East, it is a forced growth, an importation,

---

[21] Ibid., p. 99.
[22] Carlton, *Anthony Eden*, p. 348.
[23] Eden, *Full Circle*, pp. 256–7.

and foreign to the soil. Consequently, it needs many years more to develop and many more to grow to be understood by the people.[24]

But such views had not really been characteristic of Eden at any point during his long service at the Foreign Office. And any close scrutiny of Eden's conduct during the last six months of 1956 will not suggest that patrician 'Blimpishness' had suddenly returned to his thinking. For example, he did not respond to Egypt's nationalisation coup in July with an immediate declaration of war but rather with a willingness, however reluctant, to refer the issue to the United Nations and to enter into other international diplomatic efforts under US sponsorship. And in these negotiations he seems to have been prepared by mid-October to acquiesce in principle to a compromise settlement based on a six-point programme negotiated between British Foreign Secretary, Selwyn Lloyd, and his Egyptian counterpart, Mohammed Fawzi. What may well have destroyed the prospects for this deal was that Eden concluded that 'hawks' in his Cabinet, led by Chancellor of the Exchequer Macmillan, would reject it, would resign if defeated and would brand him an appeaser. The situation was not helped by the fact that the Conservative Party Conference, by chance meeting in mid-October, was also in a belligerent mood. So Eden chose instead to opt for the now well-known, and by any normal standards dishonourable, collusion with France and Israel. The sequel was the abortive attack on Egypt that had to be humiliatingly halted when Macmillan, who, like Churchill but unlike Eden, had an American-born mother, suddenly became a 'dove' in the face of a US-instigated run on sterling. Incidentally, either before or after the ceasefire no fewer than four Cabinet Ministers, Macmillan himself, Butler, Lord Salisbury and Monckton, had disloyal dealings with the American ambassador in London, Winthrop Aldrich, without the knowledge of either No. 10 or the Foreign Office. So, with colleagues capable of such duplicitous conduct, 'damned if he did and damned if he didn't' was probably what awaited Eden once the Canal coup had taken place. But his ultimate choice of the doomed French option rather than that urged by Washington shows us where Eden's long-term strategic thinking was taking him. And it is of interest here that in retirement he was frequently to be an honoured private guest of de Gaulle in Paris. So it is with a consideration of Eden's eventual alignment with France that we may most appropriately end this review of the place of his premiership in British history.

For some, Eden's fatal compact with France really only began at Chequers on 14 October 1956 with the visit of Albert Gazier and Maurice Challe, suggesting collusion; was carried forward by Eden himself in Paris on 16 October; and was cemented with the sojourn of a Foreign Office team in Sèvres from 22 to 24

---

[24] Carlton, *Anthony Eden*, p. 18.

October. On this reading it could be seen as a mere improvisation by a leader at his wits' end. And there may be some truth in this – particularly given the emerging threat that Israel was making to invade Jordan, raising the prospect of Britain, under its treaty obligations to Amman, finding itself at war on the same side as Egypt! Yet there is another way of looking at matters. It is to see Eden as far-sightedly attempting to align Britain with a more reliable long-term ally than, as he saw it, the United States could ever be. And the strongest case for arguing this has only recently received much scrutiny. It is that as early as September 1956, that is, before the Suez Crisis had become desperately acute, Eden responded positively to a remarkable demarche from French Premier Guy Mollet, who suggested a far-reaching pooling of British and French sovereignty. While inevitably not ready for a complete and immediate union, Eden was sympathetic to France being allowed to join the British Commonwealth, to France acknowledging Queen Elizabeth II as head of state and to the French being accorded 'common citizenship on the Irish basis'.[25] This was a variant of Churchill's famous proposal made to France during the last days of the Third Republic in June 1940. And Eden, with some apparent enthusiasm, instructed officials to explore the detailed implications. Nothing, of course, came of the idea after the British Cabinet let France down by forcing a premature ceasefire on 6 November. But had the bold plan of Mollet and Eden to topple President Gamal Abdel Nasser not been scuppered by Eisenhower and by Eden's Cabinet colleagues, the Entente Cordiale could have developed along quite spectacular lines during 1957. For there might have been no great nostalgia for the 'Special Relationship' in London's political circles. After all, in the aftermath of the ceasefire no fewer than 127 Conservative back-bench MPs signed a Commons motion criticising the United States for 'gravely endangering the Atlantic Alliance'. And there can be no doubt that many Labour MPs also had reservations about the desirability of subordination to Washington – though usually for rather different reasons from those motivating the 127 Conservatives.

Some will reply that Eden could never have been serious about pooling sovereignty with any continental country. After all, had he not set his face against European quasi-federalism to an even greater extent than Churchill? In January 1952, for example, he told an American audience at Columbia University:

> If you drive a nation to adopt procedures which run counter to its instincts, you weaken and may destroy the motive force of its action ... You will realise that I am speaking of the frequent suggestions that the United Kingdom should join a federation on the continent of Europe. This is something which we know, in our bones, we cannot do.[26]

---

[25] *The Guardian*, 16 January 2007.
[26] Carlton, *Anthony Eden*, p. 311.

And, on his own watch as Prime Minister, Eden sent Russell Bretherton, a comparatively junior civil servant, to make clear to those negotiating what became the Treaty of Rome, or European Economic Community, that British participation was out of the question. According to Jacques Delors, Bretherton took the following line:

> The future treaty which you are discussing has no chance of being agreed; if it was agreed, it would have no chance of being ratified; and if it were ratified, it would have no chance of being applied. And if it was applied, it would be totally unacceptable to Britain. You speak of agriculture which we don't like, of power over customs, which we take exception to, and institutions, which frighten us. Monsieur le president, messieurs, au revoir et bonne chance.[27]

But perhaps for Eden, at least until the US-induced ceasefire of 6 November 1956, making moves towards a merger with France was quite distinct from joining a multinational quasi-federation starting with six states, or seven if Britain were to be included, with no defined limit to future enlargement – and the European Union now comprises 27 member states. In short, for Eden, Monnet 0, Mollet 1.[28]

---

[27] Roy Denman (1966) *Missed Chances: Britain and Europe in the Twentieth Century*, Cassell, pp. 198–9.

[28] A curious evolution in Eden's thinking in the aftermath of 6 November 1956 appears to have occurred, as has been most helpfully pointed out to me by Geoffrey Warner. For, in an assessment of the lessons of Suez, written shortly before his resignation, the Prime Minister concluded: 'While the consequences of this examination [of Britain's world position and domestic capacity] may be to determine us to work more closely with Europe, carrying with us, we hope, our closest friends in the Commonwealth in such development, here too we must be under no illusion. Europe will not welcome us simply because at the moment it may appear to suit us to look at them. The timing and the conviction of our approach may be decisive in their influence on those with whom we plan to work' (quoted in Dutton, *Anthony Eden*, p. 310). But this may not mean that we can safely say that in Eden's mind the score had now become Monnet 1 Mollet 0. Rather, it may mean no more than that he favoured making a tactical and temporary adjustment given the near-certainty that Mollet would be bound to lose interest at least for a time in forging close bilateral ties with London after the way in which Eden had unilaterally capitulated to Eisenhower on 6 November. At all events, throughout his long political retirement, Eden pointedly refrained from identifying himself, whether on the point of principle or on tactical aspects, with those favouring ever-closer British integration into the European Economic Community, with what he saw as its long-term quasi-federalist agenda. In 1962, for example, he drafted a speech – apparently not delivered but clearly not intended to be helpful to the British government – in which he warned that Macmillan's ill-fated attempt to secure British admission to the European Economic Community would be unsoundly based

For half a century Eden's vision of a Franco-British pooling of sovereignty has had no following at all on either side of the Channel. But might Eden's hour on this, as on some other themes we have examined, at last be approaching? There would appear to be two preconditions. The first is that the 'Special Relationship' should effectively end rather than merely enter upon a period of coolness. If this is to happen the initiative will probably not come from London. For, even at the depths of the disillusionment over Iraq, the House of Commons strongly endorsed Blair's wish to sign up to a new Trident agreement with Washington – with not a voice raised in favour of an alternative arrangement with Paris. But the 'Special Relationship' may be in jeopardy all the same. For in the wake of a massive apparent defeat in Iraq, which now seems inevitable, and also in the entire Greater Middle East – more speculative perhaps – the United States, as a broken-backed hyperpower with less than 5 per cent of the world's population, could turn in disillusionment to a hemispheric security approach, retaining some residual interests in the other hemisphere only in parts of Africa, as a source of oil, and in East Asia.

A second precondition for a belated triumph for Eden's strategic vision – if we may call it that – would be for the European federal project to collapse and for great parts of the continent to be rebalkanised. Pointers in this direction could be the rejection by the French and the Dutch people of the proposed European constitution; growing asymmetries between France and Germany in energy dependence on Russia; and the evident tensions between different parts of Europe concerning the policies pursued by the European Central Bank in the management of a single currency still not in sight of being underpinned by a single system of taxation.

Neither precondition seems likely to be met in the near future, or indeed at all. All the same, the odds against may now be rather shorter than at any time since Eden's resignation more than 50 years ago. Suppose that a Franco-British merger did again become a proposition seriously discussed by Heads of Government in Paris and London? The leading role would surely no longer be automatically reserved for Britain, as it was assumed would be the case in both 1940 and 1956. For in half a century the Commonwealth has been greatly devalued, and it is difficult to imagine any French President accepting a member of the House of Windsor as head of state. France has also meanwhile become a truly independent nuclear weapon state, while Britain's status in this respect, having been fully independent in 1956, is one of ever-increasing dependency

---

if it were not clearly understood that a federal Europe was what the founders had in mind. 'What we must not do,' he wrote, 'is to join any organisations without a full understanding of its implications and then find ourselves being swept further than we intended – Better clarity now than recriminations a few years hence.' (quoted in Dutton, *Anthony Eden*, p. 311).

on the United States. And the French have enviable supplies of peaceful nuclear energy. But the British still do have something massive to offer a partnership. I refer, of course, to the City of London, which, notwithstanding its recent travails , has no conceivable equivalent in France.

Half a century after the Suez Crisis there are no statues of either Eden or Mollet in London or Paris – though there is a modest bust of the former in the British Foreign and Commonwealth Office. Might there be such statues by the middle of the present century? Stranger things have happened in the modern era. And many of them have been a good deal less agreeable.

4
Harold Macmillan, 1957–1963

D.R. Thorpe

At one minute before 10 o'clock on the evening of the General Election on Thursday 8 October 1959, for polling in those days ended at nine, the High Sheriff of Essex stepped outside the counting hall in Billericay and announced in record time the first result. Billericay was of double significance. Not only the first seat to be declared, as it had been in 1955, it was then regarded by psephologists as the archetypal constituency, a demographic microcosm of the entire country, and thus the most accurate pointer to the eventual outcome. In the General Election of May 1955 the overall Conservative majority under Sir Anthony Eden had been 60 seats, with the Billericay majority just over 4,000 votes. The figures declared at Billericay that evening in October 1959 showed that the Conservative candidate had won the seat with an increased majority of just under 5,000 votes. Although 629 seats were still to be declared, when Hugh Gaitskell, the Labour Leader of the Opposition, heard the figures from Billericay, as the chimes of Big Ben sounded at the start of the radio and television election results programmes, he said to his closest aides: 'We've lost by a hundred seats.' When the final result was declared from Orkney and Shetland (the Liberal leader's, Jo Grimond) at Saturday lunchtime, Gaitskell's prediction was fulfilled. Harold Macmillan had led the Conservatives to victory with an overall majority of exactly 100. It was the greatest political triumph of Macmillan's career, the equivalent moment for him to that on the afternoon of 29 June 1919 when King George V, abandoning protocol, greeted Lloyd George at Victoria Station on his return from the signing of the Versailles Peace Treaty and drove with him in an open carriage to Buckingham Palace, handing him a laurel wreath. For Macmillan it was all a far cry from that day in January 1957, in the wake of the Suez Crisis, when he had been invited by the Queen to form an administration and had warned Her Majesty that his government in all likelihood would not last six weeks. In fact, his time as Prime Minister was to last six years and nine months, and in terms of the changes Britain experienced in those dramatic years it proved one of the most formative and influential of the post-war era, its ramifications still felt today. In short, it was a premiership that made a difference.

The Macmillan years from 1957 to 1963, under the ever-present shadow of the Cold War, were characterised by several important initiatives. First and foremost, the rebuilding of the Anglo-American relationship after Suez was for Macmillan a priority accomplished by skilful use of his close wartime association with Eisenhower in North Africa. The great mistake in dealing with the Americans, Macmillan believed, was to treat them as though they were Anglo-Saxons. Like Henry James, a Macmillan author, he knew what was absent from the texture of American life. In his essay on Hawthorne, writing on nineteenth-century American civilisation, James declared that the Americans had 'No State, in the European sense of the word and indeed barely a specific national name. No sovereign, no court, no aristocracy, no diplomatic service, no castles, nor manors, nor old country houses, no cathedrals nor abbeys, no Oxford, nor Eton, nor Harrow – no Epsom, nor Ascot.' But he knew, like James, that a good deal remained, and was more adept at understanding that specific American character than many of his political contemporaries. After all, like Churchill, he had an American mother. As a result, in his years in No. 10 (and temporarily in Admiralty House), Macmillan ensured significant British support for the United States at key moments such as the Berlin Crisis in 1958 and the Cuban Missile Crisis in 1962, whilst the United States supplied Polaris, ensuring Britain a place at the nuclear top table. Secondly, belated steps were taken to apply for membership of the European Economic Community, an attempt, unsuccessful initially, to atone for the lost opportunities of the Messina conference in 1955. Macmillan was not alone in finding de Gaulle more difficult to deal with, 'the almost impossible ally' in the title of Peter Mangold's study of the relationship.[1] Not for nothing did Macmillan describe de Gaulle as possessing 'all the rigidity of a poker without its occasional warmth'.[2] Thirdly, Macmillan presided over the second post-war phase of the ending of Empire, a process hastened by sympathetic Colonial Secretaries such as Iain Macleod and Reginald Maudling, however unpopular this made them or Macmillan with Conservative backwoodsmen. Churchill, for one, was horrified by the 'Winds of Change' speech Macmillan made in South Africa in 1960. Fourthly, Macmillan – in his Disraelian guise – presided for most of his premiership over a period of economic stability, full employment and a vast improvement in 'the condition of the people'. In his famous Crystal Palace speech of 1872 Disraeli proclaimed that the people of England would be foolish 'if...they should not have long perceived that the time had arrived when social

---

[1] Peter Mangold (2006) *The Almost Impossible Ally: Harold Macmillan and Charles de Gaulle*, I.B. Tauris.
[2] Harold Macmillan (1972) *Pointing the Way*, Macmillan, p. 410.

and not political improvement is the object which they ought to pursue'. It was not a mistake Macmillan was to make between 1957 and 1963. At the time of the 1959 election, *The Times* observed: 'People are prosperous; prices are steady; unemployment is low.' Only when the economic climate deteriorated in 1961 did the political tide begin to turn and the troubles begin. Macmillan's antennae were so finely tuned that he was one of the first to see the unsustainability of much of this material progress, as shown in his infamously misinterpreted Bedford speech of July 1957 about the British never having had it so good. 'What is beginning to worry some of us,' he actually warned, 'is "Is it too good to be true?" or perhaps I should say "Is it too good to last?"'[3] On 28 May 1962 he admitted to his Cabinet that his dream of keeping in the air the four balls of full employment, stable prices, a strong pound and a balance of payments in surplus was doomed to failure.

Enoch Powell has famously written that 'all political lives, unless they are cut off in midstream at a happy juncture, end in failure, because that is the nature of politics and of human affairs.'[4] In retrospect, 8 October 1959 can be seen as the moment when Macmillan's political life began a slow, almost imperceptible, descent from its achieved peak, through spectacular political terrain no doubt, and with moments of skilful technical achievement in traversing myriad difficulties, but inexorably ending in the mundane base camp of a hospital bed in the King Edward VII Hospital, an outcome announced at 9.41 p.m. on 8 October 1963, almost four years to the exact minute since he had won 49.4 per cent of the popular vote at the 1959 Election. Despite such important developments as the rapport Macmillan struck up with Eisenhower's successor as American President, the youthful John F. Kennedy, and lasting achievements such as the Test Ban Treaty in the summer of 1963, the period after the 1959 General Election was characterised by reversals in different forms, the 'events, dear boy, events' that Macmillan saw as defining political activity and response. These included such diverse and damaging moments as the collapse of the Paris Summit in the summer of 1960, the Orpington by-election of March 1962, the Night of the Long Knives in July 1962, and, in January 1963, the death of Hugh Gaitskell (which brought Harold Wilson to the leadership of the opposition) and de Gaulle's veto of the British application to join the EEC. 1963 also saw the report of the Vassall Spy Tribunal in April, which led to the imprisonment of two journalists for refusing to disclose their sources, and the Profumo scandal in June 1963. Though sensationally seized upon at the time, the Profumo scandal, far from hastening the end of Macmillan's premiership, actually prolonged it. If the Profumo affair had not blown up, Macmillan might well have resigned in the summer of 1963, an option he was considering

---

[3] Harold Macmillan (1971) *Riding the Storm*, Macmillan, p. 350.
[4] Enoch Powell (1977) *Joseph Chamberlain*, Thames and Hudson, p. 350.

with increasing seriousness, in which event his successor would almost certainly have been the Chancellor of the Exchequer, Reginald Maudling, thus avoiding many of the controversies of the infamous Blackpool Conference of October 1963, when Lord Dilhorne, the Lord Chancellor, canvassed opinion, in Rab Butler's vivid phrase, 'like a large Clumber spaniel sniffing the bottoms of the hedgerows'.[5] The Vassall Tribunal was actually far more damaging than Profumo, as it turned the press inexorably against the Macmillan Government, and thereafter no opportunity of hounding Macmillan personally was missed. By comparison, the satirical outpourings of *Beyond the Fringe* (Macmillan loved Peter Cook's impersonation of him in the famous globe sketch) and *That Was The Week That Was* were affectionate. He specifically warned his Postmaster General not to order the BBC to withdraw *TW3* from its schedules, as it was better to be mocked than ignored.

Macmillan's career, like Churchill's, thus had its elements of the steeplechase. What sets it apart from those of most of his peers is that Macmillan had to wait an inordinately long time for one of the great offices of state. Stanley Baldwin and Neville Chamberlain, both relatively late starters in high politics, had to wait 12 and 5 years respectively from entering Parliament for such preferment; Macmillan had to wait 31 years. To be right before the war on both the key issues, unemployment and the appeasement of Nazi Germany, and to be articulate in his criticisms, was not the quickest way to the inner governing circles of his party. (When told that Geoffrey Dawson, editor of *The Times*, supported Chamberlain's appeasement policy, Macmillan observed: '*The Times* is always wrong, and every twenty years or so publishes the next volume of its official history to demonstrate the fact.')[6] Eden, whom he succeeded as Prime Minister in January 1957, was three and a half years his junior, yet had 20 years of experience in the great offices of state on retirement, against Macmillan's then 20 months. As a result one of Macmillan's defining political characteristics was that of, if not 'an old man in a hurry', then an experienced man making up for lost time. Inevitably this meant taking risks, being willing to gamble.

'To succeed pre-eminently in English public life,' observed Malcolm Muggeridge, 'it is necessary to conform either to the popular image of a bookie or a clergyman.'[7] Macmillan undoubtedly belongs to the former category, just as surely as, say, Attlee belongs to the latter. In fact, if one looks at the first 10 post-war prime ministers – from Attlee through to Major – it is interesting to note that 10 Downing Street, thanks to Wilson's two spells, is occupied

---

[5] Entry on Lord Dilhorne in *Dictionary of National Biography, 1971–1980* (1986), Robert Blake and C.S. Nicholls (eds), Oxford University Press, p. 546.

[6] Private information.

[7] Malcolm Muggeridge (1973) *The Infernal Grove*, Collins.

alternately by a clergyman, then a bookie, and so on, from 1945 right up to the present day with Gordon Brown, not only a clergyman, but a clergyman's son.[8] But, to return to the first post-war prime ministerial clergyman, one can hardly imagine Attlee allowing, or Sir Stafford Cripps being willing to introduce, Premium Bonds, which so enraged Archbishop Fisher in 1956 after Macmillan's only budget. Nevertheless, Attlee regarded Macmillan as the most radical politician he had ever encountered, and once claimed that, had it not been for the war, Macmillan would have ended up by leading the Labour Party. Macmillan's relations with Archbishop Fisher, who had clashed with the Government over Suez in 1956, tell us much of his political style. When Fisher retired from Lambeth Palace in 1960 he was dismayed to learn, in the manner of retiring Archbishops, that the Prime Minister was not intending to appoint Fisher's favoured successor to Canterbury (the Bishop of Bradford or, failing him, the Bishop of Peterborough), but Michael Ramsey, then Archbishop of York. In an unavailing late attempt to change the decision Fisher called on the Prime Minister. 'Dr Ramsey is a theologian, a scholar and a man of prayer. Therefore, he is entirely unsuitable as Archbishop of Canterbury,' adding, as what he hoped would be the final *coup de grace*, 'I have known him all my life. I was his Headmaster at Repton.' 'Thank you, Your Grace, for your kind advice,' replied Macmillan. 'You may have been Dr. Ramsey's headmaster, but you were not mine.'[9] In fact, educational similes featured prominently in Macmillan's political vocabulary. Budget day, he said, was rather like speech day, a bore but something one had to get through. After his creation of life peers in 1958, he said the newcomers were 'like day boys', and, when anti-Etonian sentiments were aired with ever-increasing frequency (this happened even before the days of Gordon Brown), Macmillan observed: 'Mr Attlee had three old Etonians in his Cabinet, I have six. Things are twice as good under the Conservatives.'[10] As befitted a publisher, literary references abounded too. Over the appointment of Michael Ramsey, Macmillan said: 'I rather enjoy patronage. I take a lot of trouble over it. At least it makes all those years of reading Trollope seem worth while.'[11] Allusions to Dickens also proved useful code, as references to, say, Pecksniff or Uriah Heep left a sense of uneasiness among those so described, as not all knew their Dickens as well as Macmillan, and may not have been sure whether they were being complimented or castigated.

---

[8] Tony Blair from 1997 to 2007 is not the exception that proves Muggeridge's rule, but its complete validation – a bookie masquerading as a clergyman.

[9] Lord Ramsey of Canterbury to the author, 21 August 1985. Also in Peter Hennessy (2000) *The Prime Minister: The Office and its Holders since 1945*, Allen Lane, p. 250.

[10] Anthony Sampson (1962) *The Anatomy of Britain*, Hodder and Stoughton, p. 175.

[11] Ibid., p. 322.

Many factors contributed to Macmillan's complex personality and approach to politics. I first met him on St George's Day 1975 at Birch Grove, with the daffodils in full bloom, when he had willingly agreed to help me with research into my first book. He shuffled to the door, for all the world like Chekhov's aged retainer Firs in a Sussex production of *The Cherry Orchard*, and took me through to the book-lined study. On the table was a copy of his family firm's recent publication, Robert Skidelsky's life of Oswald Mosley. 'Of course,' he said, indicating the book, 'for all his brilliance, Mosley never grasped one essential point about the British people – they will never vote for extremism.' Recollections of Mosley's Memorandum, the New Party and the battle between economic orthodoxy and economic unorthodoxy in the 1931 financial crisis poured forth and the past lived again. Then he paused. 'But of course, you are not here to talk about all that. How can I best help on *your* book?' I told him I was writing on those 'uncrowned Prime Ministers' of Conservative Party history, Sir Austen Chamberlain, Lord Curzon and Rab Butler, all of whom he had known, and all of whom had attained the penultimate, but not the expected final rung in the political hierarchy. 'Oh, I see,' he said, after a pause, 'kind of failed BAs', before adding: 'Of course if you want to make it a more amusing book you could always have a fourth section on George Brown.'[12] Then for two hours the recollections poured forth; the memory is still as vivid as it was over 30 years ago. Later that year when I interviewed Rab Butler, he asked me in a slightly querulous manner whether I had spoken to Macmillan. When I confirmed – or perhaps admitted – that I had, he said: 'And how was he that day? Was he the crofter's great-grandson, or the Duke of Devonshire's son-in-law?' The truth is that he was both – and more. But in this lay the appeal he had for much of the British electorate for so long.

Macmillan may have been a political bookie, but he was also an intellectual, the first, and only, premier since Balfour who could be so described. His life was full of such contrasts – radical yet traditional; gownsman yet swordsman; classicist yet populist; the list is endless – and this was one of his political strengths in winning power. He appealed to so many different constituencies. He knew that politics is a vulgar business. He had an intuitive feeling for what appealed to the electorate, and for the way in which power operated. He once said that his son Maurice had not got as far in politics as he should have, because he was not ruthless enough. As Eden was preparing to bow out of the Foreign Office, prior to entering No. 10 in the spring of 1955, Churchill asked him, as Eden recorded in his diary, how he 'had got on with Harold Mac in Paris. I said "Very well, Why?" He replied, "Oh, he is very ambitious". I laughed.'[13]

---

[12] Harold Macmillan to the author, 23 April 1975.

[13] Cited in D.R. Thorpe (2003) *Eden: The Life and Times of Sir Anthony Eden, First Earl of Avon, 1897–1977*, Chatto and Windus, p. 425.

Macmillan himself often said that, as an older man, he posed no threat to Eden's position; at such moments Eden's friends advised him to start counting the spoons. Harold Macmillan understood the machinery of Government and how to crank it into action. He was combative and knew that in politics one had to be a salesman; it was not in the mid-twentieth century (was it ever?) a gentlemanly profession, which is why he was always so assured when facing Gaitskell, whom he once described as 'a sanctimonious Wykehamist, with gestures like an Armenian shopkeeper',[14] and so much more wary and respectful when facing Harold Wilson across the despatch boxes. No one is given the keys to No. 10 on a velvet cushion, again a political truth Macmillan – and his successor Alec Home – understood intuitively.

The list of those to whom Macmillan appealed was a remarkably broad cross-section of British society: the deferential working class who thought in those far-off days that the governing class knew their business, and that it was best to let them be about it; to the military veterans who admired his Great War record, in an age when MPs who had seen active service were referred to in the House of Commons as Honourable and Gallant; the aspiring lower middle class, who wanted their children to have educational opportunities denied to themselves in pre-war days; the Rotary Club members in his Bromley constituency, who thought him the last British prime minister who actually looked like a prime minister; the left-of-centre Keynesian economists, who saw him, with his deficit financing and authorship of *The Middle Way*, not only as one of themselves, but also one with the political will and acumen to achieve manageable fiscal expansion; the intellectuals and university world, who admired his undoubted intelligence and seriousness (or at least the Oxbridge world – he once asked one of his Cabinet colleagues, a bemused alumnus of the London School of Economics, if he had had a Sligger Urquhart); the business world, which respected his years of commercial experience; Disraelian One Nation Conservatives, who wanted 'Tory men and Whig measures', and who agreed with him that 'Toryism has always been a form of paternal socialism;' the literary world, who were in reverence at his personal links with Hardy and Kipling; the religious community, who saw him as second only to the Queen in his loyalty and devotion to the Church, reading the lesson each Sunday at St Giles, Horsted Keynes whenever in Sussex (his successive private secretaries had instructions to let the vicar know if he was unable to read the lesson; otherwise it was taken for granted); the patriots who applauded his unambiguous pursuit of British interests (and the ease with which he discomfited a shoe-banging Khrushchev at the United Nations); the internationalists who appreciated his shrewd acceptance of the second phase of decolonisation; the aristocrats, who saw him as one of their own, though he had married into the aristocracy, rather

---

[14] Harold Macmillan to the author, 23 April 1975.

than being an aristocrat in himself. Of the maze of Chatsworth, he once said one had to throw a double six to find the way out. Only when he had seen off a Cecil, in 1957, in the shape of Bobbety Salisbury, over Archbishop Makarios and the Cyprus question, did he feel he had finally come to terms with the aristocracy. In essence he remained a Scottish bourgeois, as he knew himself. He had an acute sense of 'placement'. Macmillan described Lord Home, the 14th Earl, in his 'Tuesday Memorandum' to the Queen in October 1963 on the Tory Leadership, as 'a right-down regular peer', whereas Lord Hailsham, the Second Viscount, like officers who had risen to fill the gaps in the Great War, he described as 'a temporary gentleman'.[15] He thought Herbert Morrison a third-rate Tammany boss and a Cockney guttersnipe, Selwyn Lloyd he described as 'a middle class lawyer from Liverpool', and the Cabinet Secretary, Norman Brook, a former pupil of Wolverhampton Grammar School, as 'having no background'.[16] Ironically, though the denizens of Chatsworth and Hatfield never knew it, on Friday evenings at Downing Street before leaving for a week-end at Birch Grove Macmillan actually took high tea first, as it was convenient and saved time before braving the rush hour traffic, something which Harold Nicolson would no doubt have regarded as 'very bedint'.

Napoleon once said that to understand a man one had to know what was happening in the world when he was 20. The fact that Macmillan was born in 1894 tells so much. He was thus 20 when he went into the trenches, one of the survivors of that lost generation and the ghosts of Oxford (from which University he said he was 'sent down by the Kaiser'). In Britten's *Owen Wingrave*, the pacifist hero, in one of the great lyrical outpourings in opera, sings of how 'In peace I have found my image.' With Macmillan it was the exact opposite. It was in war, both on active service in the Great War and in high executive position in the Second War in North Africa, that he found himself. Some of the most harrowing and moving documents in his papers are the letters he sent home to his mother from the trenches, some still bearing bloodstains, and one of 30 August 1915, after an injury to his hand, in stubby pencil markings, which somehow adds even more to the intensity of what he recalls:

Dear Mother – do not worry about me. I am very happy; it is a great experi-ence, psychologically so interesting as to fill one's thoughts. A company has just passed my house, back from a long route march, singing wonderfully the dear soldier songs, with silly words and silly tunes, but which some-how seem, sung by their great childish voices, from the depths of their very

---

[15] National Archives. Memorandum of 15 October 1962, PREM 11/5008.

[16] Peter Catterall, ed. (2003) *The Macmillan Diaries: The Cabinet Years, 1950–1957,* Macmillan, p. 82; D.R. Thorpe (1989) *Selwyn Lloyd,* Cape, p. 1; Lord Moran (1968) *Winston Churchill: The Struggle for Survival, 1940–1965* (1966), Sphere, pp. 795–6.

lovable hearts, the most delicate music and the most sublime poetry. Indeed of all the war, I think the most interesting (and humbling too) experience is the knowledge one gets of the poorer classes. They have big hearts, these soldiers, and it is a very pathetic task to have to read all their letters home. Some of the older men, with wives & families, who write every day home, have in their style a wonderful simplicity, which is almost great literature...It is all very touching...Indeed, I think there is much to be learnt from soldiers' letters.[17]

Coupled with his experience of pre-war unemployment in Stockton-on-Tees, and his three years with Dame Evelyn Sharp at the Ministry of Housing, Macmillan thus had insight into the experiences of what Lord Falconer calls 'ordinary people' that was virtually unparalleled among his political contemporaries. In *Culture and Society*, an influential book published in the second year of Macmillan's premiership, Raymond Williams observed that the fact that the working classes aspired to the material comforts taken for granted by the middle classes did not of itself mean that they also wanted to become middle-class. 'The worker's envy of the middle-class man is not a desire to be that man, but to have the same kind of possessions.'[18] Macmillan understood this; indeed, it was the driving force underlying his domestic agenda. He never had the puritan's high-minded disdain about improving material standards. Scarred by his experiences of pre-war and pre-Welfare State Stockton, he knew all too well the alternatives. Living under the flight path of Gatwick airport, he judged the noise pollution an accurate indicator of economic activity. In the summer of 1959 one of his grandsons noted complainingly the incessant drone of aircraft taking off for the continent. Macmillan told him this was a propitious sign. The people would have good holidays, they would come back happy, and in the autumn they would return the Conservatives to power in the General Election. And so they did.

He showed similar wisdom with the old. At one of the degree ceremonies over which he presided as Chancellor of Oxford University in the 1960s, an angry crowd of protesting undergraduates threatened havoc as Macmillan led the procession of University grandees from Wadham to the Divinity School. 'It'll be all right if we get past the King's Arms,' said Macmillan reassuringly to Alan Bullock alongside him. 'You see, they'll rush us as we pass the King's Arms; it was the same in the First War, the danger spots were always the cross roads.'[19]

---

[17] Macmillan papers, Bodleian Library, MS Macmillan dep. d 1/1, fol. 30.
[18] Raymond Williams (1958) *Culture and Society*, Chatto and Windus, pp. 310–1.
[19] Alan Bullock, 'Most Honoured Chancellor: A Personal Reminiscence', *Oxford Magazine*, no. 17, Hilary Term, Noughth week, 1987.

If the first problem of politics is how to win power, the second (and more difficult) is what to do with that power once it has been won. Macmillan's solution was to choose wise lieutenants, of whom three outside the Cabinet, in particular, were of seminal importance – Michael Fraser, Deputy Chairman of the Conservative Party, and, as a former Director of the Conservative Research Department, his link with Rab Butler; Freddie Bishop, his principal private secretary; and John Wyndham, at whose Petworth estate many crucial decisions were considered and finalised. It was to Fraser that Macmillan sent his celebrated memorandum asking to be told on a single sheet of paper exactly what it was the middle classes wanted, and then he would see whether they could be given it. Bishop was his rock at many moments of crisis, notably the abortive Paris summit in 1960, when Macmillan chose to take Bishop with him to his last meeting with Khrushchev in the hope of averting breakdown. 'This is government by Private Secretary,' complained Selwyn Lloyd, the excluded Foreign Secretary, as Gladwyn Jebb, the British ambassador in Paris, fumed alongside him. 'Well, the only alternative is government by politician,' replied Bishop insouciantly.[20] Macmillan appreciated such calm. Despite his reputation for unflappability ('Quiet calm deliberation disentangles every knot' was the notice he placed on the cabinet door, the original of which he gave to Bishop on his retirement), Macmillan was a pack of nerves on public occasions, whether it was presenting the prizes at his preparatory school, Summer Fields in Oxford, or addressing the United Nations in New York. At such times he recalled Raymond Asquith's words at Balliol, 'Whatever happens, remember that the sun will still rise over Wadham, and set over Worcester.' John Wyndham was a specially trusted courtier, unpaid, discreet and loyal. On his 1958 tour of the Commonwealth, Macmillan was introduced to an old, bedraggled peasant in a model village at New Delhi. 'This is one of the largest landowners in this district,' he was told by his Indian hosts. Introducing John Wyndham to the man, he said: 'And this is one of the largest landowners in *my* district.'[21]

John Wyndham was by his side, too, at one of the unrecorded moments of Cold War public relations. The 'space race' was then one of the prizes of Cold War supremacy. Initially, the Russians seemed to be the victors, with the Sputnik in 1957, then successfully sending Leica, the dog, into space, before Yuri Gagarin became the first man to orbit the earth. When Gagarin visited England in July 1961, there was much talk in Cabinet about the appropriate level of Royal hospitality. Should it be a state banquet at Windsor (no, Bulganin and Khrushchev in 1956 had only been given tea at Windsor), perhaps a visit to

---

[20] Thorpe, *Selwyn Lloyd*, p. 304.
[21] Sampson, *Anatomy of Britain*, p. 336.

the Queen Mother at Clarence House? The royal diary was very full at the time and it was a sudden request. Finally, Gagarin was invited to one of the Queen's regular Buckingham Palace luncheons – fellow guests included Bud Flanagan of the Crazy Gang, and Lord Mountbatten. Afterwards Gagarin was driven down the Mall to see Macmillan at Admiralty House, where the Prime Minister was then living whilst Downing Street was undergoing renovations. The Foreign Office came up with a special open-topped Rolls Royce – registration number YG 1 – and Gagarin drew vast crowds, waving Union Jacks and Russian flags, as his cavalcade with outriders made its slow progress through the cheering throng. London was *en fête*. Macmillan watched the noisy spectacle from an upper window in Admiralty Arch. 'Of course,' he observed to John Wyndham, 'it would have been far worse if they'd sent the dog.'[22]

The public response to the Gagarin visit showed an underlying sense of uncomplicated respectfulness that was still strong in British society. By 1963 the social climate was very different. Addressing an American audience in retirement, Macmillan drew a Biblical parallel to illustrate the contrast:

'"Do not worry too much," Adam is reported to have said to Eve as they left the Garden of Eden, "we live after all my dear in an age of transition." And, of course,' 'we always do.'[23]

All ages of history have their elements of transition, but the six years of Macmillan's premiership saw crucial changes in so many areas of public life. The introduction of life peerages in 1958 was to have profound, and at the time unforeseen, effects on the constitution. Dubbed 'day boys' at the time by Macmillan and the hereditary peers, the life peers were eventually to take over the whole school. The Preston bypass, opened in 1958, as the first section of motorway in Britain, was to be the harbinger of a complete change in road transport, just as the American-style steak houses revolutionised eating habits. On one occasion Macmillan, Lord Salisbury and Roy Strong had been invited to luncheon with Lady Diana Cooper, but found on arrival that Lady Diana had confused the dates and given her cook the day off. Undaunted, they set off on a search for food, lighting eventually on an Angus Steak House. For Macmillan, it was a revelation (and a gratification) that people could walk in off the Edgware Road and partake of such a first-class meal, and the event was accounted a great success – except by Lady Diana Cooper, who did not think that the wine list amounted to much.[24] Such social changes, as memories of

---

[22] Private information.
[23] Speech at the Wilson Centre, Smithsonian Building, 25 November 1980.
[24] Simon Ball (2004) *The Guardsmen: Harold Macmillan, Three Friends and the Wold They Made*, HarperCollins, pp. 397–8.

the age of austerity faded, were one of the defining qualities of the Macmillan years. Gastronomically, for instance, 1957 was still largely a world of Brown Windsor soup; by 1963, specialist shops were marketing silver crème brulée hammers.

Politically, Macmillan was a realist. He knew, four years before Dean Acheson famously said that Britain had lost its Empire and failed to find a role, that he was operating in an age of readjustment, which is why joining the EEC became such an important priority, and in the end the failure to do so such a damaging and fatal political moment. 'The dinosaur was the largest beast but it was inefficient and therefore disappeared,' Macmillan said in one speech. 'The bee is efficient but it is too small to have much influence. Britain's most useful role is somewhere between bee and dinosaur.'[25] So, like Churchill and Eden, Macmillan maintained the belief in the concept of three interlinking circles: America, Europe and the Commonwealth, with Britain a crucial constituent of each component. In his Manchester speech of 1872 Disraeli said: 'The very phrase "foreign affairs" makes an Englishmen convinced that I am about to treat of subjects with which he has no concern.' Macmillan knew that well-ordered international relations were crucial to national security, but from an electoral point of view he understood the primary importance of 'next Friday's grocery bill'. Foreign policy may have been his passion, and economics his hobby, but he knew that economics would determine political success. In his own brief spell as Chancellor of the Exchequer Macmillan in 1956 would have liked to bring in a full-scale capital gains tax, but was not then confident enough to take on both the Inland Revenue and his own party. Ironically, the stagnation that accompanied Macmillan's time at the Treasury was the price that had to be paid for Butler's boom. It was not a pattern he wanted repeated by his own Chancellors.

The defining figures in his premiership were, therefore, not grandees such as Bobbety Salisbury, Lord Kilmuir or Lord Dilhorne, but his four Chancellors of the Exchequer, who successively resigned, acquiesced, fell and flourished. They are the true measuring points of his years in Downing Street. Peter Thorneycroft was Chancellor from 1957, until his sudden resignation in January 1958 over the levels of public expenditure, on the eve of Macmillan's departure for his Commonwealth tour, when he was succeeded by the safe, stopgap figure of Derick Heathcoat Amory. In two long meetings at Petworth in the summer of 1960, Macmillan persuaded Selwyn Lloyd to take up the burden. This experiment ended in the tears on the Night of the Long Knives on Friday 13 July 1962. Only with the appointment of Reginald Maudling did Macmillan have a Chancellor who was committed, like him, to Keynesian expansion and 'the dash for growth'. After de Gaulle's EEC veto in January 1963, Maudling's success was

---

[25] *New York Times*, 30 December 1968.

even more crucial to the survival of the Macmillan, and subsequently Douglas-Home, governments. The last 15 months of Macmillan's premiership, therefore, was, economically, a crucial watershed in post-war politics, the moment when inflation became institutionalised as a method of paying for the growing demands of a socially conscious electorate.

Of Macmillan's four Chancellors, the two most similar were Thorneycroft and Selwyn Lloyd, in that both wanted to impose severe financial constraints, and as a result finally fell foul of Macmillan, ironic in that Macmillan's own spell as Chancellor was far from expansionist. (Macmillan cut government spending by £100 million in his only budget). After a moderate budget in the spring of 1957, Thorneycroft had to deal in September with a sterling crisis and run on the pound. Thorneycroft responded by raising bank rate from 5 per cent to 7 per cent. Thorneycroft relied on Enoch Powell, his Financial Secretary, and Lionel (Lord) Robbins for economic advice. Both believed that control of the money supply would curb inflation, a view Thorneycroft, a converted monetarist, came to share, and thus a moment of immense long-term significance for British politics in the final third of the twentieth century. Macmillan relied more on Roy Harrod's advice and invariably sent Harrod's sceptical letters to Thorneycroft ('The idea that you can reduce prices by limiting the quantity of money is pre-Keynesian'). Thorneycroft's eventual resignation on 6 January 1958 was famously dismissed by Macmillan, about to depart on his Commonwealth Tour, as 'a little local difficulty'. It was far from that, and in the longer term can be seen as one of the first stirrings of what later became known as Thatcherism.

With his aeroplane virtually waiting on the Heathrow runway, Macmillan had to move very quickly, and as a result took the decision to promote Derick Heathcoat Amory from Agriculture to the Treasury, as the only means of avoiding a major reshuffle. The appointment of Heathcoat Amory, whom Macmillan thought rigid and not over-clever, was essentially a holding operation, though Amory proved willing to finance inflation, whilst at the same time claiming that there was no departure from previous policy. By October 1958, even Roy Harrod was warning Macmillan: 'I have an uncomfortable feeling that all the excellent things you have achieved in the past few months will still not add up enough to prevent a serious growth in unemployment in the time ahead.'[26]

Amory did not want to stay in politics in the long term (he had business and charitable interests in Devon to which he felt pledged to return) and, once the 1959 election was successfully surmounted, Macmillan turned to thoughts of a major reconstruction. In the summer of 1960 he moved Selwyn Lloyd from the Foreign Office to the Treasury, a fateful decision for both men. Selwyn Lloyd proved less pliant than Macmillan anticipated, and when economic difficulties

---

[26] British Library, Harrod papers, Mss. Add. 72742.

arose in 1961 there would be only one eventual outcome. Macmillan was primarily concerned with the political consequences of his Chancellor's policies, whereas Lloyd, to his credit, continued to be preoccupied by the economic ones. Reflecting after his dismissal, with six other Cabinet Ministers, on Friday 13 July 1962, Lloyd recorded that Macmillan's biggest mistake was 'thinking unemployment a worse enemy than uncontrolled inflation'.

Selwyn Lloyd's misfortune was to become Chancellor as these inflationary pressures began to build. The 'pay pause' he had introduced in the sharply deflationary July measures of 1961 was particularly unpopular with nurses and teachers, who had a large measure of public support, and contributed to a series of by-election reverses for Macmillan's government, the most spectacular being the Orpington by-election on 14 March 1962, when a Conservative majority at the previous General Election was overturned by a Liberal majority of 7,855. Orpington entered the political vocabulary as a symbol of the rebellious, disenchanted commuter and his wife, as the financial pressures began to mount.

A remarkable play, now sadly neglected, premiered on 16 May 1962, midway between Orpington and the Night of the Long Knives, encapsulates perfectly the contemporary mood of middle-class financial disenchantment. *Everything in the Garden* by Giles Cooper is set in an ordinary suburban Home Counties house, somewhere on the A3 between Surbiton and New Malden. 'Everything in the garden' seems lovely, but it is far from so. The pressures of maintaining the former standards of living are seemingly insurmountable, school fees are rocketing, the car needs changing, and the bank manager is calling in the overdraft. There seems no way out of the impasse, until, almost by accident, the bored housewife finds herself offered afternoon work in a discreet, high-class London brothel, where she soon begins to earn vast sums of money. The author was present on the first night and remembers that the sound of the seats flipping up as people left at this moment was like rifle fire. By turns black comedy and high fantasy, the play takes a tragic turn, but at the end money and outward respectability remain the driving motive. 'The garden of the house,' says the housewife, 'must be kept up...we can't afford to let it go. You notice them from the train, the gardens that people have let go. You know at once there's something wrong in the house. Ours must look like all the others, don't you think?'[27] In Britain in 1963 people had grown accustomed to wanting everything in the garden to look lovely; Maudling was the man whose job it was to provide the wherewithal, by his economic policies after Orpington and related reverses, to realise that goal.

---

[27] Giles Cooper (1963) *Everything in the Garden*, New English Dramatists 7, Penguin Books, pp. 220–1.

Maudling's brief from Macmillan was to be as unlike Selwyn Lloyd as possible, in short to finance an expansionist programme to curb unemployment, but this proved easier in theory than practice, and initially Maudling was cautious in his approach. But he was in a stronger position than Amory or Lloyd in that Macmillan was increasingly preoccupied with battalions of other political sorrows (one Cabinet was even taken up with examining and considering photographs of members at one of the Duchess of Argyll's louche parties), and he could hardly sack another Chancellor after the events of July 1962. *That Was the Week That Was* became less cosy. One sketch, after Maudling had met a delegation of the unemployed, ended with the Chancellor saying, as he left, 'Well, I've got work to do, if you haven't.'[28] By July 1963, however, unemployment had fallen below 500,000 and, as Macmillan's myriad difficulties increased, Maudling was seen by many as his most likely successor. The French veto on Britain's EEC application had left the government directionless, difficulties skilfully exploited by the new Labour leader, Harold Wilson, relishing his role as Leader of the Opposition, and the press were baying for blood after the Vassall Tribunal, and the imprisonment of two journalists. The visit of the young American President John F. Kennedy to Birch Grove in June gave some respite from domestic problems, and showed Macmillan, the statesman, once more confident on the international scene. But it was illusory. Before the autumn leaves had turned, Macmillan had resigned and Kennedy was dead by an assassin's bullet; thereafter Macmillan always wrote to Kennedy's widow, Jackie, on the anniversary, 22 November.

One of the great mysteries about the last months of Macmillan's premiership is why Maudling did not succeed him in No. 10. A certain raffishness counted against him in some circles, epitomised when he arrived at an evening function at Downing Street, sporting a light blue velvet dinner jacket, which he thought the height of fashion, until Macmillan greeted him with the words: 'Ah Reggie, playing the drums at the 100 Club again tonight, I see.'[29] But what really did for Maudling was the Profumo scandal. Macmillan could hardly resign at the height of that furore, yet, had he departed in the summer of 1963, as he had been seriously considering, Maudling would have been the strongest of all the candidates. At that moment, that list could not have included, in Anthony Howard's phrase, 'Mr Home and Mr Hogg', the Lords Home and Hailsham, as the Peerage Act, allowing existing peers to disclaim their titles, did not come into force until 31 July 1963. Yet, in some strange way, Maudling let the ball slip from his hands. For a start, the 'Profumo affair' spurred Macmillan into renewed and determined action, and he expected other party workers to react

---

[28] Cited in Lewis Baston (2004) *Reggie: The Life of Reginald Maudling*, Sutton Publishing, p. 188.

[29] Reginald Maudling to the author, November 1975.

likewise. Central Office at his instigation sent a message to all approved candidates for the next election, reminding them, as they went out to canvass countrywide, of G.K. Chesterton's approach to a pre-war speaking visit to a Northern town. 'Looking forward to meeting you,' had telegrammed the host mayor. 'Brass band will meet you at station.' 'Brass band unnecessary,' replied Chesterton. 'Am bringing own trumpet.'[30]

The last months of Macmillan's premiership, nevertheless, had important consequences. In international affairs, the Test Ban Treaty was a lasting achievement, though the legalistic performance of Lord Hailsham at the negotiations in Moscow so annoyed the American delegation, in particular Averell Harriman, that Macmillan was warned at the time of his resignation that if Hailsham succeeded him as Prime Minister it would mean the end of the special relationship. Life peerages now became a relevant factor in the resolution of the Tory leadership crisis in October 1963. Two false myths still persist about that dramatic month: firstly, that Macmillan, according to the account of events given by Iain Macleod in his notorious *Spectator* article, had been determined from the first to deny Butler the succession and had even falsified the result of soundings to the Queen to achieve that aim; and, secondly, that in the initial absence of his regular doctor in the Lake District Macmillan regretted resigning almost as soon as he had done so, as his prostate condition proved to be benign.

Rab Butler was never going to get the Tory leadership in 1963. He knew it, and, though the eventual outcome was hard to bear, nothing Butler did could have altered it. He had been told by John Morrison, Chairman of the influential 1922 Committee in the summer of 1963, that 'the chaps won't have you,' and shortly afterwards, as Maudling told me in 1975, one day, as he left his Hans Place apartment, by chance he had met Butler in the street, and, after some small talk, Butler taking him by the arm, had suddenly said: 'Of course, I will be very happy to serve under you, Reggie.'[31] When Lord Home was attempting to form his Cabinet, he told Maudling that if he, Home, failed in forming a government, the Queen would send for him, Maudling, not Butler. The most damaging point that Macleod made in his article, however, was actually a less regarded one, towards the end of his article: 'we have confessed that the Tory Party could not find a Prime Minister in the House of Commons at all.' Macmillan's advice to Home was that, if Macleod persisted in this line, Home should say that it reflected ill on the profession of journalism that they could not find an editor for the *Spectator* from within its own ranks, but had to resort to choosing Iain Macleod.[32]

---

[30] Election file. Conservative Party Archives, Bodleian Library, Oxford.
[31] Reginald Maudling to the author, September 1975.
[32] Harold Macmillan to author, 23 April 1975.

In October 1963, as Macmillan prepared for surgery at the King Edward VII hospital, the thoughts of the summer returned again. The game was no longer worth the candle; his time had passed. 1963 had indeed proved, in Bill Deedes's words, 'a horse carrying more lead than it could manage'. David Badenoch, son of the surgeon who operated on Macmillan, recorded that 'the histology of the prostate showed benign hyperplasia and Macmillan was aware of this fact. At no time was he encouraged to resign by his medical attendants and indeed when he did resign he expressed great relief that he had reason to leave the political crises which he faced. He termed this "an act of God".'[33] To those who attended him in the aftermath of his operation, including his Parliamentary Private Secretary, Sir Knox Cunningham, who recorded all the details in his important, but as yet unpublished, memoir, Macmillan's decision to resign came to him as a relief; he was at ease in his mind, saying that he had been looking for a way out and that events really might have been providential.[34]

Nevertheless, all Conservative leadership contests since that in October 1963, including the present one, have been directly influenced by the party's experiences at that traumatic time, both in the codifying of changing rules and in the manner in which those rules have been implemented. The royal prerogative, too, has changed irrevocably. As both the major parties elect their leader, it would be difficult to imagine circumstances in which the Queen would not accept the decision of the governing party at a time of vacancy, confirming as her First Minister the accepted and democratically chosen leader of the party commanding a majority in the House of Commons. Again, it was very different from January 1957, when the Queen did ostensibly have a genuine choice, though she was happy to be guided by the advice of those she consulted. In October 1963, it was made quite clear by the Palace from the outset that the procedure to be followed was what was described as 'You Choose, We Send For.'[35] In his letter of resignation to the Conservative Party Conference in Blackpool, Macmillan hoped that 'the customary processes' for choosing a new leader would now begin. In fact, there were no 'customary processes'; that was part of the difficulty. In future, there were.

Macmillan's 12 years in Cabinet – from 1951 to 1963 – spanned an era of profound change in British society, a period comparable to the transformation of society in the early Victorian years with the advent of the railways. 1951, despite the green shoots implicit in the Festival of Britain, was still largely a world of rationing, reserve and radio news. By 1963, consumerism had replaced food coupons, popular culture was the complete antithesis of reserve, and television

---

[33] David Badenoch, letter to *The Times*, 12 January 1994.

[34] Knox Cunningham, *One Man Dog: The Memoirs of Harold Macmillan's Private Secretary*, in the possession of the Drapers' Company.

[35] Sir Edward Ford to the author, July 1993.

gave a new immediacy to global news. For an Edwardian, Macmillan adapted brilliantly to the challenges of the television age – 'that deep probing eye', as he described the camera – just as Baldwin had used the wireless so effectively in his day, and Macmillan's regular retrospects with Robert McKenzie, on the occasion of the publication each of the six volumes of his memoirs, became unmissable television events. Both Macmillan and Baldwin understood that, although mathematically they were speaking to a potential audience of millions, actually they were speaking to a small family unit, a skill which Harold Wilson was also to exploit so effectively.

Macmillan's premiership was the link between the age of austerity and the age of affluence, which it did so much to bring into being, but at long-term cost. 'This long run is a misleading guide to current affairs,' Keynes famously remarked. 'In the long run we are all dead.'[36] For monetarists, therefore, Macmillan will always be the spectre at the feast, and during the Thatcher hegemony his name was not revered; especially when ennobled, as the first Earl of Stockton, his sense of nonagenarian mischievousness remained undimmed. 'First of all the Georgian silver goes, and then all that nice furniture that used to be in the saloon,' he observed of privatisation. 'Then the Canalettos go.'[37] The critique proved, as he intended, very damaging. 'The image of ministers,' wrote Thatcher's biographer, John Campbell, 'like a lot of dodgy housestrippers, knocking down the nation's heirlooms at a cost well below their true worth subtly undermined Mrs. Thatcher's carefully created reputation for thrifty housekeeping.'[38] As a businessman, Macmillan knew it was against all the rules of economic husbandry to spend the proceeds of such asset-stripping on consumption, not investment.

Yet, looking at the overall sweep of history, Macmillan had helped to pave the way for Thatcher – and for other developments that could not possibly have been foreseen in 1963: devaluation, a belated entry into Europe (Macmillan's chief negotiator, Edward Heath, not missing out a second time), the winter of discontent and the rise of monetarism in fiscal policy, which in its turn led to the demise of old-style Socialism, to Tony Blair and New Labour.

So when the High Sheriff of Essex declared the Billericay result that October evening in 1959 he was not only announcing a Conservative victory in an individual seat (and for the cognoscenti the overall result itself), but marking the beginning of a new phase of British politics. Macmillan had exorcised the memories of Suez; in the preferred phrase of a recent prime minister, he had drawn a line under the past, and could now move on. Whether, as he moved

---

[36] Robert Skidelsky (2000) *John Maynard Keynes, Fighting for Britain, 1937–1946*, Macmillan, p. 479.

[37] Speech to the Tory Reform Group, 8 November 1985.

[38] John Campbell (2003) *Margaret Thatcher*, vol. 2: *The Iron Lady*, Cape, p. 240.

on, Macmillan presided over the acceleration of eventual decline is a problem that will probably exercise economists rather than political historians, for their science is more measurable. Whatever the ultimate verdict, though, Macmillan will always remain one of the most individual, subtle and beguiling of prime ministers, and a constant attraction for those who make a study of what Stanley Baldwin lovingly called the endless adventure of ruling men.

5
Alec Douglas-Home, 1963–1964
D.R. Thorpe

After Andrew Bonar Law's funeral in Westminster Abbey in November 1923, Herbert Asquith observed: 'It is fitting that we should have buried the Unknown Prime Minister by the side of the Unknown Soldier.'[1] Asquith owed Bonar Law no posthumous favours, and intended no ironic compliment, but the remark was a serious underestimate. In post-war politics Alec Douglas-Home is often seen as the Bonar Law of his times, bracketed with his fellow Scot as an interim figure in the history of Downing Street between longer-serving premiers: in Bonar Law's case, Lloyd George and Stanley Baldwin; in Home's, Harold Macmillan and Harold Wilson. Both Law and Home were certainly 'unexpected' Prime Ministers, but both were also 'underestimated', and they made lasting beneficial changes to the political system, on both a national and a party level. The unexpectedness of their accessions to the top of the greasy pole, and the brevity of their premierships (they were the two shortest of the twentieth century: Bonar Law's one day short of seven months, Alec Douglas-Home's two days short of a year), are not an accurate indication of their respective significance, even if the precise details of their careers were not always accurately recalled, even by their admirers. The Westminster village is often another world to the general public. Stanley Baldwin was once accosted on a train from Chequers to London, at the height of his fame, by a former school friend. 'It's Baldwin, isn't it?' he asked. 'Harrow, '84?' Baldwin paused in his perusal of *The Times* crossword and confirmed the details. His friend leant forward. 'And what are you doing now?' The equivalent moment for Alec Douglas-Home came in retirement, travelling back to Berwick-upon-Tweed, when he was engaged in conversation in a railway carriage by an elderly couple. 'My husband and I think it was a great tragedy that you were never Prime Minister,' said the lady,

---

[1] Robert Blake (1955) *The Unknown Prime Minister: The Life and Times of Andrew Bonar Law, 1858–1923*, Eyre and Spottiswoode, p. 13.

as they parted. 'As a matter of fact I was,' replied Home, with his customary politeness, adding: 'but only for a very short time.'[2]

Home owed the possibility of that very short time indirectly to Tony Benn, erstwhile the Second Viscount Stansgate. Following Benn's determined campaign in the early 1960s for the right to renounce his title, the Peerage Act came on to the Statute Book on 31 July 1963. In January 1963 the Government had promised that the Bill should 'become law in time to take practical effect at, but not before, the next General Election.'[3] But this did not satisfy supporters of the Bill. Further discussion led to the Lords' declaration on 8 May 1963 that 'Surrender should not extinguish the peerage itself' (a crucial factor for Home). The Opposition amendment of 16 July 1963, proposed by Lord Silkin, some think with the encouragement of Lord Salisbury, astute king-maker, which the Lords endorsed by 105 votes to 25, was that the Act should become operative on receiving the Royal Assent. This followed a fortnight later. Existing hereditary peers now had a window of 12 months in which to disclaim their peerages if they so wished. The second Viscount Stansgate disclaimed his at once.

As the leadership of the Conservative Party was increasingly a matter of speculation in the summer of 1963, this Act, and the date of its implementation, subtly altered the ground rules. Both Lord Hailsham and Lord Home, who had discussed the matter in May 1963, were theoretically potential future candidates, if they so wished, but only, it seemed, after the next election, when the matter would have been resolved one way or another without their participation. One of the myths of this time is that the Profumo affair shortened Macmillan's premiership. In fact, it did precisely the opposite. In the summer of 1963 Macmillan had been seriously thinking of stepping down, in which case his successor would almost certainly have been Reginald Maudling, then on a political high. The Profumo affair removed that possibility. It would have been seen as an admission of failure by Macmillan to have gone in the midst of that furore. Macmillan decided to stay on and to fight the next election. Only his prostate condition in October – 'the stroke of fate' as Macmillan called it – led him to resign, almost welcoming by then the opportunity of a way out.[4]

At this moment, thanks to the amended Peerage Act, Hailsham and Home were now *papabile* – and without the years of scrutiny that had attended figures such as Rab Butler, Reginald Maudling or Edward Heath, though at that stage only Hailsham was considered a possibility for a future disclaimer. Although Home and Hailsham were senior figures, they were fresh faces in this particular

---

[2] D.R. Thorpe (1996) *Alec Douglas-Home*, Sinclair-Stevenson, p. 8.

[3] CC (63) 6, minute 6, 24 January 1963.

[4] Harold Macmillan (1973) *At the End of the Day*, Macmillan, p. 505.

race. 'Enter Mr Hogg and Mr Home,' as Anthony Howard put it in the New Statesman, an article which concentrated Home's mind on the options.[5]

The subsequent Conservative leadership contest in October 1963 is still surrounded by many inaccurate myths. Suffice it to quote Vernon Bogdanor: 'The outcome, the selection of Lord Home, cannot be said seriously to have misrepresented Conservative opinion at the time.'[6] Criticism of the Queen, too, is unfounded. To quote Vernon Bogdanor again: 'If the Conservative Party was divided, as it clearly was, the Queen could only compromise the position of the monarchy if she were to take part in that conflict.'[7] The point often overlooked is that not only was Rab Butler not going to get the leadership, but he knew that himself, which is why he dreaded the moment of Macmillan's retirement. John Morrison, Chairman of the 1922 Committee, had told Butler in the summer of 1963 that 'the chaps won't have you,'[8] and when, that autumn, Butler met Maudling by chance in the street outside Maudling's Hans Place apartment, he said to him in the course of the conversation: 'Of course, I'll be very pleased to serve under you Reggie, when the time comes.'[9] Hailsham's candidature was ended in part by the Americans, who let it be known through the British ambassador in Washington, Lord Harlech, that Lord Hailsham as Prime Minister would be the end of the special relationship.[10] The two serious candidates by October were Home and Maudling, and, after a trawl of the whole party inside and outside Parliament, Home was given what was in essence the 'first option'.

Crucially, Lord Home did not kiss hands when he was called to the Palace, but agreed to see first if he was able to form a government. The acceptance of the Foreign Office by Butler, the central figure, established Home as Prime Minister. So Rab Butler, mindful of Peel and the split over the Corn Laws in the 1840s, made Home Prime Minister, not Harold Macmillan. By then there was no point in Hailsham, or Maudling, being *plus royal que le roi*, and, in Lord Beaverbrook's vivid observation, 'He has got the loaves and the fishes. There is no stopping him now.'[11] When Home asked Maudling to stay on in the Treasury, he also told him that if he (Home) were unable to form a Government, then Maudling would be the politician the Queen would invite to try to form an

---

[5] *New Statesman*, 14 December 1962.

[6] Vernon Bogdanor (1995) *The Monarchy and the Constitution*, Oxford University Press, p. 96.

[7] Ibid., p. 98.

[8] Philip Goodhart (1973) *The 1922: The Story of the Conservatives' Backbenchers' Parliamentary Committee*, Macmillan, p. 196.

[9] Reginald Maudling to the author, September 1975.

[10] Thorpe, *Alec Douglas-Home*, pp. 298–9.

[11] A.J.P. Taylor (1974) *Beaverbrook* (1972), Penguin, p. 846.

administration.[12] Although Iain Macleod and Enoch Powell declined to serve, Home was able to form a government without them.

If Home's entry into Downing Street was unusual – the nearest parallel was Queen Victoria's invitation to Lord Hartington in 1880 to try to form a government – the first few weeks were constitutionally unprecedented, as, for a short time after Home had disclaimed his title to seek election in the by-election at Kinross and West Perthshire, the Prime Minister of the United Kingdom was a member of neither House of Parliament, a position to be repeated, regarding the Foreign Secretaryship, between October 1964 and January 1965, after Patrick Gordon Walker had lost his seat at Smethwick at the General Election. Home ensured then that the Conservatives did not make political capital of this constitutional anomaly, as, in a way unimaginable today, Labour had let the matter take its natural course when he was seeking election to the Commons.

Home had a difficult legacy. The Conservatives had been in office for 12 years, and third term governments, rare phenomena in any case, are by their very nature often unpopular, as Tony Blair admitted towards the end of his premiership. Although the Conservatives still had a comfortable majority from their 1959 General Election victory, despite some dramatic by-election losses, notably Orpington in March 1962, there was an atmosphere of damage limitation. Home faced in Harold Wilson, a formidable Leader of the Opposition, a figure wholly in tune with the Zeitgeist of the age. An election was due within a year, and few expected many fresh initiatives. They were to be proved wrong. From his first day in Downing Street, Home concentrated on putting the Conservatives in a position to win what would then have been an unprecedented fourth term. In the event he failed by the narrowest of margins: a few hundred votes judiciously redistributed in the most marginal seats would have altered the overall result. The Conservatives were 11 percentage points behind Labour when Alec Home became Prime Minister; 12 months later they suffered defeat by only 0.7 per cent; indeed, the Labour share of the vote (at 44.1 per cent) was only 0.3 per cent higher than in October 1959, when they had lost by 100 seats.

Home's Cabinet contained a blend of experienced figures and the leading politicians of the next generation. But it was not a Cabinet that was always at ease with itself. The events of October 1963 cast a long shadow and there was a sense of jostling for post-election positions, probably in Opposition. Rab Butler became Foreign Secretary, the post he had wanted in 1957, and which made him then only the second politician after Sir John Simon to have held all

---

[12] Reginald Maudling to the author, September 1975; Lord Home to the author, August 1990.

three of the great offices of state below the premiership.[13] But the appointment was not the one for which his career will be remembered. He was moving into the political arena where the Prime Minister had acknowledged expertise, and in which he had relatively little experience, apart from his unhappy pre-war spell as Under-Secretary at the time of Munich, a point he acknowledged in his first major speech in the Commons as Foreign Secretary: 'I know that I shall greatly profit by the Prime Minister's own experience and great skill as Foreign Secretary in conducting my own duties as Foreign Secretary in succession to him.'[14] Butler, his spirit crushed by three failures to become Prime Minister, in 1953, when both Churchill and Eden were ill (with hindsight Butler thought this his best opportunity[15]), 1957 and 1963, was demob-happy, and even more prone to his famous Rabbisms. 'Mind you, Alec's a good man, really,' he would say at meetings.[16] And, when he visited Moscow University on his Russian tour, he amazed his hosts by asking through the interpreter: 'Is this university state-aided?'[17] More seriously, just before the election in October Butler told a reporter that 'things might start slipping in the last few days,' adding, inaccurately as it proved, 'they won't slip towards us.'[18] When Home published in retirement what proved a bestselling political memoir, Butler offered it to weekend guests at his home at Stanstead, asking if they would care 'to look at this book on fishing'.[19]

Maudling continued as Chancellor of the Exchequer, and Henry Brooke as Home Secretary. Hailsham was Lord President and later, in addition, in charge of Education and Science. Duncan Sandys, Peter Thorneycroft, Freddie Erroll and Geofrey Rippon were also prominent figures. Two of the key figures were in non-departmental jobs. Selwyn Lloyd was recalled to the Cabinet as Leader of the House and Lord Privy Seal (he had been the principal victim of Macmillan's Night of the Long Knives in July 1962), and provided Home with not only support and encouragement, but also the riposte about Harold Wilson being 'the 14th Mr Wilson'.[20] John Hare, now Viscount Blakenham, was Chancellor of the Duchy of Lancaster, and Party Chairman. Blakenham was the principal advocate of an early election, so much so that he was dubbed 'the March Hare'.[21] Home, rightly, decided to follow Harold Macmillan's advice and play it as long as possible constitutionally, even into November. He later

---

[13] James Callaghan became the third in 1974.
[14] Anthony Howard (1987) *RAB: The Life of R.A.Butler*, Cape, p. 326.
[15] Lord Butler to the author, November 1975.
[16] Thorpe, *Alec Douglas-Home*, p. 320.
[17] Howard, *RAB*, p. 332.
[18] Thorpe, *Alec Douglas-Home*, p. 368.
[19] Ibid., p. 453.
[20] D.R. Thorpe (1989) *Selwyn Lloyd*, Cape, p. 388.
[21] Thorpe, *Alec Douglas-Home*, p. 343.

regretted not going to the country even later than 15 October. But the key figure in terms of the legacy the Home government would leave was, in fact, the man destined to be Home's successor as Party Leader: Edward Heath, the President of the Board of Trade.

With his combination of reforming zeal and determination to modernise, Heath had published a bill in January 1964 to abolish resale price maintenance. Its effects can be seen today in the cut-price stickers on the piles of books in any high street Waterstone's. The free-market concept was an ideal banner for the Conservative modernisers, but it threatened the livelihood of many small shopkeepers. A vociferous campaign, orchestrated by Lord Beaverbrook's *Daily Express*, fuelled sectional protests and a back-bench rebellion. On 11 March 1964, 21 Conservatives voted against Heath's bill and 17 others abstained. In a later division the government had a majority of only one. The issue lay at the heart of the old tensions between free traders and protectionists in the Conservative Party. Modernisers saw a system that legitimised an anticompetitive structure, at levels fixed by the manufacturers of branded goods, as incompatible with the radical business restructuring needed for Britain's trading survival. Caution was urged by those who had the interests of the traditionally Tory shopkeepers in mind. Home, who believed industrial modernisation was vital, backed Heath, even though the Cabinet, as it had been in 1959 when the issue had last been raised, was divided. 'The government had committed themselves to a policy of modernising Britain and promoting a more efficient use of resources,' Home told the Cabinet on 14 January 1964. 'This policy would fail to carry conviction if they were to tolerate the continuance of a practice so manifestly at variance with it.'[22] After much controversy and backbench revolts, the Bill passed its third reading on 13 May. The main impact of the abolition was positive. It showed that the government had not run out of new ideas and was not prepared to have economic policy dictated by vested interest groups, even if these were traditional Conservative supporters, and as such it was the harbinger of even more decisive changes in the future. Many Tories feared that the whole issue would be electorally disadvantageous, but this proved statistically unfounded. 'Once past the House of Commons,' David Butler and Anthony King concluded in their book on the 1964 Election, 'the bill aroused little further controversy, and resale price maintenance figured hardly at all at the election.'[23] Another example of Home's decisiveness was his tough stance on trade unions, giving no legislative help over the Rookes v. Barnard case in January 1964, when the House of Lords upheld the right of a BOAC employee at Heathrow Airport to damages for unfair dismissal because

---

[22] Cabinet minutes, 14 January 1964, National Archives, CAB 128/38.
[23] David Butler and Anthony King (1965) *The British General Election of 1964*, Macmillan, p. 23.

of a closed shop policy by the Association of Engineering and Shipbuilding Draughtsmen. He also made regulation 6 of the 1920 Emergency Powers Act a permanent legislative tool, ironically to prove a great help to Harold Wilson during the 1966 seamen's strike.

Within a few weeks of entering Downing Street, Home had to coordinate the British response to the news of President Kennedy's assassination. There were no indications that 22 November would prove such a dramatic and tragic day. Home had been to the TUC headquarters in the morning to view and discuss an education presentation, and he followed this with talks on Northern Ireland with the province's Premier, Captain Terence O'Neill. At 5.15 he was then driven to Arundel Castle, with his wife Elizabeth, for his first weekend break since taking office. He was met at Arundel Castle by the breathless Duke of Norfolk, who informed him of the breaking news from Dallas. The BBC were already in contact with Arundel Castle, and after a hurried supper Home was driven back to London to the BBC's Lime Grove studios, where his speech on behalf of the British nation was simple and dignified, unlike that of George Brown, the Deputy Labour leader, who, in the words of one his civil servants, 'declined in efficiency as the day progressed'. It was the moment when Home really established himself as the public face of the nation, as became clear from correspondents from many parts of the country, and not all by any means Conservative voters.

Home met the new American President, Lyndon B. Johnson, after Kennedy's funeral, but his first substantive talks with the new American President came in a visit to Washington in February 1964. Johnson, the Texas bruiser, was rather wary of the new British premier, as he was for Johnson such an unknown quantity. The Beatles were taking America by storm at the time and Johnson attempted humour initially. 'I like your advance guard,' he quipped. 'But don't you think they need haircuts?' If Johnson thought that Home would be a pushover in talks – especially, for him, on the contentious issue of the sale of British Leyland buses to Cuba – he had a rude awakening. Harold Macmillan had famously described Home to the Queen as 'steel painted as wood', and this certainly became clear in Washington that week. 'There is no question of dictation by the United States Government to this country over commercial relations with Cuba,' said Home. 'This is a subject which is decided solely by the British Government.' And so it was, to Johnson's undisguised fury. When Butler was in Washington two months later, the matter still rankled, and Johnson waved a wad of dollar notes at Butler, saying that, if Britain was so hard up that she needed to trade with Cuba, he could pay for the cancelled order himself. But the deal was concluded. Home showed similar steel in his second spell at the Foreign Office in 1971 with Andrei Gromyko – the abominable no-man – over the expulsion from Britain of 105 Russian spies.

At the forefront of Home's mind was always a possible post-election fourth term. He saw no reason why this should not be achieved, and ordered Cabinet ministers to conduct business on the expectation that they would be returned to office. During the course of his year in Downing Street he promised Christopher Soames, then the Agriculture Minister, the reversion to the Foreign Secretaryship if the Conservatives won. Enoch Powell was pencilled in to return to the Cabinet with a brief to reform Whitehall. No plans were made to recall Iain Macleod, certainly not after the *Spectator* affair in January 1964, an episode that in Home's view tipped the balance against the Conservatives in October 1964. In January 1964 Randolph Churchill published *The Fight for the Tory Leadership*, an insider's account, with material from Harold Macmillan, of the previous autumn's political upheavals. Iain Macleod, by now editor of the *Spectator*, in addition to his back-bench responsibilities, was outraged. On 17 January he published a review under the title 'The Tory Leadership', describing the book as 'Mr Macmillan's trailer for the screen play of his memoirs'. But the phrase that went at once into the political lexicon was that about the supposed 'magic circle' of Old Etonians who had conspired to make one of their own Conservative leader, over and above better-qualified candidates, notably Butler, Macleod's candidate. Alec Home was deeply saddened by the ensuing row, which raked up all the controversies of October 1963, not for his own feelings or reputation but because of what he considered the irreparable damage to the Conservative Party's chances in the next election. Macleod, surprisingly for one with sharp political antennae, did not anticipate the furore he would cause. 'He was not forgiven,' *The Times* wrote on his premature death in 1970. 'It was a political failing on his part that he took so long to appreciate that he had disqualified himself for the highest office.'[24] Home took advice from Harold Macmillan on what he should say if Macleod persisted in his attacks, notably the point that the Conservative Party had not been able to find a leader from within its own ranks in the Commons. Macmillan advised Home to say that it was a sad reflection on journalism that the profession had not been able to find an editor of the *Spectator* from within its own ranks, but had had to resort to Iain Macleod.[25]

The Macleod article came at exactly the wrong moment – but what would have been the right one – as the Conservatives were picking up some momentum, particularly on the domestic front. In the week of the article, Home was in South Wales on a pre-election tour, when statistics showed that fewer than one family in three had owned their home in 1951 when the Conservatives had come into office. Now it was nearly half. 'A property owning democracy is becoming a reality,' Home said in his speech in Swansea, a reference

---

24 *The Times*, 22 July 1970.
25 Harold Macmillan to the author, 23 April 1975.

to his mentor in pre-war days, the Unionist MP for the Scottish Universities, Noel Skelton, who had first advocated the principle in his book *Constructive Conservatism* in 1924. 'Until our educated and politically minded democracy,' wrote Skelton, 'has become predominantly a property-owning democracy, neither the national equilibrium nor the balance of the life of the individual will be restored.'[26] It was a message that was taken up by Skelton's two principal protégés, Anthony Eden and Alec Home, future prime ministers both. Not that it was necessary to remind Alec Home, but on the eve of the 1964 campaign Eden, by then Earl of Avon, wrote to Home as the manifesto was being written, reiterating: 'A property-owning democracy is the aim.'

In the Cabinet room, Home proved a formidable chairman, pushing the agenda onwards, being crisp in his summings-up and shrewd in his preparation of the agenda. One of the first things he did was to cut a swathe through the ever-burgeoning number of ad hoc Cabinet Committees, many of which had now run their natural course. This reorganisation was symptomatic of the pragmatic approach Home brought to his task as Cabinet Chairman. Indeed, no less a distinguished mandarin than Sir Burke Trend, who was Cabinet Secretary under four prime ministers, believed that Alec Home was the most orderly and efficient of all in his conduct of Cabinet business.[27] Another underestimated change that Home introduced was the so-called Douglas-Home rules whereby the Civil Service is permitted to talk with Opposition leaders in the lead-up to a general election, so as to expedite more efficiently changes of policy in the event of a change of government. This is now such an established part of the political procedure that it is often forgotten how relatively recently the system was introduced, and by whom.

Home was courteous and brisk with memos. Colin Cowdrey, the England cricket captain, and a notable slip fielder, wrote to him once on MCC matters as 'Sir Alec'. Home replied, 'You can drop the Sir, if you ever drop anything.'[28] Above all, there was never any masquerading or spin by Alec Home. What you saw was what you got. Even his political opponents acknowledged that his integrity was absolute, another similarity with Bonar Law, of whom Lloyd George said, during the 1922 General Election campaign, that Law was 'honest to the point of simplicity', which proved a telling advantage with the British electorate after six years of Lloyd George. Home was the embodiment of Walter Bagehot's ideal, 'Sensible men of substantial means are what we wish to be ruled by.'[29]

---

[26] Noel Skelton (1924) *Constructive Conservatism*, Blackwood, p. 17.

[27] Trend served Macmillan, Home, Wilson and Heath as Cabinet Secretary between 1963 and 1973.

[28] Thorpe, *Alec Douglas-Home*, p. 395.

[29] Walter Bagehot (1872) introduction to the second edition of *The English Constitution*, in 'The Collected Works of Walter Bagehot', *The Economist*, 1974, vol. 5, 181.

Prime ministers fall into many categories. As Prime Minister, Home may not have been an innovator, changing the political landscape, like Margaret Thatcher, or a reformer, bringing about a major change of direction in policy, like Clement Attlee. He was certainly not an egoist, living for the adrenalin of office, like Lloyd George and others. He did not change the political weather, as Churchill said of one who never even became Prime Minister, Joe Chamberlain. Home was in a different category of prime ministers, as a balancer chosen to bring different wings together, a role that was second nature to Stanley Baldwin or James Callaghan. Just as Bonar Law was chosen as Conservative leader because he was not Walter Long or Austen Chamberlain, so Alec Home was chosen because he was not Rab Butler or Quintin Hailsham. But, like James Callaghan, he was a prime minister who came at the tail-end of a long period of dominance by his party, a position not enviable in politics, and one that both Home and Callaghan shared with Lord Rosebery in the 1890s.

The inevitable problems faced by Rosebery, Home and Callaghan at such an unpropitious time in the electoral cycle were thus exacerbated by the perceived view that they were not destined to be in office for long. Of these three premiers, Home was by far the most successful, leaving his party best equipped to regain power, something it did less than five years after he gave up the leadership, whereas for the Liberals at the turn of the century the process took 10 years, and for the Labour Party at the end of the century 18 years. Although the change did not take place whilst he was Prime Minister, but in February 1965 in his short period as Leader of the Opposition, Home's review of the procedure for choosing the Conservative Party leader was to have a profound effect on the party, and on the executive's relationship with the sovereign at a time of vacancy. It is often claimed that this new system, which itself has undergone many changes in subsequent years, was the brainchild of the back-bench MP Humphrey Berkeley. But Berkeley, with his own proposals, courteously considered by Home, was knocking at an already open door, as Berkeley himself acknowledged.

The first public surprise about Home's early days in No. 10 was the extent to which he was interested in and knowledgeable about domestic affairs. For those who knew of his time as resident Minister of State at the Scottish Office from 1951 to 1955, this was only to be expected. In those years, when Home travelled the length and breadth of his native country, from Cape Wrath to John O'Groats, past Bettyhill on the Northern seaboard, through the Highlands and Islands, as well as the great industrial conurbations, there were few domestic concerns that at some stage did not cross his desk in St Andrews House in Edinburgh. He followed a path of which Noel Skelton, who had died prematurely in 1935, would have approved. In Mull, he had talks on the reorganisation of local government; at the Turnberry Hotel in Ayrshire he met on a regular basis with the Scottish Farmers' Union to discuss their manifold problems. He worked on questions of crofting and depopulation in the Highlands and Islands. He had a sharp eye for administrative detail. Once a civil servant handed him a draft that spoke of proposed changes to the system of tied cottages 'by regulation'. Home, the experienced parliamentarian, swiftly changed this to 'by legislation'. The rating system, schools, transport, unemployment and health care were all problems with which he was concerned in these years. Even Home's opponents admitted his profound knowledge of foreign affairs, from his days at the Commonwealth Office and the Foreign Office between 1955 and 1963; what they had not expected was his expertise in the niceties of domestic policy. For one whose original mentor had been Noel Skelton, the originator of the concept of the 'property owning democracy' among One Nation Tories, this was only to be expected. Satisfyingly, one of the earliest projects he had worked on with James Stuart, the Secretary of State, in the early 1950s had been the proposal to build a Forth Road Bridge, which was finally accomplished in the closing days of his premiership.

Foreign events also loomed large – Cyprus, where civil war had broken out, Rhodesia and the growing threat of a rebel breakaway, a topic which involved Home in his second spell as Foreign Secretary in the early 1970s, clashes on the borders of Yemen and Aden, and a row with Spain over frigates. In July Home chaired the Commonwealth Prime Ministers' conference in London, in which the question of Southern Rhodesia was of central importance. Clashes between America and North Vietnam in the Gulf of Tonkin also contributed to the volatile atmosphere that summer. Home showed a sure hand in all these crises – Rab Butler was quite happy to leave the day-to-day response to Downing Street, a rare example of the Foreign Office not being discomfited by No. 10's involvement in foreign affairs. Gradually Conservative fortunes and morale were on the rise. 'The government could be seen to be governing,' was one Press comment at this time. There was a growing feeling that, against all the odds, the Tories might just win another term.

After Parliament had risen on 31 July, the first anniversary of the Peerage Act becoming law, Home wrote to all Cabinet Ministers warning against complacency over the summer months. In his first six months in office Home had given 64 'full dress' speeches and 150 whistle-stop homilies. A pre-election tour in Yorkshire in the summer had included a visit to Huddersfield, Harold Wilson's birthplace. The announcement of the election date was made on 18 September, with polling day set for 15 October. This would be five years and one week since Macmillan's victory on 8 October 1959, so the parliament was the longest since the interval between elections had been reduced to five years in 1911. The result – Labour 317 seats, Conservatives 304, and Liberals nine – was also the closest in living memory, an overall majority of three once the Speaker had been re-elected.

Even then three events on 15 October 1964, had they taken place 24 hours earlier, would almost certainly have guaranteed a Conservative victory. As the polls closed, at 9 p.m. in those days, which is why Wilson successfully arranged with the BBC for the popular TV comedy, *Steptoe and Son*, to be delayed till later than its usual slot in the Thursday evening's schedules, news came of the downfall of the Russian leader, Nikita Khrushchev. Indeed, the early election broadcasts were far more concerned with this dramatic and unexpected breaking news than with the exit polls. There was also news of the successful Chinese nuclear explosion. Either of these global events could well have induced a sense of 'Safety First' that would have denied Wilson victory had they happened earlier. A more parochial event, if handled more subtly, could also have helped to change the result. The Labour victory could have been even narrower if the Conservative MP for Brighton Kemp Town had not arranged for 200 of the ladies from his constituency organisation to travel on an all-day cross-channel shipping trip to Boulogne, leaving at 6 a.m. and returning in the small hours. Labour won Brighton Kemp Town, its first ever seat in Sussex, by seven votes after seven recounts. Subsequently, Home always said Boulogne, not Calais, would be forever engraved on his heart, that and Iain Macleod, towards whom his private anger was unbridled. Home shrewdly realised in his disappointment that the narrowness of defeat was actually a far worse result than a loss by 20–30 seats, as it guaranteed another election before long, at which, such are the vagaries of the electoral system and voters' feelings, Wilson would certainly be given a larger majority. Indeed, Wilson increased his majority to 97 in March 1966, by which time Home was no longer Conservative leader.

Home stood down in July 1965, one of the few party leaders to leave with dignity and at a time of his own choosing – Harold Wilson was to prove another 11 years later – and, in the first outing for the new rules he had established, Heath was elected leader, defeating Reginald Maudling and Enoch Powell. But this was not the end of Home's story in the upper reaches of the Conservative Party. Lord Rosebery once said that an ex-Prime Minister in the Commons was a danger to shipping, and that to include such a figure in a Cabinet was for the successor 'a fleeting and dangerous luxury'. There was never any question of Heath flinching from such a choice, and in June 1970 Home became Foreign Secretary for the second time, a figure of ballast and stability in Heath's administration, particularly over the Rhodesian rebellion. Few Prime Ministers have had such a useful post-No. 10 career. The nearest parallel is Balfour, who also served as Foreign Secretary after his spell in No. 10.

Home showed all his successors as party leader absolute loyalty; there was no sniping or tacit criticism whatsoever, not of Heath, Thatcher or Major. When Mrs Thatcher became Conservative leader in February 1975, she at once engaged in a lengthy correspondence with Home on foreign matters, on which she confessed ignorance that she needed to rectify. Home obliged and was a vital help during the four years of opposition Mrs Thatcher endured before entering No. 10. In the early 1990s, during the first Gulf War, he was rung up on a regular basis by the Foreign Secretary Douglas Hurd to be kept in touch with developments. Home lived longer than Churchill, dying in October 1995 at the age of 92.

Home may have been Prime Minister 'for a very short time', but in that time he added a quiet dignity to British public life, despite the ridicule of the modish satirists, and he surprised pundits and politicians alike by his sense of clarity, efficiency, firmness and patriotism at a time when society seemed to be on an inexorable downward path. After his years at the Commonwealth Office and the Foreign Office, he had a clear understanding of Britain's place in a transitional post-war world. He knew that the former American Secretary of State Dean Acheson had spoken an unpalatable truth when he said that Britain had lost an Empire and failed to find a role. 'We have shed a terrible lot of power,' he wrote reflectively over the Christmas recess in 1963 to Sir Michael Fraser of the Conservative Research Department, 'but it is useless to cry over spilt milk.'[30] In the days of the Cold War, he was completely unsentimental about the Soviet Union and consistently pursued a policy of firmness, best evinced by the expulsion, during his second spell as Foreign Secretary in 1971, of 105 Russian spies from Britain. This attitude conditioned his views on African issues, notably the Congo, especially during its first 18 months of independence, when he emphasised the need for 'a government which will keep order and prevent a Communist takeover'.[31] 'Had he been of another generation, he would have been of the Grenadiers and the 1914 heroes,' observed Harold Macmillan. 'He gives that impression by a curious mixture of great courtesy, and even of yielding to pressure, with underlying rigidity on matters of principle.'[32]

Home's premiership was a one-off, as Britain stood on the cusp of profound social change, and was of a kind never to be repeated. There were failures and misapprehensions, inevitably. On his return to the Commons in November 1963, Home was shocked by the changes that had come about in parliamentary procedure since he had last spoken from the front bench in July 1951, and by the sheer rudeness of many members. In the face of heckling, even abuse from the Opposition benches, he never established himself as a domineering parliamentarian. Nor did he ever fully come to grips with the demands of television and the autocue. Both were areas where the Leader of the Opposition, Harold Wilson, excelled. Interestingly, Home's most successful television broadcast

---

[30] National Archives, PREM 11/5006. 'My philosophy', Lord Home to Sir Michael Fraser, 30 December 1963.

[31] National Archives, FO 371/154941.

[32] National Archives, PREM 11/5008. Memorandum of 15 October 1963.

was on the death of President Kennedy, when he spoke from the heart, not from the autocue the backroom boys had provided for him.

As Dominic Sandbrook has shown in his study of this period, *Never Had It So Good*, society in the early sixties was not one headlong rush to hedonism. There was a silent majority who wanted the old values, who were mistrustful of trend-setting and the lowest common denominator world of the media. For such people, in particular, Home appeared as a Prime Minister with an innate inner calm, well fitted to represent Britain's interests. Home had many of the good points of his predecessors without their downside – like Balfour, he was willing to serve in Cabinet after having held the top post, but, unlike Balfour, he was never aloof and indecisive; like Bonar Law, who freed the Cabinet Secretariat from its Lloyd George Garden Suburb connotations, but without his sometimes angular responses, he renewed the system of Cabinet committees, a progeny of the Secretariat, and liberated the Civil Service from its purdah regarding the Opposition; like Baldwin, but without his long periods of inactivity, he represented a kind of country viewpoint that saw Westminster as a part, a necessary part, of public life, but by no means the be-all and end-all. Just as Baldwin really did like leaning over a fence in Worcestershire and scratching a pig, so Home was most at ease, with his labrador, fishing on the Tweed, as his portrait in the National Portrait Gallery shows him. He was never seduced by the metropolitan world. As Selwyn Lloyd said, without any sense of irony, of the Conservative Party's difficulties in the late 1960s, 'the only real provincials are Alec Douglas-Home and myself.'[33] The world that followed was a more technocratic, even soulless one. Like Attlee, Home was a down-to-earth figure of common sense, who left flashy charisma to others, got on with the job and made time for the cricket scores, as befitted the only prime minister to have played first class cricket.

Home was the last flourishing of a particular strand of British public life, 'an utterly authentic evocation of deep, traditional, landed Toryism', in the words of Peter Hennessy. 'He was like the very last of the steam locomotives which were on their twilight journeys at exactly this time. Perhaps he was a kind of human Coronation Scot. Or more likely, given his country pursuits, he was Mallard, pulling one last express from King's Cross to Edinburgh and sounding its distinctive whistle in a plaintive farewell as it crossed the Royal Border Bridge above the River Tweed at Berwick.'[34]

---

[33] Thorpe, *Selwyn Lloyd*, p. 409.
[34] Peter Hennessy (2000) *The Prime Minister: The Office and its Holders since 1945*, Allen Lane, p. 285.

6

Harold Wilson, 1964–1970, 1974–1976

Philip Ziegler

In a recent poll professing to measure the public's assessment of the success enjoyed by post-war prime ministers, Harold Wilson and John Major came equal bottom. Whether this poll was in any serious way representative of public opinion and what criteria were adopted in deciding what constituted 'success' remains uncertain: one cannot pretend, however, that the conclusion was encouraging to anyone concerned for Wilson's reputation. Students of the period have for the most part treated him with indifference, if not contempt. It would, indeed, be difficult to claim that his years as prime minister were radiantly successful: I would maintain, however, that, given the problems he faced and the atmosphere in which he was required to solve them, he deserves to be treated with far greater respect than is customarily allowed him.

It is hard today to recall the euphoria which greeted Wilson's accession to power after the election of 1964. In that campaign he had brilliantly, if to a considerable extent unfairly, characterised his opponent, Alec Douglas-Home, as an amiable but tweedily ineffective aristocrat, wholly out of touch with the contemporary world. He had set out his own stall at the party conference at Scarborough in October 1963. For 45 minutes he kept a hard-boiled, sceptical and jaded audience enthralled as he set out his vision of the future. Under Labour there would be a second industrial revolution, creating 10 million new jobs by the mid-1970s by: 'Planning on an unprecedented scale to meet automation without unemployment; a pooling of talent in which all "classes" could compete and prosper; a vast extension of state-sponsored research; a completely new concept of education; an alliance of science and socialism'. Only by central planning could the full potential be realised: 'Because we are democrats, we reject the methods which Communist countries are deploying in applying the results of scientific research to industrial life but, because we care deeply about the future of Britain, we must use all the resources of democratic planning, all the latent and under-developed skills of our people, to ensure Britain's standing in the world.' The Tories had proved themselves incompetent to meet this challenge. They said Britain would have all the scientists it needed by 1965: 'Of course we shall – if we do not use them. We shall have all the bull-fighters we need by 1965.' They believed in amateurism at a time when even the MCC had abolished the distinction between amateurs and professionals; 'in science and industry we are content to remain Gentlemen in a world of Players'. But Labour, too, must be prepared to rise to new challenges: 'There is no room for Luddites in the Socialist Party. ... The Britain that is going to be forged in the white heat of this revolution will be no place for restrictive practices or for out-dated methods on either side of industry.'[1]

That speech, in effect, provided Wilson's platform for the 1964 election. It caught the nation's imagination and won their votes. An overall Tory majority of over 100 was turned into a Labour majority of five. But, though the result was impressive, it left no room for overconfidence. The big winner in the election had been the Liberals, who had secured two million extra votes. Mainly these had been taken from the Conservatives, but the Labour vote was still down in comparison with 1959. A majority of five, even though the Liberals were unlikely to make common cause with the Conservatives in the immediate future, was uncomfortably, even unmanageably small. Wilson knew that he was only marking time until the moment seemed propitious for him to go back to the country. A sensible rule for any incoming prime minister is to introduce as quickly as possible any measure which is necessary but is likely to prove unpopular with the electorate. Wilson had no such period of grace; from the start he knew that another election might be just round the corner, at the most round the next corner but one. He could not afford to alienate even a small part of the electorate in case a snap election was forced on him and there were enough extra malcontents to wipe out his majority.

Wilson announced proudly that he would not allow his precarious position to deter him from pushing forward with the promised programme. The Queen's speech at the opening of Parliament in November 1964 showed that he was going to be – or at least was going to try to be – as good as his word. Prescription charges were to be abolished, the iron and steel industry was to be nationalised, a major review would be launched in the field of social security. It was a full-blooded socialist programme, but introduced by a government which claimed that it could work with business, that it understood and could ride with the tide of international economics in a way unknown to the Conservative amateurs who preceded it. A few people might be temporarily worse off because of the government's activities, but in the not-so-distant future the country would be vastly more prosperous. Everyone would benefit from Labour's policies.

---

[1] The text of this speech can be found in Harold Wilson (1964) *Purpose in Politics: Selected Speeches*, Weidenfeld and Nicolson, pp. 16–28.

Wilson might have got away with it. The first few months of his administration did show a welcome energy and efficiency. But almost before he had taken possession of 10 Downing Street the economic storm was beginning to rage, driving the ship of state disastrously off course and threatening to swamp it altogether. The most immediate problem was the trade deficit, which seemed to be running at £800 million a year, twice as bad as Wilson had deemed likely in his most gloomy moments. Some economists have questioned these figures, but Wilson himself believed in them and convinced not only his colleagues but the foreign bankers and investors that Britain was in a desperate plight. There were various ways of tackling the problem. The most dramatic would have been devaluation. Before the election this option had been firmly excluded. 'There will be no devaluation. You would water the weeds as well as the flowers,' Wilson declared.[2] If the economy was really in as dire a state as now appeared, it was obvious that the possibility would have to be reconsidered. It was, but only to be dismissed again. Wilson concluded that the certain risks were greater than any possible gains and that 'socialist' policies could cure the balance of payments problem.

It has often been maintained that the rejection of immediate devaluation, when it could plausibly have been presented as the result of 13 years of Tory misrule, was an egregious blunder. At least as many economists, however, doubt whether devaluation would have achieved the hoped-for result. The Bank of England opposed the move both in principle and because it feared that a Labour government would squander whatever benefits there might be. To the layman it seems as if the balance of economic argument tips narrowly in favour of devaluation, but that the point is, in any case, academic since politically such a step was inconceivable. Wilson was haunted by the fact that he had been involved in the last devaluation in 1949; if he did the same thing in 1964 he feared that Labour would be forever stamped as the party of the easy option. He saw sterling, said Denis Healey, 'as a sort of virility symbol'; to let its value fall would be proof of British weakness.[3] Discussion of the possibility was banned, even in the most privy conclave.

If Britain were not to devalue it must deflate; that at least was the judgement of the Treasury and the Bank of England. Up to a point Wilson accepted the logic; but he could not tolerate the price that society would have to pay, particularly in unemployment. He sought a third way, holding the economic line by a series of stopgap measures such as the curbing of imports and the cancellation of a few ambitious and expensive programmes, but sticking to his guns

---

[2] Peter Kellner and Christopher Hitchens (1976) *Callaghan: The Road to Number 10*, Cassell, p. 47.
[3] Philip Whitehead (1985) *The Writing on the Wall: Britain in the Seventies*, Michael Joseph, p. 3.

over the main items in his projected social revolution. The further development of Concorde was a tempting target for a cut, but when the possibility was
broached with the French the response was so hostile that the idea was hastily
abandoned; in the end the economy drive achieved little beyond a few minor
savings in the running of Whitehall. Callaghan's first budget, a week after
the Queen's speech, increased social benefits and national assistance as well
as introducing a capital gains tax. The results were damaging, verging on the
catastrophic. The international bankers panicked at what they saw as Labour's
improvident and inflationary policies. Lyndon Johnson, American President
since the assassination of J.F. Kennedy, who was temperamentally well disposed towards the new government, was almost equally alarmed. 'The British
decision has shaken us some,' he admitted.[4] There was a hectic run on sterling
and the reserves were dangerously depleted. Lord Cromer, the Governor of
the Bank of England, managed temporarily to extricate the government from
its difficulties by raising a guarantee of $3,000 million to protect sterling, but
the first fine careless rapture of Wilson's administration had been for ever dis-
pelled. From now on, until he finally resigned nearly 12 years later, he was
doomed to live from hand to mouth, perpetually strapped for cash, peering
apprehensively into an uncertain future, forced to chop and change his policies to suit the dismal economic circumstances which prevailed.

It was because such tactics were forced on him that he acquired the reputation of a trimmer, a man without principles or convictions who would abandon any friend or policy without hesitation if it seemed to him expedient.
Up to a point, the charge has some validity. Wilson believed that it was his
prime responsibility to keep the Labour government in office; any conduct
that seemed likely to defeat this object, however commendable in itself, must
therefore be eschewed. A prime example of what to him seemed the merest pru-
dence, yet to others appeared a betrayal of principle, was his attitude towards
the nationalisation of the steel industry. This piece of legislation was enshrined
in the manifesto and Wilson could, therefore, not discard it altogether, but
privately it seemed to him unlikely that it would contribute much towards
the nation's prosperity. Certainly it was not worth going to the stake for. Yet it
looked as if that was where he might end up, because a handful of Labour MPs,
notably Desmond Donnelly and Woodrow Wyatt, were strongly against the
project. In normal circumstances they could have been ignored and crushed if
they stepped out of line. So small was the Labour majority, however, that the
rebels, if they persisted in their opposition, could bring down the government.
Wilson devoted endless time and energy to the search for a compromise which
would satisfy Donnelly and Wyatt yet not alienate the rank and file of the

---

[4] Lyndon Johnson Library. NSF files of McGeorge Bundy. Memos for the Record – 7
December 1964.

party. It proved a thankless task, which earned him little credit with anyone involved. Wyatt claimed to have found him 'totally cynical'. Wilson, Wyatt recorded, kept repeating that he was a pragmatist and protested: 'I don't think there are ten votes in the country in steel one way or the other but I'm stuck with it.'[5] When Wilson told the cabinet what he had been doing, Crossman accused him of being 'without a touch of vision – no Kennedy touch, not even the dynamic of Lyndon Johnson.'[6] The Queen's Speech of November 1965 omitted any reference to steel; proof that no compromise had been discovered. In the eyes of much of the parliamentary Labour party this meant that the government had shirked its clear responsibility; the blame, they believed, must lie with Wilson.

Steel was only one of a myriad of problems which beset him during his three administrations. Wilson recorded his years as prime minister in two volumes of memoirs, which are notable for their crushing tedium even in a branch of literature not renowned for its liveliness.[7] Yet at the same time they are among the most valuable and, in their own way, most fascinating records ever left by a senior minister. They report, in often otiose detail and with a flatness memorable for its refusal to distinguish between the important and the trivial, the permanent and the ephemeral, the events of each day as they happened. When, for instance, the developing crisis in Rhodesia deserved all his attention, Wilson would find himself grappling simultaneously with a run on sterling, a furious Minister of Defence complaining about a projected cut in spending, a left-wing revolt over the nuclear deterrent, an American President demanding support for his policy in Vietnam, not to mention a row between his political and his private secretaries, a scandal involving an MP's improper use of inside information and all the routine matters that by themselves fill the life of a prime minister to overflowing. Worse still, these problems were interrelated: if he made no concessions to the left wing over the deterrent they would be more likely to revolt over Vietnam; if he did not do what the American President wanted over Vietnam the run on sterling might become a stampede. Wilson could, of course, have left some at least of these problems to other members of his government, but, like so many prime ministers, he found it hard to delegate, being confident that on every issue there was a significant contribution which only he could make. The consequence was that each day, and all too often a great part of each night as well, was spent on a roller-coaster

---

[5] Woodrow Wyatt (1985) *Confessions of an Optimist*, Collins, p. 3.

[6] Richard Crossman (1975) *Diaries: Minister of Housing, 1964–1966*, Hamish Hamilton/ Cape, p. 321.

[7] Harold Wilson (1971) *The Labour Government, 1964–1970: A Personal Record*, Weidenfeld and Nicolson, and (1979) *Final Term: The Labour Government, 1974–1976*, Weidenfeld and Nicolson.

of recurrent crises, which left no opportunity for calm reflection, let alone serious strategic planning.

This was the more to be regretted because the administration over which he presided was crowded with exceptionally able ministers who, if only he had felt able to trust them, would have been well capable of looking after their designated fields. A government which was led by a prime minister who could boast, and frequently did boast, that he had been awarded the most distinguished First in PPE of his year, perhaps of his decade, and which included such men as Roy Jenkins, Denis Healey, Anthony Crosland and Richard Crossman, was intellectually streets ahead of anything the Tories of the day could offer. James Callaghan and, when he was sober, George Brown were outstandingly efficient administrators capable of arguing a case with eloquence and conviction. Tony Benn and Barbara Castle threw themselves into whatever task they had been allotted with a passion and energy that ensured they would leave a mark, if not always precisely the mark that Wilson had envisaged when he appointed them. The problem was that two at least of these felt that they should have been at No. 10 instead of the present incumbent; Crossman was a professional trouble-maker and plotter who could never resist a chance to stir up dissent within the Cabinet; and as for the others, loyalty and a readiness to toe the party line were not conspicuous among their attributes. Wilson believed in 'creative tension', a healthy rivalry between ministers and the evolution of policy by rational argument and the eventual victory of the stronger case. Unfortunately, given the personalities involved it was inevitable that the tension would often be destructive rather than creative and that victory would be won not by those who had the stronger case but by those who were most unscrupulous in their tactics and who possessed the bigger guns and the louder voices when the issue came to Cabinet.

One of the very few causes for which Wilson seemed prepared to fling compromise and party unity to the winds and fight his battle to the verge of the last ditch was the reform of the trade unions. By the end of 1968 he had long been convinced that unofficial strikes were Labour's biggest electoral handicap. In Barbara Castle he had a Minister of Labour who fully shared his ideas and had the courage and energy to try to put them into practice. *In Place of Strife*, the White Paper on which the reform of the trade unions was to be based, was hardly a revolutionary document, but it contained certain clauses which the unions found it very hard to swallow – notably those giving the Secretary of State powers to impose a pause for conciliation and to order a ballot before a strike could begin. If he had had a united cabinet behind him Wilson might still have got away with it, but James Callaghan, partly from a sense of loyalty to the unions, partly perhaps in pursuit of a more self-interested agenda, came out in forthright opposition to the proposed reforms. For a time it seemed that there was no possibility of a compromise, still less of the surrender of the

Prime Minister, but, when it became clear that Wilson and Castle were almost isolated within the cabinet, the advantages of a patched-up settlement became suddenly more obvious. The unions eased his passage by entering into a 'solemn and binding' undertaking that they would scrutinise the government's proposals on unofficial strikes ('Solomon Binding – sounds like a character out of George Eliot', remarked an irreverent official) and Wilson, with some relief, hailed this as a noble victory and abandoned *In Place of Strife* for his Conservative successor to revive in new clothes a few years later.

The loss of reputation involved in this debacle must have been one of the factors in Wilson's unexpected electoral defeat in 1970. He himself blamed it above all on the iniquities of the BBC and the irrational nature of women voters. Some assumed that his retreat from 10 Downing Street would quickly be followed by his surrender of the leadership of the party, but Wilson had no such intentions. Instead he devoted himself to writing the history of his term of office and planning his return to power. There were those among his followers who saw things differently and would happily have seen him replaced, preferably by themselves, but they were too divided, too jealous of each other, to unite in forcing a change of leader. Wilson was still in charge when the crisis caused by the Yom Kippur war and the coal miners' strike forced the Conservatives into a premature election. His victory was as unexpected as had been his defeat in 1970. He found that all the old problems still existed, many of them exacerbated, and that a new one had arisen. Britain was now part of Europe and Wilson was going to have to decide what to do about it.

Though Wilson eventually found it necessary to entrust the Foreign Office to George Brown and then to Callaghan, it is noteworthy that the Foreign Secretaries of his first choice, Patrick Gordon Walker and Michael Stewart, were not among the more dynamic of his appointments. The reason was that he saw foreign affairs both as providing a global stage on which he would rejoice to play a starring role and as posing problems on which he had strong views which he was determined to impose upon his colleagues. The country would probably have been better served if he had devoted more of his time and energy to economic affairs and the development of Britain's industrial base and less to such issues as Vietnam, Rhodesia or the British presence East of Suez. That, however, was not how he saw his responsibilities. The tragedy for him was that, on almost every major issue, political, economic and military realities forced him to follow a course almost directly contrary to his deep convictions.

Churchill once remarked that he had not been appointed Prime Minister to preside over the dissolution of the British Empire. By the time that Harold Wilson found himself in Downing Street the process of dissolution, irreversible even when Churchill stated his position, was far advanced. Logically and emotionally Wilson was prepared to accept, indeed enthusiastically agree, that the day of empire was over, but in his eyes it did not necessarily follow that this entailed any marked diminution of Britain's status in the world. He had not been elected, he would have maintained, to preside over the exclusion of Britain from the table of the great powers. So far as he was concerned, the 'Great' was still in Great Britain and ever more would be so. When left-wing – or just realistic – members of his party argued that it was folly to waste vital resources keeping forces in such far-flung relics of empire as Hong Kong or Singapore, he retorted that such people 'would like to contract out and leave it to the Americans and Chinese, eyeball to eyeball, to face this thing out…. It is the surest prescription for a nuclear holocaust I could think of.'[8] In another context he would have substituted Russia for China and allotted Britain the same mediatory role. He was ridiculed for absurdly overstating the role that Britain could play in resolving, or at least palliating, any dissension between the great powers, not to mention his own personal influence with the leaders of Russia, China or the United States. And yet he was not being entirely foolish. He was surely right in thinking that there was a real contribution to be made, if only as a conveniently positioned honest broker, and that the potential to serve in that role should not lightly be discarded.

Two underlying considerations were always in Wilson's mind: the need to keep the Commonwealth united and the vital importance of the Anglo-American alliance. That these two aims sometimes seemed incompatible was an additional, vexatious strand in the complex web of commitments and respon-sibilities. One point, however, on which the two were entirely compatible, and yet over which Wilson eventually found himself reluctantly compelled to dis-oblige both the Commonwealth and the United States, was the British military presence East of Suez. When Lee Kuan Yew told him that the retention of the British base in Singapore was essential for the survival of democratic socialism in the area; when the Australians used such words as 'treachery' and 'betrayal'; when the American Secretary of State threatened dire consequences if Britain reneged on its commitments, Wilson found himself entirely persuaded that they were right. Britain's frontier was on the Himalayas, he once pronounced grandiloquently. It took three years of economic crisis, three years in which the ever more straitened British armed forces became more and more obvi-ously unable to perform the tasks imposed on them, to convince Wilson of the harsh reality. Either Britain must pull out of the Far East and the Persian Gulf or it must drastically reduce its commitment to the defence of Germany: any other course would lead to national bankruptcy. The first choice was infinitely disagreeable; the second – with the Cold War still at its most dangerous – was impossible. Later Wilson was to say that he felt clinging on to the East of Suez role had been one of his worst mistakes as Prime Minister: he was, he said, one

---

[8] Quoted in Andrew Roth (1977) *Harold Wilson: Yorkshire Walter Mitty*, Macdonald and Jane's, p. 52.

of the last to be converted, 'and it needed a lot of hard facts to convert me. Others of my colleagues, left-wing and pro-European alike, were wiser in their perceptions.'[9] The occasion was memorable as being almost the only time in a long and not wholly unblemished career that Wilson admitted he had been wrong. It is only fair to Wilson to say that this is once more than is the case with certain other prime ministers who come to mind.

By withdrawing from East of Suez Wilson knew that he would incur the displeasure of the Americans. This was a particular cause for lamentation. As is not entirely unknown among leaders of the Labour Party, Wilson invested the special relationship with almost mystic significance and consistently believed that by staying close to the president of the day he could exercise a significant influence on the evolution of American policy. He assured the American ambassador, David Bruce, that Britain 'solidly supported' US policy in Vietnam, though hoping that military action would be matched by willingness to negotiate.[10] Left to himself, it is perfectly possible that he would have manifested that support more overtly, conceivably even by committing British forces to the campaign. Mercifully, he was not left to himself. The left wing of the Labour Party, indeed a majority of Labour moderates, believed that it was not enough merely to refuse to support American military action; American policies should be roundly denounced and attacked in the United Nations. When Wilson visited Washington at the end of 1964, President Johnson took him for a walk in the rose garden of the White House and in these seductive surroundings pressed him to send the Black Watch to Vietnam; even a single piper would be better than nothing. Wilson did not respond. The talks had been 'very successful', he told George Brown; he had accepted no new commitments as regarded Vietnam.[11] For the rest of his time as Prime Minister he conducted a singularly skilful operation designed not to cause undue offence to the Americans while throwing a sop from time to time to the potential rebels to his left. His strength lay in his weakness: the Americans knew that he was under genuine threat from his left wing and that anyone who replaced him was bound to be more hostile to their interests. When the aerial bombardment of North Vietnam, and American use of gas and napalm, exacerbated Labour disapproval still further, Wilson told his Foreign Secretary, who was in Washington, that the Americans should be left in no doubt about the strength of feeling in Britain and about the difficulties he was facing. There was, he said, a danger of widespread anti-Americanism and of America losing her moral position. 'Should the President try to link this question with support for the pound,' he added menacingly, 'I would regard this as most unfortunate.' Such behaviour would

---

[9] Wilson, *Labour Government, 1964–1970*, p. 243.
[10] Lyndon Johnson Library. NSF. Memos to the President, vol 8. 1/1. 28 February 1965.
[11] Philip Ziegler (1993) *Wilson*, Weidenfeld and Nicolson, p. 222.

'raise very wide questions indeed about Anglo-American relationships'.[12] In the end the Americans accepted the unpalatable fact that no Labour Government could be expected to lend them military assistance in Vietnam. It is curious to reflect that if Tony Blair had only had a more vociferous and independently minded left wing he might now be able to share with Wilson the credit for keeping Britain out of an ill-considered and unnecessary war.

But no amount of left-wing huffing and puffing was able to affect Wilson's support for that ultimate virility symbol, the nuclear deterrent. Before he became Prime Minister Wilson told the American Secretary of State for Defense, Bob McNamara, that, while he was not a nuclear disarmer, he was all for integrating the British deterrent with a common, European effort. The trouble was, he said, that the issue had become 'highly electoral' and the idea of a British deterrent had 'an emotional appeal to the man in the pub'.[13] Once he was in power it soon became apparent that the issue remained 'highly electoral', in his eyes at least, and, what is more, that when it came to the point he shared with the man in the pub an emotional attachment to the deterrent. The fact that Britain's continued possession of what was somewhat hopefully described as an 'independent' deterrent was entirely dependent on American goodwill and continued technological support was, of course, an extra reason for Wilson to tread carefully when affronting American susceptibilities in other fields. In defiance of the strongly expressed opposition of his left wing, Wilson contrived to retain four out of the five Polaris submarines commissioned by the Conservatives without any significant changes being made to the chain of command by which they were controlled. Even more dexterously, he managed so to present this as to leave the impression that he was itching to place the deterrent under multilateral control and had indeed to all intents and purposes achieved this laudable end. It was, said his admiring Chief Whip, Ted Short, 'sheer wizardry. He was the cleverest politician for many a long year – by far'.[14] Regretfully, the Americans accepted the inevitable. The British deterrent had escaped the economy axe, the President was told by the State Department in mid-1966. The reason given was simple: the nuclear deterrent was the most important of the great power symbols still in British possession. Although Wilson was theoretically committed to giving it up, the President's briefing went on, he had so far shown no disposition to do so. He was still showing no such disposition when he finally retired.

Wilson as champion of the Commonwealth was a familiar figure; Wilson the ardent pro-American was almost as well known; Wilson the European remained an enigma until almost the end of his period in office. Between the election of

---

[12]   Wilson to Stewart, 23 March 1965, Wilson papers, box 54 at the time of writing.

[13]   Lyndon Johnson Library. NSF Country File. UK box 213, 17a.

[14]   Edward Short (1989) *Whip to Wilson*, Macdonald, p. 97.

November 1970, when Labour had been defeated by a Conservative party led by Edward Heath, and Wilson's return to power at the head of a minority government in February 1974, Heath had taken Britain into Europe. Would Wilson now take it out again? His line when Britain entered the Common Market had been that, quite apart from the issue of principle as to whether Britain did or did not belong in Europe, on which he kept an open mind, the terms accepted by Heath were damaging to British interests and must be renegotiated. Only then should the issue of British membership be put to the electorate – probably in a referendum. Formally, this remained his position when he again became Prime Minister. As late as July 1974, he remarked in Cabinet that he thought the odds were against Britain staying in the Market. Nobody took him seriously, and with good reason. By then Wilson was clear in his own mind that he wished Britain to remain in Europe; that the only way this would be acceptable to the Labour Party would be if a clear majority of the British people had shown that such was their wish; that since both parties were split on the issue an election would achieve nothing and a referendum was essential; that he proposed to recommend British membership when the time came for a vote to be taken; and that the only way he could reconcile this attitude with the line he had adopted while in opposition would be by ensuring that the terms for British membership were in some way varied so that he could plausibly maintain that the balance of advantage had changed.

It was a hand that had to be played with much patience and consummate skill. At the time of entry a large majority of the parliamentary Labour Party had been strongly opposed to British membership; by the time renegotiation began hostility to Europe was less pronounced, but most Labour members would probably still have favoured withdrawal. They had somehow to be convinced that things had changed. Barbara Castle was sceptical whether any new terms could possibly match up to the requirements in the party manifesto: they would end up, she predicted, with 'a messy middle-of-the-road muddle'. 'I'm at my best in a messy middle-of-the-road muddle,' retorted Wilson.[15] He meant it as a joke but he knew that the joke contained a lot of truth. The middle of the road, messy or not, was indeed where he felt most at home. When I was discussing with him the possibility of my writing his official biography I said that I was perhaps unsuitable because, though over the previous 25 years I had more often than not voted Labour, I was far from being a committed or doctrinally pure supporter of the party. 'That's lucky,' said Wilson. 'Nor am I.' Again it was a joke; again it contained much truth. In the case of Europe, however, he contrived until close to the end to give the impression of being in the middle of the road while in fact being totally committed to the continuance of British membership. Renegotiation, wrote Roy Jenkins balefully, 'was a

---

[15] Barbara Castle (1980) *Diaries 1974–1976*, Weidenfeld and Nicolson, p. 289.

largely cosmetic exercise, producing the maximum of ill-will in Europe and the minimum of result (except for a smoke screen under which both Wilson and Callaghan could make their second switch of position of Europe in five years).'[16] Some significant gains were in fact achieved, though not nearly enough to win over the hardened Europhobes. It was enough for Wilson, however; his last doubts were stilled when Michael Manley, the Jamaican Prime Minister, without overmuch prompting, made a statement to the effect that continued British membership of the Common Market would be in the best interests of the Commonwealth as a whole. This declaration immeasurably eased Wilson's conscience. The prime minister had never previously been able wholly to reconcile his almost atavistic respect for the Commonwealth with his new-found faith in Europe. Now the two could be happily harmonised. He returned to the battle with renewed heart and vigour. When 67 per cent of the electorate finally voted to stay in, even *The Daily Telegraph* admitted that the result was 'quite frankly a triumph for Wilson'.[17]

He could legitimately take pride in this achievement, but he would not have described it as his finest hour. If there was one success story during his time in office which gave him unequivocal satisfaction, it was the Open University. This was a bold attempt to give a chance of higher education to those who had missed out on university. Wilson had told Callaghan even before he became prime minister that this was going to be one of his priorities and that he would need money for it, and he jealously defended it when every other sacred cow was suffering in the crises of 1965 and 1966. Aneurin Bevan's widow, Jennie Lee, was put in charge of the enterprise. Without her energy and enthusiasm it would have got nowhere, but without Wilson's continued support she would have had no chance to do what she did. It is easy to see why it appealed so strongly to Wilson: his reverence for academic achievement and his genuinely egalitarian instincts both attracted him to a project which would extend the joys of Oxbridge – however much diluted – to a class which had hitherto been denied them. The fact that the most conspicuous beneficiaries turned out to be underemployed middle-class housewives surprised and mildly disappointed him, but never led him to doubt that his initiative had been worthwhile.

His last year as Prime Minister was marked by his physical and mental deterioration. His prodigious memory began to fail him; he became obsessed by the conviction that he was being spied on, that the security service which was supposed to guard him was instead working to destroy him. There were probably a few shreds of reality behind his fantasies; a handful of mavericks in MI5 and MI6 seem to have concluded that he was a danger to the state and saw it as their duty to bring him down. They were almost entirely ineffective, however;

---

[16] Roy Jenkins (1991) *Life at the Centre*, Palgrave Macmillan, p. 494.
[17] *The Daily Telegraph*, 6 June 1975.

Wilson could well have afforded to ignore them and, in happier circumstances, would certainly have done so. His judgement was no longer what it had been, however; the first traces of the senile dementia which wholly overwhelmed him some 15 years later were beginning to make themselves apparent. His decline should not be overstated. Compared with Winston Churchill in the closing stages of his term in office or with Eden at the end of 1956, he was a model of lucidity. But he must have known that he was not the man he had been, and the knowledge preyed on him. Even a year before he would not have prepared, or allowed others to prepare, the infamous Resignation Honours List, in which distinctions were lavished on a range of recipients who were generally deemed unsuitable and whose claim in several cases seemed to be only that they had been or were likely to be financially useful to Wilson or to members of his entourage.

The resignation itself is mainly surprising in the surprise it caused; not just among the general public but in those inner circles where anyone who paid attention should have known what to expect. So many people had been warned, so many hints had been dropped over so long a period, that the secret had been opened as wide as any barn door; yet still when it happened the reaction was stunned incredulity. The main reason for this was a failure to believe that a man as totally wrapped up in politics as Wilson, who had striven so hungrily for office, who had few other interests to pursue, who was under no immediate challenge in his position, should voluntarily surrender power. Nobody ever had. The only prime minister to have resigned in the twentieth century, except after electoral defeat, on the insistence of his colleagues or for pressing reasons of health, was Stanley Baldwin, and he was 69 years old, tired and very deaf. Wilson was not yet 60 and apparently fit. When he announced in Cabinet that he was going, the immediate reaction, even among those who should have known better, was that there must be some hidden reason: incipient physical collapse, perhaps, or some hideous scandal which was about to be revealed. Some suggested the whole thing was bluff: Wilson believed that he was indispensable and thought that his colleagues would soon be forced to plead with him to return. In boring fact, when Wilson became prime minister again after the first election of 1974 he had told his most trusted intimates that they could not expect him to remain more than another two years in Downing Street. Six months before his resignation he had notified both the Queen and the Secretary to the Cabinet of the planned date for his departure. Minor changes were made to the calendar but substantially he stuck to his plans. His retirement came as a shock to his associates and, still more, to the world at large, but it was long premeditated and certainly unprovoked by any fear of scandal.

The Open University is a worthy monument to anybody's memory, but Wilson would not have been pleased to think that it was the solitary great achievement of his eight years as prime minister. To have kept Britain out of the Vietnamese war, to have kept it in Europe, certainly mattered greatly to the country, but could hardly be classed as dashing political initiatives. His years as Prime Minister, for reasons, one can argue, largely beyond his control, were singularly lacking in striking achievements. Wilson would have maintained that that was beside the point. The Abbé Sièyes, when asked what he did during the French Revolutionary Terror, replied simply: 'I survived.' If asked what he had done during his years in office, Wilson might have replied: 'I kept Labour in power.' After 13 years in the wilderness he won four out of five general elections and made Labour respectable as the party of government. In so doing he preserved the unity of a party rent by fissures which under his predecessors had seemed unhealable, and managed to retain the cohesion of a Cabinet composed of relentlessly warring prima donnas. He did so because party unity was essential if he were to remain prime minister, but he was not actuated by mere self-interest. He believed strongly in social justice. He was resolved that the lot of the poor and the underprivileged should be improved; that education and technical training should increase the chances of all citizens to realise their full potential; that the barriers of class should be whittled down and the right of the employer to ride roughshod over the employed should be curbed and regulated. He was convinced that movement in this direction was more likely under a Labour than a Conservative government, and that his first duty was, therefore, to keep Labour in power. If Labour split over some ideological difference, then the Tories would gain or retain power and nothing would be achieved. There *might* be issues of such significance that this result had to be accepted – the reform of the trade unions at one moment seemed to him almost to qualify – but on the whole he doubted whether political suicide could ever be a proper course for the leader of a great party. So far as nationalisation, Europe or almost any other issue was concerned, the prime consideration was to evolve a policy which would accommodate all but the most irreconcilable of partisans, and so far to blur the controversial points that confrontations could be avoided. As a style of government, Wilson's perhaps lacked both glamour and nobility. In the long term it could sometimes lead to disaster, when unresolved problems festered unseen and then erupted in a form exacerbated by neglect. In the short term it usually worked. A succession of Wilsons as leaders would doom any nation to decline; a Wilson from time to time to let the dust settle while the demolition squads of the radicals gather strength for their next enterprise can be positively beneficial.

7
Edward Heath, 1970–1974

Philip Ziegler

Like Harold Wilson, Edward Heath was born in 1916. Those preoccupied by the stratification of British society have suggested that Wilson's forbears, northern lower middle-class, were slightly grander than Heath's manual labourers, but in their upbringing they can both be described as lower middle-class. Both progressed by way of scholarships to Oxford where they excelled – though in contrasting ways. Both aspired to a career in politics from an indecently early age, and prided themselves on their no-nonsense, classless approach, with a heavy emphasis on efficiency and scant respect for the more picturesque traditions. Yet in other respects the two men could hardly have been more different. Wilson was the supreme tactician, little preoccupied by grand strategy and untroubled by principle except in so far as he believed that Britain would be most likely to evolve into a humane and civilised society under a Labour Government. Heath was quite as clear that a Conservative Government offered the best chance of providing a Britain fit to live in, but he scorned the intricate manoeuvring which was Wilson's favoured means of operation and held passionately to certain principles, above all the conviction that Britain's future lay in Europe. Events forced him radically to adapt certain of his policies, but his fundamental political credo was clearly stated and obstinately maintained.

It was his similarities with Wilson which led to his becoming leader of the Conservative Party. A Harrovian Prime Minister had been followed by three Etonians; the vein, it was felt, had been worked out. Douglas-Home's honesty, decency and amiability had failed to match Wilson's infighting skills; the Conservatives felt the time had come for someone tougher, cruder, more in the mould of the Labour Prime Minister. Heath had been a Chief Whip of exceptional ability, but he established his credentials as a future leader when he forced through the abolition of resale price maintenance against the wishes of the great majority of the Party and even of some in the Cabinet. He was much criticised at the time, and even accused, falsely, of losing the 1964 general election, but what remained in the memory of the back-benchers was his forcefulness and determination. When he showed the same qualities as Shadow Chancellor of the Exchequer by his ferocious and skilfully mounted opposition to the Finance Bill of 1965, his case had been fully established. When the time came to pick a successor to Douglas-Home, Reginald Maudling, highly intelligent but urbane, relaxed, gentlemanly, stood for the past. Heath was the future.

As seems to be habitual with the Conservatives, they had no sooner elected their new leader than they began to wonder whether they had not made a mistake. As Chief Whip, Heath had gained a reputation for being sympathetic, accessible, a good listener; as leader he rapidly revealed a propensity either for ignoring his back-benchers or for brusquely dismissing them. It was perhaps an understandable progression: as Chief Whip he had had to ensure that the rank-and-file would follow the party line; now he insisted that it was he who would lay down that line and that the rank-and-file would follow him. Even those who had been snubbed most ruthlessly did not contend that the Party should change leaders again after Wilson increased his majority in the general election of 1966, but from then on Heath was on sufferance. He would not long have survived a second defeat.

It never occurred to him that he might incur one. The Conservative Party in 1970 was as scrupulously well prepared to take office as any opposition can ever have been. Every sector had been the subject of careful planning, policies had been endlessly debated, new departures prepared, the machinery of government reconsidered. In a way, it could be said that there had been too much preparation; the new Conservative government came to power committed to a range of activities that did not necessarily take account of the realities of the moment. On the whole, though, the process had been salutary. It attained its apotheosis at the Selsdon Park conference in January 1970, when the finishing touches were applied to the Party's programme in preparation for what was clearly an imminent election. The conference in fact introduced little that was new: it emphasised the importance of tax cuts and trade union reform, and reaffirmed that prices and incomes should be left to find their proper level by market forces without interference by the government, but none of this came as a novelty in a Conservative platform. Nor, with the exception of tax cuts, was there anything very alluring electorally. It was with this last consideration in mind that Heath, at the end of the conference, told the press that issues of law and order had figured prominently on the agenda. Wilson seized on this to claim that there had been a sharp move to the right: he coined the phrase 'Selsdon Man' to signify the ravening beast which was emerging from the jungles of reaction to lay waste the welfare state. In the event the conceit worked against him; it turned out that the electorate was in the mood for a bit of reaction. It meant, however, that Heath found himself in power with a reputation for being a hard right-winger – a state of mind totally alien to his true inclinations.

At the time of the Selsdon conference, however, it seemed increasingly improbable that Heath would have a chance to display in office either his true beliefs or those attributed to him. During the 12 months before mid-1970 the polls had moved inexorably against the Conservatives. A clear lead for the Opposition had been reversed, and when Wilson called a general election for 18 June Labour seemed destined for an easy victory. So despondent were the Conservative grandees that Whitelaw and Maudling made secret plans to meet at Alec Douglas-Home's home, The Hirsel, after the results were known to decide who should replace Heath as leader. Heath alone remained optimistic, or at least put up a creditable display of confidence, and professed to be unsurprised when candidates throughout the country reported that the voters were far better disposed towards Conservative policies than the polls suggested. A week before the election the polls showed Labour with an 11-point lead, and Ladbrokes offered odds of 20 to 1 against the Conservatives. Only at the very last minute was there any evidence that the tide had turned. Poor trade figures, an English defeat in the World Cup, a powerful finish to his campaign by Heath: all contributed to a late swing that in fact was not as dramatic as the polls had suggested. By the time Heath drove to Buckingham Palace to kiss hands on his appointment he knew that he had an overall majority of 30.

At his first Cabinet meeting Heath declared that his government 'should be seen to adopt from the start a new style of administration and a fresh approach to the conduct of public business. They should seek to establish a practice of deliberate and considered working, avoiding precipitate reactions to events and hasty or premature declarations of policy.'[1] His words were carefully chosen to distinguish between his approach and the hectic frenzy of activity indulged in by the Wilson government in its 'First Hundred Days'. He emphasised the difference by himself almost immediately departing on holiday. When accused of irresponsibility, he claimed that he was never out of touch with the affairs of the country and could study his papers as assiduously in Cowes or Burnham as in Downing Street. In fact, however, he relished the image of the insouciant statesman defying the elements and the opposition aboard his yacht, *Morning Cloud*. The tactic was defensible but still risky; the government lost some momentum during its first three months and was thereafter constantly trying to catch up.

His government more or less formed itself: once Douglas-Home had decided that he would like to take the Foreign Office, the remaining senior ministers fell into place. The most obvious and potentially the most important appointment was that of Iain Macleod as Chancellor of the Exchequer. Macleod took some pride in not being an economist, but he had high intelligence allied to a sharp political mind and it seems certain that he would have challenged some

---

[1] National Archives. CM 1(70), 23 June 1970.

of the economic decisions made in 1972 and 1973. His premature death after only a few weeks in office was a crippling blow to Heath. Macleod was the most effective debater and orator in the government; still more, with Douglas-Home determined to confine himself to the Foreign Office, Maudling increasingly embarrassed by his financial problems and Hailsham out of the way as Lord Chancellor, he was the only minister able and willing to tackle Heath on equal terms. His replacement, Anthony Barber, was both likeable and competent, but he lacked the weight to oppose the Prime Minister. Under him the Treasury lost much of its traditional influence; Heath increasingly ignored it and relied on the advice of civil servants of his choice.

Some, at least, of the plans that had been formulated in opposition were quickly implemented. Five ministries were bundled up and reshaped into two larger units, the Department of the Environment and the Department of Trade and Industry. This reform, it was believed, would lead to a smoother process of decision-making and, at the same time, reduce the size of the Cabinet – a step Heath believed essential if Government were to operate efficiently. More boldly still, he invented the Central Policy Review Staff, or 'think-tank', a band of high-powered civil servants or hand-picked outsiders under the maverick intellectual Lord Rothschild. The CPRS's task was to think the unthinkable, to challenge accepted dogmas and to come up with solutions to any problem that ministers – in practice, almost always the Prime Minister – might care to throw at it. The value of the think-tank depended entirely on the quality of its members: some senior civil servants believed that it was a pointless irritant, but for a few years it proved a useful stimulant until, as such institutions often do, it ran out of steam and expired.

Over the first two years of his government, however, Heath was above all preoccupied with what he considered to be his first priority, negotiating the terms for British entry into Europe and persuading Parliament that this was in the country's best interests. He was accustomed to claim that he had acquired his enthusiasm for European union while serving as an artillery officer in France and Germany during the Second World War. This must not be allowed to happen again, he had concluded; only if Britain, France and Germany were inextricably bound together could the danger totally be eliminated. There is some truth in this; witness the fact that his first speech in the House of Commons had been in support of the Schuman Plan for integrating the coal and steel industries of Europe. This predilection only became an obsession, however, when Harold Macmillan, in 1960, appointed him Minister of State in the Foreign Office with special responsibility for negotiating British entry into the Common Market. That effort foundered on de Gaulle's veto, but not before Heath had established a reputation as a skilled, patient and resolute negotiator and had determined that, when the time was ripe, he would try again and this time succeed. Now, with de Gaulle gone and the new French President, Georges

Pompidou, believed to be better disposed towards British entry, it seemed that his moment might have come.

Though Douglas-Home and Maudling were both advocates of entry, Heath knew that the Cabinet was not unanimously behind him and that a substantial element in the Conservative Party was strongly opposed to British entry. Undeterred, he pushed ahead. He was rightly convinced that, in the last resort, another French veto could only be averted if he could personally persuade Pompidou that the British were good Europeans and did not propose to use their membership as a means of blocking further progress towards union. The two men met at a crucial summit in May 1971. When they began their talks, the officials waiting nervously outside would not have rated the chances of success at better than fifty-fifty; when they ended it was clear that the matter of principle had been resolved, and all that remained was to settle the details. Some of those details were both important and troublesome – particularly where the interests of the Commonwealth were concerned – but there was little doubt that, one way or another, they would be resolved.

It remained to convince the House of Commons. Somewhat opportunistically, the Labour leaders decided to oppose entry on the terms proposed, even though they had themselves advocated something very similar only a year or two before. A significant group of pro-European Labour MPs, however, led by Roy Jenkins, was not prepared to accept this volte-face. Though at first reluctant, Heath was finally persuaded that, if he put the issue to a free vote in the House of Commons, the Labour Europeans prepared to vote for entry would be at least as numerous as the rebels in his own camp. He took the risk and triumphed; the House voted by 356 to 244 in favour of joining the Community. That was not the end of the battle; the Bill was fought out clause by clause on the floor of the House of Commons, and 16 times the Conservative majority fell into single figures. It was not until 17 October 1972 that the royal assent was given and Britain became a fully committed member of the European Community.

Even this did not end the controversy. In May 1970 Heath had pledged that the Community would not be enlarged without 'the full-hearted consent of the peoples and parliaments involved'.[2] This, it was argued by some, was tantamount to promising a referendum. Heath had no intention of acceding to such a demand – both because he believed referendums to be contrary to the principles of parliamentary democracy and because he was by no means sure that he would win. But many people felt that they had been robbed of a chance to express their views. Only in 1975 were they given that chance by a Labour government. The other potentially explosive issue was whether Heath, while

---

[2] Edward Heath (1988) *Course of My Life*, Hodder and Stoughton, p. 362. Conversation with Lord Hurd of Westwell.

professing publicly that he had no intention of leading Britain down the path towards a federal Europe, did not secretly favour a far higher degree of political integration than he would admit to. Heath was certainly careful to play down the long-term issue of unification, but his words, though sometimes equivocal, were never dishonest. A degree of unification must come, he insisted, but it would take time and must evolve rather than be forced arbitrarily on the participants. Nobody can doubt that he would be sadly disappointed by the Europe that exists today.

He was sometimes accused of being anti-American. It would be more true to say that he was pro-European, and believed that an exclusive relationship with any outside country was incompatible with full membership of the European club. Kissinger maintained that President Nixon was anxious to reinforce the special relationship but that Heath rebuffed him: 'After talking with Heath, Nixon felt somehow rejected and came to consider the Prime Minister's attitude towards him as verging on condescension.'[3] Records of the conversations between the two men, whether from British or American sources, do not support this thesis; Nixon and Heath were quick to consult each other and spoke frankly about common problems. Heath, however, believed that the Americans had never fully accepted the fact that Europe existed and must now be considered as an entity. 'Apparently Dr Kissinger did not like having a Dane speaking for Europe,' he told a group of American correspondents. 'Well, he will have to get used to it.'[4] But it was not until the Yom Kippur war in the Middle East, when the United States energetically supported Israel and a – distinctly fragmented – Europe took a far more conciliatory line towards the Arabs, that the strains on Anglo-American relations became fully apparent. 'The special relationship is collapsing,' Kissinger told the British ambassador. British entry into the Community 'should have raised Europe to the level of Britain. Instead it had reduced Britain to the level of Europe.'[5] The relationship would no doubt have improved once the war was over, but by then Heath was not there to undertake the task.

Inevitably British entry into Europe made more difficult her relationship with the Commonwealth as well as with the United States. British prime ministers – particularly Conservative prime ministers – in the second half of the twentieth century tended to find Commonwealth relations, most of all Commonwealth Conferences, a painful chore. All too often they were set up as Aunt Sallies for their third-world colleagues to take to task. Heath was as afflicted as any of them. Arms for South Africa proved a particularly virulent casus belli. The previous Labour Government had suspended all sales to the apartheid regime; the

---

[3] Henry Kissinger (1999) *Years of Renewal*, Weidenfeld and Nicolson, p. 602.
[4] National Archives. PREM 15 1989.
[5] National Archives. PREM 15 2232.

Tories, while dutifully deploring the policies of the South African government, had maintained that there was an obligation under the Simonstown agreement to supply certain weapons to the South African navy. Such weapons, they claimed, could in no way be used to suppress the black and coloured communities, but were essential if South Africa was to play an effective role in countering the growing incursions of Russian vessels into the area. How far Heath himself believed this argument is hard to establish; certainly his disapproval of apartheid was sincere, but the commercial arguments for supplying the arms were brought forcibly to his attention and his right wing would have been outraged if he had continued to follow Labour's policy. He managed to postpone a final decision until after the Commonwealth Conference in 1971, and in the end no country left the Commonwealth in protest or even came close to doing so. Indeed, Hastings Banda of Malawi applauded his decision. 'There can be no doubt that Mr. Heath is a strong Prime Minister,' he wrote. 'I, for one, like him for it. I do not like weaklings in men at the head of affairs.'[6]

Rhodesia was another issue that brought the wrath of the Commonwealth on Heath's head and, still more, caused an embarrassingly obvious split within the Party. Ian Smith had made his Unilateral Declaration of Independence in November 1965. The Labour government imposed sanctions while continuing, in a desultory way, to conduct negotiations with the rebel regime in the hope of finding some face-saving solution which would enable it to give Rhodesia independence without betraying the African majority. When the issue was debated in the House of Commons, the Conservative leadership rather ignobly called on its members to abstain. More than 80 members refused to do so: 50 voted against sanctions while 30 supported the government.

When Heath became Prime Minister he found the Party no less divided. His advisers pointed out that to enrage the left wing by selling arms to South Africa while causing equal offence to the right wing by continuing sanctions against Rhodesia was to get the worst of both worlds. 'I agree,' Heath minuted gloomily, but he did not find the comment particularly helpful.[7] His personal inclination was to disengage as far as possible, but he could not bring himself to accept Smith's *fait accompli*, while to hand the affair over to the United Nations would have outraged every section of his Party. He shillied, and, when that served no useful purpose, shallied; one of the few consolations of losing first the election of February 1974 and then, in 1975, the leadership of the Party was that the poisoned chalice of Rhodesia was left for someone else to drain.

The Party was almost as badly divided over immigration. Heath was by instinct a liberal on the issue and had had no hesitation in dismissing Enoch Powell from the Shadow Cabinet when Powell made his notorious 'Rivers of

---

[6] January 1971. Heath papers. Reference at time of writing 3 2/20.
[7] 23 January 1971. Heath papers 3 2/20.

Blood' speech in Birmingham in May 1968. Powell undoubtedly commanded substantial support in the country, but it seemed that the problem could be contained without too much dissension until, in August 1972, Idi Amin, the alarmingly eccentric dictator of Uganda, announced that he proposed to expel 57,000 Indian Ugandans, nearly all of whom had British passports and therefore the right to settle in the United Kingdom. Worse still, there was reason to fear that Kenya, where even larger numbers of Indians were involved, might follow suit in the not-too-distant future. Heath accepted that Britain was in honour bound to accept any Ugandan Asians who were resolved to come, but sought to mitigate the impact by persuading other Commonwealth countries to take a proportion of the refugees. 'My main concern has been to avoid the erosion of communal harmony in this country,' he told Mrs Gandhi. 'This is a duty which we owe to the people of this country as a whole and particularly to the immigrants who are already settled here.'[8] 'The erosion of communal harmony' was certainly at the forefront of his mind; so, too, was the erosion of harmony within the Conservative Party. He had good reason for concern. A group of malcontents never forgave him, and at one moment even engineered a defeat for the government on immigration rules. A significant number of those who finally voted for his eviction from the leadership could trace their hostility back to the line he took over the Ugandan Asians.

They saw more to applaud in his attitude towards the Persian Gulf. Heath had visited the area in 1968; had been impressed by the eagerness of the local rulers – with the conspicuous exception of the Shah of Iran – that Britain should maintain a military presence in the area; and was convinced that, on both economic and strategic grounds, the Labour government was making a grave mistake by pulling out. He came to power pledged to reverse the process, certainly in the Gulf and possibly even in Singapore, but quickly found that unscrambling the omelette would be both too complicated and too expensive. In the end he could do no more than marginally slow up the retreat, but the noises that he made while he did so satisfied the imperialist fringe of the Party that, whatever the final result, his heart, in this case at least, was in the right place.

They were less sure when it came to Northern Ireland, over which some Conservatives and an increasing number of Ulster Unionists felt that Heath was far too ready to do deals with the government in Dublin and to betray the interests of loyal British subjects in favour of would-be secessionist Roman Catholics. Heath's preoccupation with Europe meant that he did not really come to grips with the Irish problem until after Brian Faulkner had become Northern Ireland's Prime Minister in March 1971. By that time violence had become a way of life in Northern Ireland, and Faulkner, after an attempt at

---

[8] 24 January 1973. National Archives. PREM15 1641.

reconciliation, advocated ever more drastic measures to bring peace, including the internment of suspects without trial. Gradually Heath lost faith in this policy, and the massacre of Bloody Sunday early in 1972 convinced him that there must be a new approach. It came with the suspension of the Northern Irish parliament and the introduction of direct rule, with Whitelaw, Heath's most trusted troubleshooter, sent to Belfast as Secretary of State. Faulkner was dismayed, and the Ulster Unionist Party, once solidly supportive of any Conservative government, became ever more hostile. Heath accepted this with equanimity. 'Personally,' he told the Party Chairman, 'I do not believe that we can continue to maintain an alliance with a sectarian party based on and largely controlled by the Orange Lodges.'[9] This attitude was to cost the Conservatives dear in the 1974 elections, but in the long-term interests of achieving a settlement in Northern Ireland it was both courageous and far-sighted. Heath almost achieved the impossible. At Sunningdale in December 1973 he bullied or cajoled the various leaders into accepting a form of power-sharing which led to a new power-sharing executive being formed in Belfast and devolved government being restored. His efforts were in vain. When it came to the point, the moderate Northern Irish leaders found few willing to follow their lead. Extremists on both sides prevented the new system working. Even before Heath lost power the Sunningdale Agreement was proving impossible to apply. Once again Heath's conviction that reason must prevail had been brutally disproved. It was to be more than 30 years before the principles which Heath had urged at Sunningdale were put into practice with what seemed some possibility of success.

Though Europe was the issue closest to Heath's heart, and Ireland the one that caused him the greatest anguish, it was the economy and industrial relations which dictated the course of his government. He had come to power with a programme drawn up on sternly Conservative principles: the reform of the trade unions; the acceptance of market forces; abstention from any interference with the regulation of prices and incomes; a steadfast refusal to rescue industrial lame ducks in the belief that, if they were allowed to fail, more vigorous and agile ducks would quickly take their places. Heath was less adamantly committed to such policies than certain members of his Cabinet, but it was the platform on which he had been elected. It was not long before he found that it was one on which it was uncomfortable to stand.

Industrial relations provided the first battlefield. Only a year before, Wilson and Barbara Castle had tried to reform the unions and had been defeated. Even though their measure, *In Place of Strife*, did not provide everything that Heath felt desirable, one can see in retrospect that the Conservatives would have been well advised simply to adopt it and re-present it as their own. This

---

[9] 14 August 1972. National Archives. PREM 15 782.

would have put Wilson in an impossible position: either acquiescing in legislation antipathetic to many of his most reliable followers or disavowing a cause
which he had championed only a short time before. Trades union reform, however, was an issue to which the Conservative planners had devoted much time
and thought, and the government had no intention of accepting a second best.
The main purpose of its Bill was to bring the unions within the law by making it possible for them to be taken before a new Industrial Relations Court if
believed guilty of certain malpractices. The Bill was ferociously opposed by
Labour, but Heath believed it was so manifestly desirable, and that the benefits to be gained by the unions if they registered under the new system were
so significant, that they would put up only a token resistance. He was sadly
mistaken. The unions would have opposed the legislation whoever had proposed it; they were doubly suspicious because the initiative came from the
Conservatives; and they were additionally incensed because the measure was
presented as a fait accompli, with only the most token effort being made to
ascertain their views in advance. The larger unions frustrated the law by refusing to register under the Act. When the new Industrial Relations Court was
invoked to deal with various forms of misconduct, the government found itself
in the embarrassing position of having to put strikers into jail and thus turning them into martyrs. In the end they found themselves having to invent
far-fetched expedients so as to secure the strikers' release.

Before things came to this point, however, Heath's government had already
made the first of the dramatic U-turns which came to mark its economic policy. John Davies, a former Director-General of the Confederation of British
Industries, who had been brought in to run the newly created Department
of Trade and Industry, made a powerful statement at the Party Conference in
October 1970 of the Government's intention never to intervene if businesses
got themselves into financial trouble. 'Perhaps John was trying too hard to
prove his credentials and those of the government,' speculated Heath 20 years
later.[10] Certainly he went far out on a limb that was soon to snap under him.
A few months later the aircraft division of Rolls Royce found itself in trouble
when the engines it was contracted to supply to the giant American company,
Lockheed, proved far more expensive than had been expected. Rolls Royce
was on the brink of bankruptcy. There were plenty of reasons for treating it as
a special case. Rolls Royce flew the flag of excellence in British engineering;
to let it founder would gravely damage the nation's reputation. Furthermore,
important defence contracts would be jeopardised and serious harm done to
Britain's relationship with the United States. All the same, the government
was being required to fly in the face of its own policy. 'They would need to
take hard-headed and, if necessary, hard decisions,' Heath told his Cabinet

---

[10] Heath, *Course of My Life*, pp. 329–30.

colleagues, but the eventual decision that the Government should, in effect, nationalise Rolls Royce's aircraft division was notably soft.[11]

Rolls Royce was wholly exceptional, it was claimed; its rescue would not be repeated in other cases. It soon was, of course. In the middle of 1971 Upper Clyde Shipyards was on the brink of bankruptcy. UCS, Heath stated, had 'become the symbol of an ailing enterprise, bedevilled by bad labour relations and poor management, in whose future there could be little confidence'.[12] It was the quintessential lame duck, crying out to have its neck wrung as speedily as possible. But, if Heath's attitude towards Europe had been shaped by his wartime experiences, so his economic views were moulded by still earlier memories of pre-war unemployment. There were already far too many people out of work on the Clyde; if UCS closed, with the resultant damage to all the ancillary businesses that depended on it, the total of unemployed would be swollen unacceptably. The government might still have stuck to its guns, but a skilfully stage-managed work-in forced a rethink. In spite of some blustering, the surrender, when it came, was complete: it was necessary, the Cabinet concluded, 'to suspend, for the time being, the application of the established policy of accepting that, when concerns ceased to be viable, they should be allowed to go into receivership'.[13]

On the central plank of its economic policy – that market forces must prevail and prices and incomes find their own level – the Government hoped it could still stand firm. Something had to be done, however, to restrain the ever-higher wage settlements which were fuelling inflation. The Government's aspiration was that each pay rise should be below the level of the previous settlement, thus eventually forcing rises down to an acceptable level. In the private sector it could do no more than make encouraging noises, but where the nationalised industries were concerned it was better placed to enforce its will. In the case of the miners that would have entailed a pay rise of some 8 per cent; in fact they demanded 45 per cent.

At first the Government believed that the threat of a strike did not need to be taken too seriously. The miners had chosen their time ill-advisedly; stocks of coal were high and the industry was anyway in recession. A year before, the government had confronted and overcome the postal workers; it might take longer, but with determination the miners, too, could be defeated. Their optimism was quickly proved ill-founded. The President of the National Union of Mineworkers, Joe Gormley, left to himself would quickly have done a deal, but the extremists, particularly Arthur Scargill of the Yorkshire miners, took control of the operation. Flying pickets roamed the country, cutting off the

---

[11] 15 October 1970. National Archives CM 30 (70).
[12] 15 June 1971. National Archives CM 31 (71).
[13] 4 November 1971. National Archives. CM 53 (71).

supply of coal to the power stations. A crucial confrontation at the giant coke depot at Saltley Gate in Birmingham became the symbol of the government's problems. The police had vowed that they would keep the depot open; the strikers forced it to close its gates. By now the country was in a pitiful plight: electricity was only available to house owners for a few hours a day; most of industry was on a three-day week. Heath faced stark reality: he could order the police to reopen the depots at whatever the cost, he could call in the troops to reinforce their efforts, or he could surrender. It seems improbable that he ever contemplated violent action; he abhorred confrontation and even had a sneaking sympathy for the miners, who were doing an exceptionally disagreeable and sometimes dangerous job and had indeed lost their place among the best-rewarded workers. Their case was referred to a Court of Enquiry headed by Lord Wilberforce, who was celebrated for his earlier generosity to the power workers in a similar investigation. Wilberforce reported within three days and gave the miners virtually all they had asked for. Even then they chose to inflict fresh humiliation on the government by demanding still further concessions before they returned to work. Present it how they might, everyone knew that the government had suffered a crushing defeat.

Heath still believed that the union leaders could be convinced that it would be as much in their interests as everyone else's if they would curb their wage demands and keep inflation down to a tolerable level. He was encouraged in this belief by Vic Feather, the conspicuously moderate General Secretary of the Trades Union Congress, who was almost as alarmed as the Prime Minister by the activities of some of his more extreme colleagues. With the somewhat nervous backing of the Cabinet, Heath embarked on a series of tripartite meetings, in which trade unionists, employers and ministers met together under his chairmanship to try to thrash out a common policy. It was a bold attempt and deserved more success than it achieved. Heath was at his best in such a situation. Jack Jones, leader of the giant Transport and General Workers Union, was far from being a moderate; indeed, he and Hugh Scanlon were generally seen as standard-bearers for the extreme left. At first Jones had thought that Heath represented the 'hard face of the Tory Party', but he quickly changed his view. 'No Prime Minister,' he wrote, 'either before or since, could compare with Ted Heath in the efforts he made to establish a spirit of camaraderie with the trade union leaders and to offer an attractive package which might satisfy large numbers of work people ... Amazingly, he gained more personal respect from union leaders than they seemed to have for Harold Wilson or even Jim Callaghan.'[14] But it was not enough. In the end the moderates were not able to carry with them the extremists or even the rank-and-file, and in November 1972 the TUC withdrew from the tripartite

---

[14] Jack Jones (1986) *Union Man: The Autobiography of Jack Jones*, Collins, pp. 261–2.

talks. Like it or not, the Government was going to have to intervene directly to curb the inflationary fury.

So began the most dramatic of Heath's U-turns. Repeatedly and categorically he had ruled out the possibility that the government might impose statutory control on prices and incomes. Now that was what he had to do. It was a purely temporary measure to meet an emergency, he protested; once inflation had been conquered market forces would resume their sway. Such assurances did not satisfy the little band of die-hard monetarists, but when a 90-day freeze on wages and prices was announced in the House of Commons only Enoch Powell voted against it and a handful of malcontents abstained. The freeze lasted till April 1972, at which point Stage Two of the policy was intro- duced; the total ban on price or wage increases was relaxed, but there were still rigid controls on the level of change that was permitted. The measure was, of course, opposed by the unions, but not with much passion; every element of society had been alarmed by what seemed to be out-of-control inflation, and the fact that some decisive steps were being taken was generally well received. By the time that the details of Stage Three were announced in the autumn of 1973 it seemed that inflation had been, if not conquered, then at least controlled. Some time in 1974, it was blithely concluded, the way would be open for statutory controls to be removed and the normal processes of wage bargaining resumed.

By then, if Heath had had his way, the economy would have expanded to such an extent that a new flexibility would have been possible. An annual 5 per cent growth rate was his target and, in the first half of 1973, it seemed that he might achieve it. The spring budget of that year pumped money into the economy at a rate which to many seemed hazardous. Among the doubters was the Chancellor of the Exchequer, Anthony Barber. To a remarkable extent, British economic policy in 1973 was controlled by the Prime Minister, working closely with a handful of civil servants, most notably William Armstrong, a former Permanent Secretary to the Treasury, who was now Head of the Home Civil Service and had time on his hands. Armstrong was so close to Heath that he was known, with mingled derision and alarm, as the 'Deputy Prime Minister'. Certainly he had more influence over Heath than anything enjoyed by Barber. This was the moment when Macleod's presence was missed most sorely: Heath had decided that the Treasury officials were cowards and con- genital pessimists; he ignored their warnings about the weakness of sterling and dismissed their argument that it was essential to raise interest rates so as to prevent the economy running out of control. By the Industry Act of 1972 – a measure described by one prominent member of the opposition as being more socialistic than anything Labour would have dared introduce – the govern- ment was already committed to pouring money into British industries in the hope that they would be able to compete by the time they were exposed to full competition within the Common Market.[15] By the middle of 1973 the 'Barber boom', as it was unfairly styled by those who thought that the Chancellor was in charge of the British economy, was raging furiously.

Though the Treasury had every right to be sceptical, the policy might have worked. Until the early autumn of 1973 growth seemed to be more or less on target; inflation was under control. Heath's dash for growth was undone by two forces, either of which separately would have been hard to overcome and which together proved fatal – the Arabs and the miners. The Arab–Israeli war, with the resultant shortage of oil, strained the unity of Europe, but it was the quad-rupling of the price of oil, coming on top of a sharp rise in the cost of almost all the raw materials essential for the running of an industrialised state, which made impossible the control of prices in the United Kingdom. The government might still have survived, however. No one could reasonably claim that they were responsible for this turn of events; the United Kingdom had, in fact, suf-fered less severely than some of its continental partners, and the public might have been prepared to accept sacrifices when the alternative was so clearly cata-strophic. The miners, however, had no such inclination. Even before the war in the Middle East they had formulated new pay demands which would have made nonsense of the prices and incomes policy. At that time it looked as if they had a difficult time ahead of them. There was only limited sympathy for them in the rest of the trades union movement and among the general public, and a second confrontation with the government might have proved harder to sustain than had the first. The rocketing price of oil, however, enormously strengthened their hand; if you are prepared to pay a vastly increased price for oil, asked the NUM, why are you not prepared to pay a bit more for the only home-produced material which can reduce our dependence on the Arab world?

Heath accepted personal responsibility for resolving the crisis. While Derek Ezra and the Coal Board were theoretically in charge of the negotiations – and played their part with some ineptness, offering the miners at an early stage all that it was in their power to give away and thus depriving themselves of any room for bargaining – Heath conducted secret talks with the miners' leader, Joe Gormley. The talks were reasonably encouraging, but, as Heath was soon to discover, Gormley could not carry his wild men with him. The NUM was not interested in any settlement that could remotely be reconciled with the Government's prices and incomes policy. On 12 November 1973 an overtime ban was declared by the miners' leaders.

It was back to a state of emergency and the three-day week. On one side a fringe of right-wing zealots clamoured for confrontation – the unions must be smashed before they took over the country altogether. On the other, Mick McGahey and a few other left-wing extremists admitted that their aspiration

---

[15] Edmund Dell (1995) *Contemporary Record*, vol. 9, No. 1, p. 9.

was not just to secure a massive pay increase but to bring down the government. Most people, however – with Heath pre-eminent among them – were anxious to find some formula which would satisfy the miners yet leave the fundamentals of the government's policies intact. At one point it seemed as if it might have been established; the TUC volunteered that any settlement reached with the miners would not be used as a precedent by the rest of the labour movement. The government was tempted, but concluded that the TUC could not deliver what they promised; some union or group of workers would be certain to ignore the agreement and insist that they had a right to be treated as generously as the miners. In retrospect it would probably have been better for the government if they had accepted the TUC's offer and given the miners exceptional treatment. It was a finely balanced decision, however, and it was not unreasonable for ministers to conclude that to give way would display a fatal weakness which must in the end lead to the collapse of the government's policy.

From an early stage of the crisis a section of the Party had been clamouring for a general election, which would show that the country supported ministers against the miners and would thus immensely strengthen, morally at least, the government's position. Heath's favourite means of reaching a decision was to listen inscrutably to every point of view and then to make up his mind and stick obstinately to his conclusion. In this case the points of view seemed exceptionally incompatible and Heath was unusually irresolute. Everyone, including the Labour leadership, seemed to agree that the Conservatives would be likely to win an election on the platform of 'Who Governs Britain?', but even if they did would it necessarily make a settlement with the miners any easier? To call an election would be to divide the country more radically than was already the case, and to the very end Heath hoped that some compromise could be conjured up. Besides, accepted wisdom had it that an election intended to be fought on a single issue rarely remained so restricted; the electorate got bored and began to look elsewhere. To the question 'Who Governs Britain?' the voters might reply that the present government was clearly not doing so or it would not have landed the country in its present mess.

For several weeks the battle to win Heath's mind was vigorously pursued. By mid-January 1974 the hawks thought that they had won. Heath almost promised that he would ask for a dissolution the following day; then Whitelaw took him out to an à deux dinner and swung him back into irresolution. Only on 7 February, by which time the NUM had declared that it proposed to transform its go-slow into an all-out strike, did he finally commit himself to an election. No one can prove that if he had gone to the country a month or even a fortnight earlier the Conservatives would have won, but the tide was on the turn and the evidence suggests that they lost a golden opportunity to increase, or at least maintain, their majority.

Even as it was, the polls at the outset of the campaign pointed towards a Conservative victory almost as unequivocally as they had indicated a Labour victory in 1970. Once again there was a late swing, stimulated by various gaffes in the Conservative camp and the publication of a new set of – substantially misleading – figures, which suggested that the miners were still lagging behind the other main industrial groups. The result was desperately close: the Conservatives had a larger share of the popular vote but Labour narrowly won more seats. Neither party enjoyed an overall majority. For 48 hours Heath hung on, trying to patch up an alliance with the Liberals, but to the relief of many of his followers no basis for a coalition could be found. On Monday 4 March he finally resigned. Though he was not prepared to admit it, even secretly to himself, it heralded the end of his time as leader. There could be no question of replacing him immediately, with Wilson, heading a minority Government, obviously poised to go back to the country as soon as he decently could; but, after the second election of 1974, in October, resulted in a decisive win for Labour, he found himself forced into a leadership contest. His almost wilful disinclination to do anything to ingratiate himself with his own back-benchers, something he could get away with when things were going well, told fatally against him. Much of the grass roots support on which a Conservative leader could normally depend was now denied him. The Party saw him as a loser, and he lost. In February 1975 he was defeated in the first ballot by Mrs Thatcher and retired from the conflict.

No Prime Minister who survives only three and a half years, loses three general elections out of four and is then dismissed by his own party can be deemed an unequivocal success. It would be unfair, however, to dismiss Heath as a failure. On the issue to which he attached overriding importance, the entry of Britain into the Common Market, he succeeded triumphantly – his personal contribution had been decisive; without his passionate enthusiasm, his patience, his negotiating skills, it is unlikely that the day would have been won. For the rest, he made bad mistakes but was above all the victim of unfortunate timing. His clash with the unions was premature but, from the point of view of the Conservatives, essential; if he had not waged his two unsuccessful campaigns against the miners it would have been far more difficult for Mrs Thatcher 10 years later. His dash for growth was perhaps over-bold, but not insanely so; if it had not coincided with the Arab–Israeli war it might have worked. If he had called the February 1974 election a few weeks earlier he might have won through and survived to enjoy the benefits of North Sea oil. That he contributed largely to his own downfall is obvious, but the banana skins on which he slipped were not all of his own contriving.

8
James Callaghan, 1976–1979

Kenneth O. Morgan

I first met Jim Callaghan when I chaired an election meeting at which he spoke, held in Brynmill School, Swansea, in October 1959. I recall that as a highly effective, old-fashioned election meeting, before a packed audience. Its success was largely due to Callaghan's own charismatic, and unscripted, performance that evening. I still remember his confronting a lone heckler with a question (referring to the atrocious deaths of 11 Mau Mau prisoners in a British military camp in Kenya): 'Do you want the Union Jack to fly over Hola Camp?' To an impressionable young history lecturer, albeit one rather hazy about where Hola Camp actually was, the note of idealism was irresistible, John Bright or Keir Hardie come again.

Jim Callaghan had a quite extraordinary career. He is often presented in journalistic stereotype as simply the stolid, conservative epitome of Old Labour, just a representative of the auld alliance with the trade unions, of a corporate style of government and faith in the enabling role of the centralised socialist state. This image seems exemplified by his performance before the TUC annual conference in September 1978, when a mass audience expecting a pronouncement about a forthcoming general election was instead entertained by a chauvinist old music-hall song, 'There was I waiting at the Church', actually sung by Vesta Victoria but mysteriously attributed by Callaghan to Marie Lloyd. Peter Mandelson and Roger Liddle in *The Blair Revolution* see Callaghan as symbolic of almost everything that New Labour opposed.[1] For apostles of Blairism in 1997 it was 'Goodbye to all that.' When Callaghan fell from power in 1979 there was talk of the end of an Ancien Regime, with Margaret Thatcher as an incipient neoliberal Robespierre.

But Callaghan was far more interesting a figure than that. Not least, he is the only person ever to have held the four main offices of state, Chancellor of the Exchequer, Home Secretary, Foreign Secretary and Prime Minister – even

---

[1] Peter Mandelson and Roger Liddle (1996) *The Blair Revolution*, Faber.

Churchill held only three. When I wrote his biography, I tried both to explain Callaghan's emergence as a major public figure and to set his long political career in the contest of the domestic and international history of Britain since the 1930s, so as to evaluate its significance for Britain and the world. Because, to adapt Ralph Waldo Emerson's observation on Abraham Lincoln, Callaghan's is the true history of the British people in his time.

Since my book was an authorised biography, I was granted unrestricted access to Lord Callaghan personally and his voluminous papers. Callaghan had already set down his view of his career in an autobiography, *Time and Chance* (1987), a major contribution to historical understanding. The sources for writing his biography are obviously massive and varied, as they would be for any major public figure in the later twentieth century. The public records for his career down to 1979 are now available. However, to judge from the materials in the National Archives, the retention of documents by the Cabinet Office is so widespread that the files by no means give the whole picture. Indeed, they create as many problems as they solve.

Lord Callaghan's own collections of 55 boxes of papers, letters, memoranda, minutes of meetings, press cuttings and so on, now housed in the Bodleian in Oxford, are in many ways more revealing for his career than the PREM files in the public records, particularly on such matters as, for example, party policy-making or constituency matters, which Callaghan's autobiography necessarily does not cover in great detail. I found that the often-made comment that the use of the telephone has eliminated large swathes of material from the historian's gaze is not really true. For episodes or conversations of any significance, a written record was usually preserved, including the key telephone conversations that Callaghan had with other leaders, such as Carter, Schmidt and Giscard d'Estaing, and the *aides-memoires* that were prepared for him, or that he wrote himself, no doubt with a view to his own place in future histories. Fortunately, Callaghan's career largely pre-dated e-mails and the technology of the Internet, a far more intractable matter for the would-be historian.

Then there are the newspapers, an absolutely indispensable source yet one, like all others, to be handled with care and scepticism. Journalists, as we all know, have their own agenda. Closely linked to the printed media is another vital source, audio-visual materials, which the BBC and others were generous in making available. These, too, need to be handled with caution since they can reflect the particular bias of editors or film producers, but it is nevertheless a huge asset to have physical evidence of what Lord Callaghan looked or sounded like at various stages of his career. The irritable look on his face when he said something uncomfortably similar to 'Crisis, what Crisis?' to a young woman journalist on returning from Guadeloupe in January 1979 is hugely revealing – as is the dismay on the faces of Tom McNally and other aides standing behind at that press conference. Callaghan was, of course, a product of the first television age in British politics in the 1950s, and his skill in this new medium (shown, for instance, in the television political debates 'In the News') was a major factor in his rise to eminence, as it was for Harold Wilson. The fact that Callaghan neither smoked a pipe nor, to my knowledge, wore a Gannex raincoat did not make him any less effective a communicator.

There was ample oral evidence, too, from politicians, civil servants, trade unionists, family, friends and enemies too (e.g. Barbara Castle), for which the historian is deeply grateful. Obviously, this must be used with immense caution. The fallibility or selectiveness of the human memory and political partiality can always distort the record. In my experience, a particular problem is that of interviewing people who have written their autobiographies, since they tend unwittingly to repeat their memoirs verbatim when pressed for their recollections. Even so, I found talking to Lord Callaghan's associates, including supposedly discreet civil servants now responding to public pressure for 'freedom of information', particularly fascinating and full of insight, giving life to the bare bones of the surviving written record. This applied especially to foreign dignitaries whom I interviewed, including Dr Henry Kissinger, ex-Chancellor Helmut Schmidt (a particularly memorable interviewee) and His Excellency Lee Kuan Yew, to whom I spoke on a notable occasion in the Istana Negara, the president's palace in Singapore. All of them, in different ways, were immensely helpful, not so much in terms of providing factual information as in offering perspective and showing me the significance with which Callaghan was invested from a variety of international vantage points.

The ultimate source, of course, was Lord Callaghan himself. We had conversations too numerous to count. There are those who have conveyed to me the dangers they believe to be inherent in writing objective history about someone who is alive. There are many answers to this one. One is that personal bias need not necessarily come into play with the living alone. One of the more partisan works I know is that of the late, great Professor David Douglas on William the Conqueror, who after all met his maker nearly 900 years before his biography was written. I gather from medievalists that Asser's *Life of King Alfred*, a controversial product evidently and of debatable authorship, was open to the same line of attack. History is not confined simply to people who are dead. As Litvinov said of peace, history is one and indivisible. Its critical modes, and the disciplines and sanctions it imposes on the historian, are eternal. There are also, in any case, obviously positive advantages in writing about a living person with whom one can debate and explore at length. How I would have wished, in writing earlier biographies, to have interviewed David Lloyd George or Keir Hardie.

There is one final methodological point. It arises from a famous remark of E.H. Carr's – if you want to study history, first study the historian. I am, of course, Welsh. But, even more important, I have always been convinced of the dangers and limitations of writing about a politician by confining yourself to the cloistered tranquillity of the study, the library or the seminar room. Roy Jenkins in writing on Asquith, Gladstone or Churchill, Douglas Hurd on Robert Peel, William Hague on the Younger Pitt, have shown the value and insight that can be obtained through shared political experience and understanding. I have never been a politician and have never stood for elective office. But I was a university vice-chancellor for nearly seven years. That gave me a new, and often uncomfortable, experience of public pressures, of the difficulty of making choices at a time of severe financial constraints, of maintaining morale and achieving a balance in one's objectives, in promotion of the public image, attending to public relations, and never letting the best become the enemy of the good. In some ways, I found the quasi-political aspect of being a vice-chancellor the most invigorating of all. Michael Foot once said to me that he would have written a somewhat different life of Aneurin Bevan had he done so after experiencing the pressures of Cabinet office in 1974–1979. On a more humdrum level, I know that I wrote a somewhat different and perhaps more revealing and sympathetic life of Jim Callaghan after some, admittedly parochial, experience of the exercise of power.

Jim Callaghan's political career was deeply influenced by his childhood and background. His early years were stamped by patriotism, puritanism and poverty. The patriotism came from the naval background – his father was a naval rating on the Royal Yacht – and its traditions of imperial greatness. Portsmouth, Nelson's *Victory*, and Fratton Park's Pompey Chimes were as important to Callaghan's psyche as were Plymouth Sound, the Armada and Drake's Drum to the young Michael Foot in the same period. The puritan ethic of the Baptist church was another important early influence, and one that Callaghan shared, of course, with another famous Welsh MP who also became Prime Minister – Lloyd George. But Lloyd George was a Campbellite or Scotch Baptist, a dissenter among the dissenters as it were, while Callaghan was a mainstream Baptist. Even though he later lost his religious faith, the impress of the Baptist community upon Callaghan's moral (or perhaps moralistic) outlook was a permanent one. His attacks on 'permissiveness' while at the Home Office in 1967–1970 were a sign of the Portsmouth Baptists taking on the scribes and Pharisees, and fighting back.

But perhaps the deepest impact upon Callaghan came from the poverty in which he grew up in the Copnor district of Portsmouth. His father died when he was only nine and the family, with no widow's pension, lived in some real hardship thereafter – indeed, they suffered from real physical deprivation. Young Jim (or 'Len' at that time) was both hungry and poor, in a way that is almost impossible to imagine today, living for a time on bread and dripping, supplemented by margarine and sugar given to him by members of his Baptist church, and with inevitable harmful effects on his health, especially his lungs. As a young boy he was angry at the deprivation his family suffered and the class system that had brought it about. As a 12-year-old schoolboy during the 1924 general election, he was seen running around the school playground shouting: 'We'll soak the rich – you Tories just wait!'[2] This deprivation meant that he had no chance of going to university, being one of just three post-war prime ministers not to have enjoyed that advantage – the other two were Winston Churchill and John Major (with whom he struck up a special affinity). This was something that always rankled with him, and he was highly sensitive when he felt patronised by intellectuals, especially those from Oxford (e.g. Gaitskell or Crossman). But he was widely read, being particularly influenced by Harold Laski, a great teacher on the left in his day, who warmly encouraged the young man. Callaghan was, with the possible exception of Ramsay MacDonald, the only Labour prime minister who came from the under-educated working class, and he was aware of it. The growth of social mobility and the expansion of higher education may well mean that there will never be another.

Callaghan's time as a trade union leader in the Inland Revenue Staff Federation in the thirties is also of great importance. He was a poacher turned gamekeeper, an early rebel within his union on behalf of young recruits to the clerical staff who felt that promotion opportunities were being denied them.[3] Then at 24 he became assistant general secretary to Douglas Houghton, decades later to be chairman of the parliamentary Labour Party when Callaghan was in government. Callaghan's early career shows the importance to the Labour movement of white-collar unionism, even though the coal, cotton and steel unions have usually been the dominating influences, but, although associated with the unions, he was not just a traditional union man. Indeed, members of the Inland Revenue Staff Federation were not allowed to become involved in political activity or to have political affiliations at that time. Until 1945, he was not particularly close to the unions generally, or to the trade union leadership in the Labour Party. He was never one of the block-vote barons. Indeed, he did not really become close to them until 1967, when he became treasurer of the Labour Party around the time he left the Treasury, and started to rebuild his career within the Party. But throughout his public life he always retained a respect for trade union practices, in particular for collective bargaining and an explicit negotiating style, which was noted by civil servants like Kenneth Stowe (and, indeed, which I myself detected in discussions with Lord Callaghan over sources for writing his biography). He always treasured the symbolic importance of a document like the union rule book, and criticised middle-class non-unionists like Gaitskell who missed its importance entirely.

---

2 Olive Tanton to the author, 9 March 1992.
3 Material on the New Entrants' Committee, Callaghan Papers, Bodleian Library, box 2.

Callaghan's wartime service in the navy, which took him to the Far East, also had a great impact on his later career. Labour politicians, such as Callaghan and Healey, who served in the armed forces had a different perspective from those, such as Gaitskell and Wilson, who remained in the Civil Service at home. Callaghan responded strongly to the robust social egalitarianism of the quarter-deck, and it helped him in finding a winnable seat in Cardiff South (defeating the near-pacifist schoolteacher, George Thomas). From the war experience, Callaghan also retained throughout his career an internationalist perspective. His maiden speech in August 1945 was on the post-war problems of Japan.

He became a Labour MP in the heady electoral landslide of July 1945. One of 200 new Labour members, he became a prominent back-bencher – and an unconventional and rebellious one. Even before becoming an MP, he had spoken against the Labour Party national executive at the 1944 annual party conference, urging that nationalisation should be a central priority.[4] One of his first votes as an MP was to oppose the American loan negotiated by Keynes in Washington after the end of the war. He was associated for a time with the Keep Left group of MPs, which criticised Ernest Bevin's foreign policy. In 1947, he led a major and successful rebellion to reduce the duration of national service – the only serious defeat suffered by the Attlee government during its years in office. But gradually he moved to a centrist position and served as a very capable junior minister at Transport (where he introduced 'cats' eyes' on roads) and the Admiralty. Even so, as a young minister, he was nobody's pushover. He refused to vote with the government in support of retaining capital punishment in 1948, standing up to Herbert Morrison and refusing to be bullied by him.[5] He was later to become the Home Secretary who presided over the abolition of capital punishment in 1969. When in opposition in 1954, along with his mentor Hugh Dalton, Callaghan was to oppose the leadership's position in endorsing German rearmament. Nevertheless, despite his impatience with Attlee's style of leadership, Callaghan rose up the political ladder. After Labour's election defeat in 1951, he was elected to the Shadow Cabinet, so beginning a career in the front rank of politics. He was to remain a front-bencher for the next 29 years.

There were perhaps five key phases in Callaghan's main political career. The first lasted from 1957, just after Suez, to the end of 1961, when he was shadow Colonial Secretary, a position in which he succeeded Nye Bevan. This was a tumultuous period of change, both in the Commonwealth and in the colonies. Callaghan was, in retrospect, fortunate to hold this particular portfolio at such a time, but he seized the opportunity with skill and self-belief. There

---

[4] Report of the 43rd Labour Party Conference, December 1944, pp. 160ff.
[5] Callaghan MS note, 14 April 1948, Callaghan Papers, box 28.

were ample crises in Cyprus and, to a lesser extent, in Malta, Malaysia (Malaya in the 1950s) and Singapore, and British Guyana. Above all, there was Africa. The once dark continent dominated British politics in the fifties as it had not done since the days of Livingstone and Stanley. East Africa – Kenya, Uganda and Tanganyika – was moving towards independence despite bloody events such as the war with the Mau Mau in Kenya. West Africa – chiefly Nigeria and the Gold Coast (Ghana) – had already achieved it. In Central Africa, the most critical area of all, the proposed federation of Northern and Southern Rhodesia and Nyasaland, first broached under the Attlee government in 1951, led to years of crisis, since Black African opinion was wholly opposed to it. In all these matters Callaghan was heavily involved, and his Commons exchanges with the Colonial Secretary, Lennox-Boyd, a key focus for public debate.[6]

Callaghan's approach was both balanced and careful. It sometimes met with criticism from the Movement for Colonial Freedom on the party left, and its spokespersons, such as Barbara Castle. On both economic development and constitutional advance, he pointed out the dangers as well as the opportunities. He thus gave effective voice to the outlook of a Labour movement generally of one mind on behalf of colonial independence, in contrast to internal party divisions on such issues as Clause Four and nuclear weapons. He also built up important relationships with a new generation of colonial leaders – Kenneth Kaunda, Julius Nyerere, Hastings Banda and Joshua Nkomo in Africa, and also with Tom Mboya, who was sadly murdered at a young age, Lee Kuan Yew in South-East Asia, and Michael Manley and Grantley Adams in the West Indies, all of whom were to figure in Callaghan's later career as an international states-man. Perhaps characteristically, he also became in time a personal friend of an old opponent, the white Rhodesian leader, ex-trade unionist and ex-boxing champion, Roy Welensky.[7] Africa in particular was a major point of reference for him: Lee Kuan Yew told me that he felt Callaghan was somewhat less at home in the affairs of Asia.[8] Without doubt, Callaghan gave Labour a new, coherent perspective in the aftermath of Suez and the retreat from Empire. Jimmy Carter and Helmut Schmidt were to place especial value on his expert-ise in African affairs, and also in the Middle East. In more personal terms, his effective role as shadow Colonial Secretary also widened his scope, enabling him to move beyond his early specialisms in transport and the social services, and making him a recognised major politician. His enhanced stature made it possible for him to stand for the party leadership following the death of Hugh Gaitskell in early 1963 (Callaghan's 41 votes included such influential people

---

[6] Material in Callaghan Papers, box 4 and Lord Boyd of Merton Papers, Bodleian library, Oxford.

[7] Welensky Papers, Rhodes House, Oxford, 596/5, f. 46.

[8] Interview with Lee Kuan Yew, Singapore, 21 September 1993.

as Tony Crosland), and it made him a natural choice as shadow Chancellor under Harold Wilson's leadership. He therefore moved to 11 Downing Street when Wilson became prime minister in October 1964, and an exciting new chapter of his life began.

The second phase of his career ended with the devaluation of the pound in November 1967, a pivotal episode and perhaps the lowest point of Callaghan's political career. Indeed, while he had good relations with key Treasury officials, the Chancellorship was the most difficult of the offices that he held: this was partly because he felt he had no instinctive feel for the subtleties of economic policy, and had met with some ridicule for having held seminars at Nuffield College to help him while shadow Chancellor.[9] But any Chancellor would have faced huge economic challenges throughout his three-year period at the Treasury, with endless balance of payments problems and repeated threats to the pound and foreign currency reserves. He had inherited what appeared in those days to be a massive deficit (£800 million) from the Conservatives, and gloomy forecasts from Lord Cromer, the right-wing governor of the Bank of England. In addition, there was inherent tension between the Treasury and the newly created but ephemeral Department of Economic Affairs, under the ebullient and volatile George Brown. Partly for this reason, the initials DEA were said in the Treasury to stand for 'Department of Extraordinary Aggression'. The 'concordat' drawn up in the Civil Service to delineate the boundary between the two departments could hardly have been less helpful, even with a colleague more tranquil than George Brown. The DEA, it was laid down, dealt with the long term while not excluding the short term; the Treasury would focus on the short term without excluding the long term.[10] It was a collision waiting to happen, a structure wisely avoided by Tony Blair and Gordon Brown in 1997 at the start of another Labour government. With the economy run partly by Callaghan, partly by Brown, partly by a prime minister who was a former economics don at Oxford, it could truly be said, as was famously observed by the ineffable Princess Diana about her marriage, that 'three was a bit crowded'. There was also a perennial background of wider international difficulties, with the growing weakness of the Anglo-American economic system of pegged exchange rates conceived at Bretton Woods during the war and relentless pressures on sterling as a reserve currency, the maintenance of the sterling balances, and the exchange rate of the pound.

In 1964, as soon as he became Prime Minister, Wilson decided to resist devaluation and to maintain the pound at its existing parity against the dollar

---

[9] Callaghan Papers, box 14, and files then in the possession of Prof. Ian Little.

[10] Note by the Secretary of the Cabinet, 'Co-operation between the Department of Economic Affairs and the Treasury', 16 December 1964, National Archives, CAB 129/119.

of $2.80.[11] This decision was endorsed by Callaghan and Brown. Thereafter, civil servants were not even allowed to discuss devaluation, which remained a taboo subject. The joint permanent secretary to the Treasury, William Armstrong, prepared a secret war book for the so-called FU committee should sterling devaluation ever come about by some misfortune: FU stood for Forever Unmentionable. The financial arguments for and against devaluation at that time were, admittedly, finely balanced. The majority of professional economists were against it at that time, though by 1966 many had moved in favour. Alec Cairncross, head of the Economic Section of the Cabinet since 1961, later a sharp critic of exchange rate policy in the sixties, was himself opposed to devaluing sterling at the time. So was Douglas Jay. Of Wilson's two famous Hungarian economic advisers, 'Buda' and 'Pest', Tommy Balogh opposed devaluation whereas Nicky Kaldor supported it. But for Wilson, and many of his colleagues, it was above all a political issue. After the shattering experiences of 1931 and of Labour's own devaluation by Stafford Cripps in 1949, they believed that it was politically impossible to devalue and maintain credibility as a government. In 1964 it was (wrongly) believed that the 1949 devaluation had been a failure. Further, the government was under pressure from the Americans, who tended to link financial aid with defence policy east of Suez, and to suggest that further US loans would be contingent on British military help in Vietnam. Ominously, the president's national security adviser, McGeorge Bundy, told Lyndon Johnson that 'a British brigade in Vietnam would be worth a billion dollars at the moment of truth for Sterling.'[12] Callaghan hoped to escape devaluation almost to the very end: it seemed distinctly avoidable even at the time of his 1967 budget. Only on 13 November 1967, five days before it actually happened, did he reluctantly conclude that devaluation was inevitable.[13] On 18 November, devaluation of sterling to $2.40 duly took place.

Devaluation was seen as a national humiliation. The pound was viewed as a patriotic symbol of national virility. Callaghan at once offered his resignation. One of his Cabinet colleagues, Richard Crossman, absurdly suggested that Callaghan had been the Chamberlain of the government and that Wilson was the Churchill. In fact, the decisions taken in 1964 and then in July 1966 not to devalue were as much Wilson's as Callaghan's. Peter Jay, in more scholarly mode, compared Callaghan and Wilson to Cardinal Wolsey and Henry VIII at the time of the former's dismissal and execution. But Jim kept his head in more senses than one. For a while he was deeply dejected. But his years at the Treasury had not been wholly barren. He had shown himself there to be a

---

[11] Meeting of the Economic Affairs Committee, MISC 1, 17 October 1964 (CAB 129/119).

[12] McGeorge Bundy to Lyndon Johnson 28 July 1965, President Johnson papers, University of Texas, Austin, NSF country file, box 215.

[13] MS note on 'The Devaluation Crisis', Callaghan Papers, box 24.

notable tax reformer, for instance on corporation and capital gains taxes. He was also part architect of an imaginative system of international drawing rights from the International Monetary Fund. He had tried to free up the problems of a reserve currency and defend the sterling balances, and had put in train the machinery for establishing decimal coinage. The royal mint moved from London to Llantrisant, near Cardiff, the famous 'hole with a mint'. He was later to be offered the managing directorship of the IMF, a signal that he enjoyed world-wide respect and approval. In political terms, notably in a brilliant combative speech to party conference in October 1967, Callaghan was still a major political player. James Margach of the *Sunday Times* thought his conference speech showed signs of 'near-greatness'.[14] He was also elected to the key post of party treasurer, which indicated the strong support of major unions.

So, while Callaghan's period at the Treasury was perhaps the least effective of his political career, it was very far from being a fatal one. The political obituaries of Callaghan, like those of Mark Twain, were premature. He had been defeated but he could bounce back. He was down but very far from out. Indeed, it was Harold Wilson, who had told unbelieving television viewers that 'the pound in your pocket is not devalued,' who proved to be the real victim of the devaluation crisis, not Jim Callaghan.[15]

Wilson refused to accept Callaghan's resignation after devaluation, and suggested that he moved to another department instead. Callaghan proposed the Department of Education, but apparently Wilson replied that this was not important enough! So Jim went to the Home Office. He proved to be unusual among Home Secretaries in that during his tenure of that office, so often the graveyard of political reputations, his reputation actually went up. Admittedly his years at the Home Office, down to Labour's election defeat in June 1970, were not free from difficulties. He was accused of being too pro-police during anti-Vietnam protests and too libertarian in student disorders on university campuses. He was also accused of being positively racist when he denied the rights of Kenyan Asians, who had been given British passports when Kenya had become independent in 1963. It was often said (and he deeply resented the accusation) that he was a more conservative Home Secretary than the liberal-inclined Roy Jenkins, who was himself all too inclined to see himself as a white knight on a charger, contrasting his own enlightened regime with Callaghan's authoritarianism. Yet in many ways the criticism of Callaghan was misplaced. Many thought he had achieved the correct balance between upholding the right to protest and preserving law and order. The Vietnam demonstrations in Grosvenor Square were almost a triumph for him. He also had real successes to show in an important Children's and Young Persons Act (1969), in

---

[14] *Sunday Times*, 8 October 1967.
[15] See Ben Pimlott (1992) *Harold Wilson*, HarperCollins, pp. 483–4.

helping to stop a South African cricket tour in the wake of the Basil d'Oliveira affair, and in the final winding-up of capital punishment. A product of the Baptist Church, he criticised the 'rising tide of permissiveness', especially in relation to the legalisation of the use of cannabis as proposed in the report of the Wootton committee at the end of 1968.[16] This was popular with the silent majority in middle England, which had little enough sympathy with the new regime of 'sex, drugs and rock 'n roll' and its long-haired, mini-skirted devotees.

But it was a difficult time, reinforced by his bruising clash with Wilson and Barbara Castle over her proposed trade union reforms, including the use of penal sanctions, in the white paper 'In Place of Strife'. Callaghan boldly spoke out against it, both on the National Executive and in Cabinet. This led to a conflict of wills, which Callaghan in effect won, since the proposals had to be withdrawn after meeting fierce opposition in the parliamentary party. But it added to a sense of political isolation. Nevertheless, it was manifestly Callaghan, rather than Wilson, let alone Barbara Castle, who enjoyed the broad support of Labour MPs, the trade unions and party members in the grass roots. Despite what is often said, and despite the 'winter of discontent' which destroyed his government in 1978–1979, Callaghan never believed that he had been wrong in 1969. To the end of his life, he reiterated his belief that it would have been a mistake to impose penal sanctions on trade unions, or disturb a voluntary system of collective bargaining, and he resisted all the Thatcherite legislation on the unions in his later years. He was always the One-Nation politician.

This led to the third pivotal phase of his political career – his involvement in Northern Ireland in 1969. It was then that his political recovery really began. It is a period that he has described in one of his few books, entitled, in Lincoln-like terms, *A House Divided*.[17] Neither Callaghan nor the Labour government had any particular contact with Irish affairs before 1968–1969. They were lumped into the remit of the Home Office, along with myriad other fringe issues, including the Channel Islands and the Isle of Man. All were buried in files labelled 'General'. There were no guidelines, since Northern Ireland was the responsibility of the Northern Ireland government in Stormont, not the British government in Westminster. But in the summer of 1969 the civil rights movement spilled over into massive violence between Protestants and Catholics, especially in Derry. Callaghan then acted with decisiveness and executive flair – and no little personal courage – in a visit to the Bogside. In effect, he took over command from Ulster's inbred and enfeebled Unionist

---

[16] Advisory Committee on Drug Dependence (1968) Sub-committee report, HMSO, 1969 (Wootton Report on cannabis).

[17] James Callaghan (1973) *A House Divided: The Dilemmas of Northern Ireland*, HarperCollins.

regime. He set out a programme of civil rights measures, primarily in housing and employment (as in the apprenticeships in Harland and Wolff's shipyards and Shorts Aircraft), in the 'Downing Street Declaration'. He abolished the hated B special paramilitaries, and reformed the monolithically Protestant Royal Ulster Constabulary. He also sent in British troops to protect the Catholic minority from a Protestant backlash. In a ferocious encounter, he told the Rev. Ian Paisley 'We are all the children of God,' to which Paisley responded 'No, we are all the children of wrath.' Aggressive Protestant housewives in the Shankill were persuaded to join Callaghan in singing the national anthem. As ever in Northern Ireland, progress was soon interrupted. By the time of the June 1970 general election, there was greater tension, with Provos and Paisleyites emerging. Paisley was first elected to the Commons in 1970.

But the real state of ungovernability came under Reginald Maudling, Callaghan's Conservative successor as Home Secretary. It was Maudling's regime that saw the introduction of internment without trial, the non-jury Diplock courts, and the fateful violence of Bloody Sunday in Derry. There were many civil servants at the time who felt that Callaghan's departure from the management of Irish policy after 1970 meant a tragic lost opportunity of settling the time-worn troubles of Ulster once and for all, at a time when neither the Paisleyites nor Provisional Sinn Fein were yet the force that they later became.[18] Even so, Callaghan emerged as one of the very few British politicians, since Pitt, or perhaps Peel, to enhance his reputation through the handling of Irish affairs. He re-established his stature as a commanding executive minister in Northern Ireland. Harold Wilson regarded it as a turning point for his government, its one and only political triumph after 1966. It also suggested to him that Callaghan, for all his waywardness on trade union reform, was much his most plausible successor in 10 Downing Street.

The fourth key phase of his career concerned Europe, which has been perhaps the central dilemma of Britain's post-imperial history. Callaghan had had early acquaintance with European politics and moves towards unity in his attendance at the Council of Europe at Strasbourg in 1950–1951. He was privately in favour of Britain's joining the Schuman plan for a Coal and Steel Community, but was pressured out of it by Ernest Bevin. But he had never been a Euro-enthusiast. He declared himself to be 'an agnostic' on European Union.[19] He went along with the decision to apply for EEC membership in 1967, but always regarded the economic case as an uncertain one. More generally, like Gaitskell, he had a strong attachment to the Commonwealth, while

---

[18] Kenneth O. Morgan (1997), *Callaghan: A Life*, Oxford University Press, p. 354; interview with Sir Geoffrey de Deney, 3 May 1996.

[19] Nicholas Henderson (1994) *Mandarin*, Weidenfeld and Nicolson, p. 59 (24 March 1974). Henderson says that 'agnosticism is his own [Callaghan's] description'.

his vision of Britain's geopolitical role was strongly pro-Atlanticist. He believed devotedly in the Special Relationship; hence his later close friendship with Henry Kissinger. As opposition spokesman for foreign affairs in 1972–1974, Callaghan took a broadly sceptical line towards Europe, even if one less dogmatic than those moving to the left, such as Tony Benn. In a particularly lamentable speech, Callaghan condemned attempts by the French to have their language recognised as the main language of the new Europe in place of 'the language of Chaucer, Shakespeare and Milton'. In chauvinist style, he wound up in a version of cod French – 'Non, merci beaucoup.'[20] It was not his finest hour.

Nevertheless, as Foreign Secretary his main task was the renegotiation of British membership of the EEC, for which the British people were to vote heavily in a referendum in 1973. His negotiating style was initially brusque but effective. He somewhat shocked the patrician Foreign Office mandarin, Sir Nicholas Henderson, by comparing himself to the then triumphant Welsh rugby XV saving the main effort for late in the second half in order to achieve victory.[21] He was helped by the friendly presence of the new French president, Giscard d'Estaing (who could speak English), and even more of his future close friend, Helmut Schmidt, the Chancellor of the Federal Republic of Germany. As Foreign Secretary, Callaghan built up a warm personal relationship with Schmidt, which proved to be of importance in the development of social democracy in Europe. (The garden-loving Audrey Callaghan also became good friends with Schmidt's botanist wife.) Labour claimed to be engaged in a real negotiation in Brussels. Others felt that it was cosmetic, and that the outcome was pre-ordained. There were certainly improvements in terms to Commonwealth countries on food exports, including smaller countries like Botswana, while the British contribution to the Community budget was effectively pegged. As he lectured Foreign Office advisers such as Adam Butler, it was all in accord with that crucial document, the 1974 Labour Party election manifesto.

Callaghan's pragmatism may not have been Churchillian, but it carried conviction with the country and the party. Not for nothing was Callaghan an unusually party political Foreign Secretary. Labour resolved its European dilemma without splitting, or undergoing the torments that the Conservatives were to undergo throughout the 1990s. Thereafter, as Prime Minister, Callaghan remained relatively cautious on Europe, notably over membership of the EMS and a common currency. But, manifestly, his European settlement gave him greater international stature. It made him Wilson's obvious successor. It is notable that all the pro-European Labour MPs voted for him in the leadership

---

[20] Callaghan Papers, box 1B (speech at Bitterne Park School, Southampton, 25 May 1971).
[21] Ibid., p. 62.

election in 1976 after Roy Jenkins dropped out. Jim's brand of Euro-pragmatism was far more acceptable than the apparent little Englandism of Benn or Foot.

The fifth and final phase of Callaghan's long political career was, of course, his three-year term as Prime Minister from April 1976 to May 1979. It is a premiership that is too often disregarded or seen as a mere interlude between the corporatism and moral hedonism of the Wilson era and the market-driven dogmatism of the Thatcherites. It was a desperately hard time, as leader of a minority government dependent on 'Nats and Nutters', in Denis Healey's vivid phrase, always dogged by financial crisis. Yet it was to prove Callaghan's best period. He is one of those rare cases of a politician whose reputation rose significantly after being Prime Minister. Indeed, he grew in supreme office, and surpassed expectations. Denis Healey, in a tribute at Callaghan's memorial service in Westminster Abbey on 5 April 2005, described Callaghan (in the presence of Blair and Thatcher!) as Britain's best prime minister since Attlee. In part, he succeeded by not being Harold Wilson, now irreparably tarnished by the tone of his time in office and his paranoid fears of 'moles' and 'leaks'. Callaghan's ministers preferred his more open style, the kind of genuinely collective Cabinet government which had been eroded in the sixties and which was to be again eroded after him (even perhaps totally destroyed by Tony Blair). His team of ministers felt that he inspired greater trust than Wilson, a view shared equally by Healey and Shirley Williams on the party right, and by Michael Foot and (to a degree) Tony Benn on the left. There was no kitchen cabinet of the type that had existed under Wilson, no Marcia Williams-type gatekeeper. The Policy Unit under Bernard Donoughue concerned itself with policymaking, not with party manoeuvres. Callaghan, indeed, imposed himself with powerful effect on the office of prime minister with various categories of policy advisers. There was the Political Office under Tom McNally, the Policy Unit under the donnish Donoughue, with such gifted young economists as Gavyn Davies and a clutch of Oxford economists, and the Central Policy Review Staff under Ken Berrill, with such rising stars as the young Tessa Blackstone.

It added up to a revolution in central government, to adapt Geoffrey Elton's description of Thomas Cromwell's work under Henry VIII. Yet it did not strain constitutional precedent, and special advisers did not override the traditional role of civil servants. Callaghan's press officer, a genial Scot, Tom McCaffrey, played a far more restrained and uncontroversial role than did Bernard Ingham under Margaret Thatcher, or Alastair Campbell under Tony Blair later on. In addition, the Economic Seminars organised by Harold Lever (and chaired by the Prime Minister himself) offered an alternative source of guidance to that provided by the Treasury, which Callaghan regarded with suspicion after his own bruising experiences there 10 years earlier.[22] It might be added here that

---

[22] Donoughue Papers, memos 287, 309, 364; Morgan, *Callaghan*, pp. 508–9.

Callaghan's suspicions were far from groundless, since the Treasury's figures for the size of the public sector borrowing requirement in 1977–1978 were much inflated, and the cuts in public spending that followed more severe than they need have been. Callaghan's seminars were also prophetic in making monetary policy formulation for the first time a systemic part of Cabinet government. They were indeed an innovation.

The feeling of trust that Callaghan's collegiate method inspired was shown to best advantage in the International Monetary Fund crisis of November–December 1976. After lengthy debates in Cabinet over many weeks, a consensus was reached on a programme of cuts in public expenditure. This was a triumph of political dexterity, avoiding the debacle of Ramsay MacDonald back in 1931. It was formal Cabinet government at its best, far removed from the informal style of sofa-government under Tony Blair, which the Butler Report was so to criticise. Indeed, Callaghan, who well remembered 1931, could legitimately claim that 'I have not been another Ramsay MacDonald.' At the same time, he also promoted the first questioning of the broadly Keynesian policies which had sustained the post-war settlement in Britain but no longer seemed to be working in a global economy. At the Labour Party conference in 1976, in somewhat Delphic words written for him by his son-in-law Peter Jay, he famously insisted that the country could not spend its way out of a recession.[23] This reflected his prophetic awareness that the main problem now facing Britain was not unemployment in the workforce but inflation of its currency.

For a long period in 1977–1978, a period often forgotten by journalists, who tend to wipe out memory of the 18 months between the IMF crisis and the Winter of Discontent, all went well. Output rose; unemployment and inflation both fell. Douglas Jay has rightly written of the unique achievement of the British economy at this time.[24] The pound strengthened to reach $1.90 and the reserves more than doubled to reach over $9 billion. After 'stagflation' under the Tories, the economy was growing again – with the cheerful prospect of Britain becoming self-sufficient in energy resources with the coming on stream of North Sea oil in 1980. The trade unions, given wise guidance by Jack Jones, maintained a stance of wage restraint, while a parliamentary pact with the small Liberal Party in March 1977 ensured that Labour could continue in office as a minority government. Mrs Thatcher, a neophyte Leader of the Opposition struggling in an overwhelmingly male House of Commons, seemed almost outclassed by an experienced and wily prime minister. It was a fruitful last phase of the old post-war consensus, and led, among other things,

---

[23] *The Times*, 29 September 1976.

[24] Douglas Jay (1985) *Sterling: Its Use and Misuse: A Plea for Moderation*, Oxford University Press, p. 62.

to effective regional policies in Wales and Scotland, where demands for devolution were growing.

Callaghan also branched out in foreign affairs, notably over strategic arms limitation and other defence issues, where he emerged as honest broker between Jimmy Carter and Helmut Schmidt. Their personal relationship was a difficult one: Schmidt's private comments about the US president, when I interviewed him 16 years later, were remarkably harsh.[25] In these circumstances Callaghan could claim to be acting as the genuine bridge between Europe and the United States that Tony Blair declared himself to be 20 years later. Callaghan helped Carter, in an unspectacular *sub rosa* way, to secure the Camp David agreement of 1978 between Israel's Prime Minister, Menachem Begin, and Egypt's President, Anwar Sadat, the last such for many a sad day. Callaghan knew them both well and used his contacts with much sensitivity.[26] Until late 1978, therefore, he was seen as an able and effective prime minister.

Then came an unexpected decision. Callaghan did not, as was widely expected, call a general election in the autumn of 1978. Leafing through the evidence of MORI public opinion polls in the privacy of his Sussex farm in the summer of 1978, he reached the view that the best Labour could hope for was another period of minority government. In the sensitive West Midlands constituencies, the evidence was especially discouraging, or so he thought. He consulted a quartet of Cabinet ministers, who, predictably, took the same view. They were Michael Foot, the leader of the House, anxious to stay on until North Sea oil was near to production, Denis Healey, the Chancellor, who believed that the economy would not deteriorate, David Owen, the Foreign Secretary who wanted to complete private manoeuvres over Rhodesia, and Merlyn Rees, the Home Secretary and a man of famously cautious outlook.[27] The majority in the Cabinet, however, ranging from Edmund Dell on the far right to Tony Benn on the left, all felt that Callaghan should go to the country, and most journalists seem to agree with them. The government would be impaled on the problems of Welsh and Scottish devolution, which Callaghan himself did not much favour in any case. In effect, they would be at the mercy of a dozen or so Scottish Nationalists. Callaghan's judgement can be defended – after all, as Gordon Brown showed in October 2007, prime ministers do not call an election if they believe they are likely to lose it – but the way in which he reached his decision was calamitous, including the notorious music-hall song at the TUC mentioned earlier.

---

[25] Interview with Chancellor Helmut Schmidt, 30 November 1994.

[26] Telephone conversation, President Carter and Callaghan, 14 January 1978, T11/78, transcript in Callaghan Papers, box 34.

[27] Material in Callaghan Papers; interviews with Roy Hattersley, Tom McNally and Tom McCaffrey, 25 March 1995, 26 July and 3 June 1994.

During the subsequent 'Winter of Discontent', the massive public sector and other strikes which marked the period from November 1978 to March 1979, the government seemed to fall apart at the seams. The unions rejected Callaghan's proposed 5 per cent pay norm and became almost anarchic in their approach to wages and inflation. Callaghan a tired man of 66 approaching the end of his career, confessed in retrospect that he had committed many errors at this time. The proposal for a 5 per cent pay norm had 'popped out' during an unscripted radio interview. He appeared not to respond to the genuine problems of the low-paid (admittedly, trade unionists such as oil-tanker drivers, who were anything but low-paid, did not seem to do so either). He came back to a frozen Britain, in the midst of a very cold winter, with rubbish on the streets, hospitals and schools being closed, and even grave-diggers on strike refusing to bury the dead. Returning suntanned from a conference with world leaders in Guadeloupe, he appeared to strike a false note of complacency interpreted by the right-wing tabloid press as 'Crisis, what crisis?' It may have been that he responded with some impatience to the question from a young woman journalist. During the public sector strikes in January, he did not declare a state of emergency – almost certainly a wise decision – and word spread throughout Whitehall and Westminster that the prime minister was tired and despondent. Defeatist civil servants such as Clive Rose in the Civil Contingency Unit argued against policy initiatives, since they might be seen as a provocation. A despondent mood of *anomie* appeared to grip Downing Street. Bernard Donoughue wrote later of 'a quiet despair' reminiscent of the good ship *Titanic*. The eventual St Valentine's Day document patched up with the TUC in February carried no conviction.[28] The strikes that grim winter destroyed the political effectiveness and the credibility of the TUC. They provided the platform for Margaret Thatcher's election victory.

There were manifest shortcomings in government policy. But the truth must be that the trade unions at that time were almost ungovernable, architects of their own downfall. They were surging in membership, at 13 million the highest ever. Large public sector unions such as NUPE and ASTMS had become very different in character from the loyalist unions with which Callaghan had been familiar in his youth. There had also been a change in leadership of a most damaging kind – notably in the Transport and General Workers, where Jack Jones had been followed as general secretary by the inept Moss Evans – and this proved little short of catastrophic. But perhaps the labour movement was beyond leadership at this stage. The result was that the warmest political friend the unions had ever had in government lost his position as Prime Minister. Since then, even under Labour governments, the unions have been

---

[28] *The Economy, the Government and Trade Union Responsibilities: joint statement of the TUC and the Government*, HMSO, February 1979.

marginalised. Their membership has fallen to 6.5 million, a 50 per cent drop, with an especial collapse in the public sector where once they dominated. It is a paradox that the Labour Party was created mainly by two elements – the socialists and the trade unions – and that neither of them now play much of a role within classless, rootless New Labour. Such were the long-term consequences of the fall of Callaghan and the Winter of Discontent.

In the course of the general election campaign in 1979, Callaghan spoke of the 'sea change' in politics that he now detected. In his (distinctly debatable) view, there was an abrupt collapse of the post-1945 era of consensus, corporatism and conciliation. The disarray in the Labour Party in the early 1980s seemed to confirm the transformation. Callaghan's own judgement on the last phase of his government was a sad one – 'I let the country down.'[29] It was far too harsh. Even during the election campaign itself, his standing ran up to 20 per cent higher than that of Margaret Thatcher. Big Jim remained Labour's strongest asset. But he lost power, just the same.

In surveying Jim Callaghan's eventful and colourful career, one is constantly aware of a politician of great ability. Lord Donoughue has written that, while not really an intellectual, he proved a more searching and demanding taskmaster than Harold Wilson. He also compares Callaghan's innate decency favourably with Margaret Thatcher, 'a dangerous woman' who pandered to populist prejudices about immigrants and foreigners.[30] Callaghan's premiership, indeed, is an important one, worth far more attention than it usually receives. For instance, *This Blessed Plot* (1998), Hugo Young's monograph on British relations with Europe since 1945, devotes just five of its 558 pages to the Callaghan years. But his time in Downing Street is more than simply an interlude between Wilson and Thatcher. Uniquely among Labour prime ministers, he grappled unflinchingly with arcane technicalities of global defence and international liquidity. He was intellectually as well as politically tough. But he was also emollient. He could be compared with Stanley Baldwin, someone he admired in his youth, an apostle of social peace in our time who was wont to say of himself that he was not 'a clever man' and who feared Lloyd George for being 'a dynamic force'. The clever men in the Labour Party often displayed intellectual snobbery towards Jim Callaghan. Yet his close colleagues and admirers included Evan Durbin, Douglas Jay, John Strachey and Tony Crosland, four of the intellectual giants of British socialism, to whom may be added the American savant John Kenneth Galbraith, whom I once interviewed. Callaghan was, indeed, the archetypal Labour man whose reading, friendships and ideas revolved around the history and principles of democratic socialism. By contrast, the more avowedly radical Michael Foot included

---

[29] Interview with Sir Kenneth Stowe, 25 June 1996.
[30] Bernard Donoughue (2008) *Downing Street Diary, Vol. II*, Cape London, p. 293.

among his intimates such notably anti-Labour figures as Lord Beaverbrook, Randolph Churchill and Enoch Powell, while Foot's favoured authors included Tory/Conservatives such as Dean Swift, Edmund Burke and Disraeli. No such aberrations were ever likely from Jim Callaghan, who never forgot his origins in the drab working-class terraces of Portsmouth.

Callaghan was cautious on many issues, on trade union reform, in choosing not to pursue the Bullock report on industrial democracy, on Welsh and Scottish devolution, and on European unity. Yet he was capable of great decisiveness, too: on Africa, on Northern Ireland, and on education, in his still highly relevant Ruskin College speech of October 1976, for example, which began the process of reassessing teaching standards and the assessment of quality in post-war education policy.[31] He was frequently innovative over economic policy, in what came to be seen as the post-Keynes era after 1976. He was seen amongst the electorate as both a unifying and a steadying force. The word commonly applied to him was 'honest'. Cartoonists depicted him (reflecting his earlier links as spokesman for the Police Federation) as Dixon of Dock Green, PC Jim, genially urging the citizenry to 'mind how you go'. Callaghan himself disliked this characterisation intensely, but it was undeniably part of his popular appeal.

The attempt can be made to fit Callaghan into the typology of classic Social Democratic leader. It is not straightforward. He was neither Max Weber's 'charismatic leader', as were Keir Hardie and Nye Bevan, for example, nor an intellectual like Gaitskell, nor a technocrat like Wilson; neither was he a machine organiser or local government boss like Morrison, nor can he conceivably be enlisted in Tony Blair's postmodernist vision of a New Labour party. Perhaps he can best be understood as an updated example of the classic professional politician, of whom the German socialist journalist Egon Wertheimer wrote, on the model of the German Social Democrats in a left-wing citadel like Hamburg – one reason why the sea-loving Hamburger, Helmut Schmidt, felt so much at ease with him. In this connection, Callaghan's adroit stewardship of his socially variegated Cardiff constituency from the working-class core of Splott and Adamsdown to the genteel villadom of Penarth is instructive. Over four generations, he was the most characteristic and representative Labour politician since Arthur Henderson. And, like Henderson, he combined a close affinity with the unions with a wider dimension, with a passionate interest in international issues, an aspect reflected in his retirement in important speeches on the developing world, the global economy and international indebtedness, and the problems of a controlled disarmament. He was, together with Henderson and Herbert Morrison, one of the three great organising figures who helped

---

[31] Callaghan Papers, box 32; Michael Barber, 'New Labour 20 years on', *Times Educational Supplement*, 11 October 1996.

sustain the Labour alliance, in good times and bad. He was much more than just a pragmatist managerialist on the New Labour model. He believed himself to be a democratic socialist. I once asked him, when concluding my biography of him, 'Are you a socialist, Jim?' He seemed surprised that I even asked the question. He replied quietly: 'Of course.'

His associates, friends and even opponents (e.g. Nigel Lawson)[32] all referred to him as 'a big man'. In general, the more important the man or woman, the higher, usually, is his or her opinion of Jim Callaghan. Roy Jenkins's memoirs, never particularly friendly, talk of big fish and minnows. There was, wrote Jenkins, a tone of 'defiant dignity' about Callaghan which survived his reputation as a machine politician who refused to accept the Boundary Commission proposals to redistribute constituencies before the general election of 1970 (Callaghan remembered similar events harmful to Labour before the 1950 general election), and which made him resemble a kind of British Jim Farley or Mayor Daley.[33] Never a bigoted partisan, he was always anxious, maybe with Ramsay MacDonald in mind, to escape the establishment embrace, even if, unlike MacDonald, he ended up in the House of Lords. His reputation contrasts sharply with the later standing of Harold Wilson. Unlike Wilson or Lloyd George, he was never tarnished by alleged corruption or a tainted honours list. And, unlike Baroness Thatcher, he spent his retirement contributing to British public life, especially to higher education as President of Swansea University and the Cambridge Overseas Trust Commonwealth scholarships, rather than continuing to fight old wars as an itinerant international ideologue.

Jim Callaghan's dominant ethos throughout his career was that of 'community'. His was as much an 'English Journey' as J.B. Priestley's, with something of William Cobbett thrown in. His rhetoric was often flavoured by words like 'partnership' or 'cooperation', or indeed 'social contract'. He cherished the ethos of the family and embodied in his own scandal-free private life the values of secure married life: Audrey Callaghan, unlike Mary Wilson, was at ease with the role of political wife. He reflected many of the themes of British socialist revisionism, without being himself devoid of ideology. Community for him meant a kind of moral cohesion, a social contract writ large. It seemed to him to be rooted in modern British history, reaching its apogee perhaps in the 1939–1945 war and in the post-war settlement, a settlement which, however, some of his own policies ultimately helped to undermine. For Callaghan the emotional basis of community also comprehended patriotism, a sentiment too seldom enlisted by the British left, but a feeling natural enough to a son of the imperial naval base at Portsmouth. His consensual tone contrasted with the militant tendency of a Thatcher or a Benn. His idea of community was

---

32 Nigel Lawson (1996) *The View from No. 11* (1992), Corgi, p. 12.
33 Roy Jenkins (1991) *A Life at the Centre*, Macmillan, p. 288.

rooted, not in an abstract 'centrism' as with the abortive SDP breakaway, or as in cruder interpretations of 'New Labour', but in a living broad-church labour movement centrally relevant to Britain's present and past. Peter Hennessy has cited Callaghan as seeing himself as neither Old nor New Labour but rather as Original Labour. The legacy of Callaghan's philosophy of community can be seen in what remains of the welfare state, in a spirit of social and industrial harmony unusual in much of Europe, and in a peaceful retreat from Empire.

At the same time, community for Callaghan evoked relatively conservative attitudes towards law and order, feminism, gay lib, 'permissiveness' such as televised nudity, and to most British institutions, including the royal family. He enjoyed a strong relationship with the Queen, and relished the fact that his father had served on the Royal Yacht in the time of Edward VII. Callaghan's creed was Britain's version of evolutionary social democracy, the British 'middle way', which made only a limited impact on much of continental Europe, but was an inspiration to a whole generation of Commonwealth third-world leaders after 1945. Like most of us, after all, Callaghan did believe there was such a thing as society.

Jim Callaghan's political career at one level is a parable of how a talented working-class boy, with a background more deprived even than that of David Lloyd George, could scale the heights without any compensating advantages. But it also offers clues to both the quiescence and the stability of the United Kingdom in the modern world. His career was anything but humdrum. It was full of colour and surprises. In pursuing the tortuous road, from Attlee's Middle Way to Blair's Third Way, James Callaghan, 'Big Jim', stood tall amongst the pioneers.

9
Margaret Thatcher, 1979–1990

Keith Middlemas[1]

About a figure as controversial as Margaret Thatcher, there is no point in preaching to a text. It is better to take something from Henry Kissinger: 'What we want is not more secret knowledge but the better analysis of what we already know.' The aim here is to ask questions rather than retell in detail 11 long years, starting with the basic question which affects all biographers – what did she, as opposed to her Cabinet, her civil servants, her party, actually do; and what, if anything, does 'Thatcherism' now mean in a very different world from that in which it originated in the 1980s ? From that follow other questions. What qualities did she bring to the office of Prime Minister? What was the nature of her power, in particular, in relation to the British economy, the structure of power in the state, and European and world affairs?

Nearly 20 years after she retired as Prime Minister, her memory retains the power to foment differences; there will be mutually incompatible answers to nearly every question about her. But first, one must ask: what was it that made her eligible to be Prime Minister? She had no memorable track record, like Lloyd George or Churchill. There was no loyal party or bureaucratic formation, such as supported Attlee and Wilson. In some ways, she was more like Baldwin – elevated by an accidental element. But her political formation is well known – John Campbell's biography gives a blow-by-blow account in two volumes.

One can start with her small town upbringing, rising middle-class aspirations, the influence of her father, Methodism – all of which are key themes – followed by her reaction, as a young woman, when she reached Oxford. But her Oxford was not that of Evelyn Waugh; hers was the Oxford of hard work, by an ambitious young woman reading always for a purpose, in a pre-feminist environment, imbued with an intense dislike of snobbery, of which there was plenty

---

[1] Most of this chapter is based upon private interviews with the leading figures of the Thatcher years.

in Oxford at the time. She discovered politics through the Oxford University Conservative Association, and discovered also the virtue of certainty rather than creative doubt. She married a wealthy businessman, with the result that her family lifestyle was largely absolved of drudgery. She was clever but not an intellectual, and held rather a narrow world view. She travelled little, and spoke no other language. She studied law, qualifying as a barrister, and then became a standard 1960s Tory back-bencher.

Her abilities were manifest, and she clearly merited promotion: she spent a short period as a junior minister in the Department of Pensions and National Insurance, and briefed herself well for her performances in parliament. In opposition she became the statutory woman in the Shadow Cabinet, with the post of Education. One thing made her different: by 1968, she had come to be linked to the free-market Institute of Economic Affairs, but she was still, and perhaps always would be, a listener rather than a contributor to its version of the Tory Enlightenment.

Then, in the Heath Government, she experienced three and a half years as Minister of Education, showing competence rather than brilliance. Because she abandoned the policy of free milk for primary school children, continuing the policy of the previous, Labour, government which had abandoned it for secondary school children, she was called a 'milk snatcher'. But that was an absurd taunt. Perhaps her main triumph was to have saved the Open University from closure. But she was excluded from the policymaking core. Heath did not like her, but saw her usefulness.

As a minister, she felt manipulated to some degree by her officials, and she developed techniques for the future to manage them, including sometimes roughing them up. As for general policy, she went along, as one would expect of a junior member of the Cabinet, with the statutory prices and incomes policy and entry into the European Community in 1973. But she was already coalescing with a second generation of 'new right' reformers who could well be described as ideologues – men such as Arthur Seldon, Alfred Sherman and Alan Walters – well outside the party mainstream. If an alternative approach to Heath was needed, then a distinctive ideology was coming into existence, of which she was part, with the support of a small group of like-minded enthusiasts.

After Heath had lost two general elections in 1974, his leadership, so it seemed, was doomed. But, one after another, the alternatives to Heath evaporated: Enoch Powell told his supporters to vote Labour in the February 1974 general election, and then became an Ulster Unionist; William Whitelaw feared to strike; Keith Joseph eliminated himself at the last moment. Margaret Thatcher was, therefore, an accidental leader. She opposed Heath initially as a test run, but it soon became the real thing, a reward for what, beyond argument, was her sustained determination and courage in agreeing to stand.

So she became Leader of the Opposition. She was likely to win in any case if Labour destroyed itself, and, of course, by 1979, after the Winter of Discontent, the Labour Government had destroyed itself. Her distinctive achievement, accentuated by Heath's personal hostility towards her, was to capture the Party by degrees: first, to take control of its organisation, to manipulate Central Office, and to downgrade the Research Department, to make quite sure that there was no alternative theology. The second part was the formation of a political core: Whitelaw to some extent, Peter Thorneycroft and, insofar as she considered foreign affairs, Lord Carrington. None of these were what later became known as 'Thatcherites': but those in the second rank were, and they were to be her stalwart supporters during the early years of government.

She began to develop strong links to the back-benchers, and used the annual Conservative Conference brilliantly, aided by the gifted speech-writer Ronald Millar. In public she demonstrated a blend of temperate public language on some issues, such as social and education policy. But she was tough on the Cold War and the Soviet Union, and she found the 'Iron Lady' sobriquet very useful. In private, she was definitely part of the future policy planning process, and a core member of that fount of ideas, Keith Joseph's Centre for Policy Studies, which stemmed from the Institute of Economic Affairs. But she was a pupil–observer rather than an originator of ideas; and she was cautious about the public impact. Indeed, one of the more incisive 'new right' documents of that period, *Stepping Stones*, written in 1979, was put aside as being too much for the public at that stage to accept.

By the late 1970s, however, she had fully formed views, among them four very clear convictions: first, that the corporate behaviour of the modern state, as it had developed since the Second World War, was a failure and had become an intolerable burden; second, that there should be more space for ideals of individualism, individual morality and responsibility; third, that wealth creation was a good thing in its own right, implying that property aspirations were desirable in the mixed economy; finally, that the ideal state should be seen as a benign regulator and no more.[2]

Meanwhile, the packaging went on: the voice changed, the accent changed, the hair changed and the hats changed. It was an exercise in Saatchi branding, accompanied by the brilliant slogan – 'Labour isn't working' – for the 1979 election. She had her own approach to the media by now. She did not make up to the BBC, but to ITV, and to the tabloid newspapers rather than the broadsheets. There was an element of truth in Churchill's famous remark about Attlee, that 'if you feed a grub royal jelly it will turn into a queen bee.'

By 1979, she was, in party terms, a convinced Conservative. In terms of philosophy and outlook, however, she was more of a classical nineteenth-century

---

[2] Interview, Sir Keith Joseph, 1984.

Liberal. It was no longer Methodism that drove her, if indeed it ever had been. The force animating her was a much earlier one, geographically from the same area that she came from – Grantham. She saw herself perhaps as Bunyan's Pilgrim, on a long march, and on the march she carried in her handbag a copy of Weber's *Protestant Ethic* and texts from the doyens of the eighteenth-century Scottish Enlightenment: Adam Smith, David Hume (but without his atheism), Adam Ferguson. She was, in short, a modern Puritan.[3]

What were the sources of her power as Prime Minister? A strong element of her difficult inheritance was the economic recession of 1980 to 1981, stemming partly from the massive increase of VAT in 1979 by her first Chancellor, Geoffrey Howe. It was a bad time to introduce a new governing regime. Nevertheless, the boats were very soon publicly burnt, by abandoning the crisis management modes of the 1960s and 1970s. These two years – 1979 to 1981 – were the severest test of her whole decade, and the underlying question became: would a government led by her bend when the recession got to its worst, or would it sail, like Captain McWhirr in Conrad's novel, through the typhoon itself?

She had a supportive Cabinet core, which was crucial in the early years: herself, Keith Joseph, Geoffrey Howe. In contrast, Jim Prior and Ian Gilmour, most prominent of what she would later call the 'wets', were there for other reasons, but mainly because Prior could keep the labour market and the trades unions relatively quiet.[4] Below Cabinet were the coming younger men, such as Nigel Lawson and Arthur Cockfield. Her Cabinet was actually more open than Heath's, and participatory, in the sense that Cabinet discussion did take place – the phrase 'sofa-government' would have been wholly inappropriate. But as Prime Minister she reserved the right to demur, to divert or simply ignore disagreement, hoping that Whitelaw and Carrington would see her through. Of course, she was – as all Prime Ministers are – very well briefed, but also overworked, a trait which quickly became habitual. She interfered restlessly, almost endlessly, to the eventual exhaustion of many of her colleagues. Everything had to go to No. 10, and she reserved the right, especially with the so-called wets, and later on, in different circumstances, with Lawson and Howe, to leak, to give unattributable briefings against her colleagues, and to use her press manager, Bernard Ingham, in ways which have since her day become both familiar and even more debased.

Amongst her colleagues, she inspired great loyalty, sometimes even love, but rarely, if ever, friendship. Her mission was not to bring harmony, but enlightenment. Sometimes, a certain recklessness betrayed itself, an ability to stand

---

[3] Interview with *Sunday Times*, 1 May 1981: 'Economics are the method; the object is to change the soul.'

[4] Interviews, Sir James Prior 1980–1982, and see Prior's memoirs (1986) *A Question of Balance*, Hamish Hamilton, *passim*.

aside, as if this were not her government at all. There were casualties, of course; over the decade, some ministers dropped out, others were sacked, so that she became more isolated and lonely; there is a parallel with Queen Elizabeth I in her latter years. She became more vulnerable to isolated but high-profile political quarrels such as Heseltine's management of the Westland helicopters affair, and the issue of entry to the Exchange Rate Mechanism in the late 1980s.

The Party and its Conference, however, were captured and stayed so. Once Harold Watkinson had declined her initial offer, Peter Thorneycroft became her chosen Party Chairman, and he and his successors ensured that the Party was held, right to the end. Every Conference, year on year, witnessed rhetorical triumphs. But the back-benchers themselves and the parliamentary party's faith were eroded, so that her advisers feared at the very end in November 1990 to tell her that in the second ballot on the leadership she probably no longer held the majority of MPs. As for the media, in press and television she benefited from great skills of image projection by Ian Gow and Bernard Ingham, and she relied on Ronald Millar for the speeches. ITV and the tabloids and their proprietors were, on the whole, supportive – perhaps even servile – not least because, in their own patch, their own bugbears, the print unions, needed to be demolished if they were to re-establish power over the public mind.

For Whitehall, that is, the Civil Service, it became a deeply complicated era. From the start, there was the new climate, created if not actively induced: Treasury dominance over the spending departments, marking a clear, almost a preacher's, division between those for and those against the new regime of financial control. The friendly symbiosis of ministers and permanent secretaries from the 1960s and 1970s disappeared. It was a true sea change, and it governed promotion to the top jobs, leading remorselessly over the years to the development of a mechanistic view of officials' roles and duties. They were not to be *énarques* in the French mode, or even advisers on policy, and it was not for them to define the national interest – a thesis which has become deeply entrenched among her successors. A hardline approach began at once with Lord Rayner's Efficiency Unit, and the imposition of a culture which led the former mandarinate towards assent rather than consent.[5]

That was quite different from her attitude towards what may be called the State's guardians, the military and the intelligence services, and the Bank of England, for whom she had great and continuing respect.[6] Meanwhile, the institutions of the post-war era, which some call the corporate state, lost power and, from one angle, even access. The CBI (Confederation of British Industry) had been close to her in the Opposition years, perhaps even a little too close.

---

[5] Interviews, Sir Douglas Wass, 1982–1985.

[6] Interviews, MI6 officials, Bank of England officials, Lords O'Brien and Richardson, Governors, 1985 and 1987.

But the heads of industry, even though they still had access to Downing Street after 1979, were distanced from actual policymaking by her government. The City was not yet a player, not until the late 1980s brought the financial services boom, the Single Market and the year of the Big Bang. But the great influence of the Bank of England and its gifted governor, Gordon Richardson, grew in the evolution of economic management and monetary policy.

Trades unions had no access at all, not even Len Murray, TUC General Secretary, who was desperately trying to hold out for a different role for the TUC, against the momentum of the radical left in the public sector trades unions and the National Union of Mineworkers.[7] The best the TUC could do in those dismal years was to retain their link with Jim Prior, accept his temperately argued labour market policy, and let the NUM go down to their own folly.

Finally, amongst the sources of power, there was the electorate. Much of Margaret Thatcher's electoral success derived from the Opposition's endemic disunity. There was not a lot of mileage in voting for the Labour Party during the wasted years after 1979; hence the rise and the popularity of the Alliance. Margaret Thatcher had two great advantages. She knew that the support of the white-collar workers in the Midlands and the South-East was almost certain. After all, fewer of them had voted Labour in 1979 than in any year since 1931. Secondly, there was a culture of enemies, at which she excelled, and which played extremely well in the popular press and elsewhere. Russia was an enemy, trade unions were an enemy, the bureaucrats, the IRA, the Argentine generals.

How, then, did Margaret Thatcher use this power? With ministers personally, she could out-argue, outmanoeuvre and dismiss, and sometimes, as with Geoffrey Howe at the end, dismiss with ignominy. After 1981, she no longer needed a tutorial education, even by Keith Joseph, and she barely needed advice, except on technical questions such as military matters. Witness that famous scene, before the Falklands War began; the House of Commons debate was about to take place and Admiral Sir Henry Leach came in, to a private meeting, in full uniform and she asked: 'Can we do it?' He replied: 'Yes, Prime Minister, it will not be easy, but you can.'[8]

The tactics of power embodied a strong gender element. She could, and did, use her femininity to charm her colleagues backstage. But she had no desire for what would now be seen as political sisterhood – that came with other women a generation later. Her habitual reliance on constant overwork, constant adrenaline rather than sleep, meant that power was an undiluted addiction. Finally, like most prime ministers, she was lonely, which made it

---

[7] TUC papers and minutes, *passim*, 1978–1985; interviews with Sir Len Murray, 1983–1986.
[8] Interview, senior Admiral, 1985.

vitally important that she had a husband waiting up in No. 10. She was vulnerable, but rarely so in public. This meant that she could ignore the taunts, and often, as with the Iron Lady remark, turn them to her advantage. Whether she actually looked at Scarfe's cartoons of her is not known, nor whether she heard the remark by François Mitterrand that she had the mouth of Marilyn Monroe but the eyes of Caligula. Certainly, she declared what she believed was true; a rather different stance from those who believe that what they say must be true because they say it.

The first test case, even if mundane, was the running of the economy and the changes that transformed the period while apparently cutting the trades unions down to size. She and her Treasury core had concluded that not only was the post-war state wrongly constructed, with its mistaken mandate to run the macroeconomy permanently on neo-Keynesian lines, but that its record had been proved wrong by what had happened in the 1970s. There should be an end, therefore, to corporatism, the attempts at triangular policy evolution by government, industry, labour and the financial sector, which had been demonstrably successful in both World Wars. It should be replaced by the imposition of strict budgetary rules which would preclude such negotiation and prevent backsliding – in ways which pressure groups could not defeat. It would be hard, but Ministers – not just the Prime Minister – all assumed that there would be a short initial shock, followed by a rational public response, leading to a virtuous circle.[9] The problem was that, in the very severe recession of 1980–1981, the public response turned out to be wildly variable rather than rational, and often very hostile. Even if the new enemies were clear enough – inflation, public sector costs, public sector pay – it was not a straightforward battlefield, and as time went on it became more like Tolstoy's account of the Battle of Borodino, a soldier's battle in the smoke, where one could hardly see the enemy at all. Also, monetarism (as it was called at the time) was a theory, not a rule, much in dispute among economists, who were able to use only one instrument – interest rates (the old Bank rate at this time being called Minimum Lending Rate). Even Keith Joseph's closest allies had not been certain how it would work in practice and whether to define money supply as M1, M2, M3 or M0.[10]

As such complexities bedevilled clarity, the wider Cabinet became uncertain and even appalled at the price. The theorists had already given way to the practical men who were now in charge. Indeed, after it was over, Milton Friedman criticised the whole exercise, though he had personally helped her to try to convert the 'wets' soon after the 1979 election.[11] A fixed rule replaced

---

[9] Interviews, Sir Douglas Wass, Sir Leo Pliatzkey, 1983–1985. See also Geoffrey Howe, address at Cambridge Summer School, July 1980.
[10] Interview, Sir Jeremy Morse, 1984.
[11] Interview at Stanford University, March 1985.

macroeconomic management, but it was allied to supply-side reform, long charted by Keith Joseph, which was intended to encourage deregulation and real organic growth. But this was a vast scenario – like the battlefield: desperate engagements were taking place all over the field, and the supply-side reforms actually came last, despite Keith Joseph's best efforts.

Meanwhile, Margaret Thatcher's work was focused on holding the Treasury core together and driving on. What followed was the converse of post-war crisis management, the antithesis, especially, of what had been done in the Heath period, from 1972 to 1974. It should, however, be remembered that much of this had been prepared for and partly enacted during the IMF crisis of 1976, when Denis Healey was Labour Chancellor. What the Prime Minister gave was personal and political direction, a populist imagery, an implacable language in public; and she held to it, literally, as if there were no alternative.

The shock came at once, in Geoffrey Howe's first budget, in March 1980, and what he called the medium term financial strategy (MTFS), reinforced in his second and third budgets in successive years. Of course there was uncertainty over whether she could get it through, but the wets, of whom Jim Prior was the ostensible head, had not prepared for the first budget, and they were subsequently dispersed as a potential force, primarily because they did not have a realistic alternative of their own. The same occurred in Whitehall and in the parliamentary party.

But the uncertainties remained: which rule, and what were the limits of MLR as a weapon? Gordon Richardson and the Bank of England were not much in sympathy with Margaret Thatcher's private advisers, Alfred Sherman and Alan Walters; like Prior, but from within the centre, they asked the deep and pertinent question: what is the national interest? Does Britain have a national interest in the survival of industry and in something still called full employment?

Mrs Thatcher at this point, and for a short time afterwards, should be seen as arbitrator rather than enforcer. To many of her Cabinet colleagues, beyond the wets, by the time sterling had reached $1.44 and unemployment had reached 10 per cent without remission, this was hell already. By 1981–1982, these also had the support of industry and the financial sector. So a moment of pragmatism seeped in. After all, there was still a balance of power between government and public to preserve: once, when Nigel Lawson was asked about monetarism, he replied: 'The conditions for monetarism in Britain do not exist.' 'What are they?' 'Water cannon.'

Thatcher's ultimate but narrow power base among Treasury Ministers was not enough to hold her up against the second thoughts of colleagues, combined with those of the CBI, the Bank of England and many Permanent Secretaries, even those who had initially welcomed the change. She was not blind, not Captain McWhirr, to drive straight through the middle of the typhoon. So in one sense she found herself closer to Lenin with his New Economic Policy in the early 1920s. So long as the ideal was upheld, and believed in by the public, that was redefined as the core, the irreversible change, rather than the precise definition of method. So the Medium Term Financial Strategy was actually rebased year on year, 1982 on 1981, 1983 on 1982, which in fact represented a slow but significant modification.[12] The PM forbade David Howell to face up to a miners' strike in 1981; she allowed Keith Joseph to bail out bankrupt but key companies. Most significantly perhaps, a far-reaching, radical Central Policy Review Staff report was binned in the summer of 1982, even though Geoffrey Howe had circulated it to the Cabinet. This had advocated real right-wing policy – freezing state benefits, an insurance-based National Health Service, introduction of education vouchers and the abandonment of Trident, the nuclear deterrent. Instead, the Prime Minister went on to tell the party Conference, in October, 'The NHS is safe with us,' and as a token, in November, MLR was pushed down to 12 per cent.

All generals know that the decision of how and when to withdraw is the most important one they ever have to make. There was an element of flexibility but, equally, as in the Napoleonic War when Wellington was beset by Napoleon's armies in Spain, there was a line of Torres Vedras, which was held not least because the critics inside the Cabinet were eventually dispersed and Prior, the only conceivable leader of an internal opposition, agreed to be sent to Northern Ireland.[13]

A new sort of agenda for public discourse had been set, about which three points should be made: first, and most significant, that the focus shifted to inflation and public spending and not, as in the post-war period, unemployment. Even if there was no final answer to the question of which monetary standard should be used, and even if the exchange rate was brought forward as possibly an alternative instrument, this shift of focus was established as a priority; it was only in the second half of the 1980s, when Nigel Lawson's exchange rate policy was to shadow the Deutschmark, that a fuller range of instruments was introduced.

The second point is that the state itself came into play. Some of the arguments that derived originally from the eighteenth-century Scottish Enlightenment emerged to justify practical observation. The state is not a source of direction, neither is it the sum of benign targets; it is actually a target in itself, and the 'Heath model' (because Heath had seen the state as a powerful instrument for creating both economic policy and European policy) became discredited in theory as well as practice.

The third concerns the end of post-war confidence about the capacity limits of government and the state. Thatcher and her colleagues believed that there

---

[12] Interview, Sir Kenneth Berrill, 1984.
[13] Interviews, Sir James Prior, 1982–1984.

had been a huge amount of over-optimism in the 35 years since 1944 about what economic management could do. That uncritical faith had been disproved, as most historians would now agree. Indeed, Keynes himself would probably have disagreed with much of what was done in his name after the war. Instead, this government would go back to the debates of 1942–1944 (i.e. before the war was over) to the Treasury requirement of a ten-year balanced budget as against deficit finance, and to an optimum level of five per cent unemployment – not Beveridge's three per cent or the actual 1.8 per cent of the 1950s. The tides of argument changed and this became the single most decisive episode of her 10 years as Prime Minister – even if the long-term results were not what she had really intended.[14]

Some of this would probably have happened anyway. But the price of doing it this way was high: GDP fell, in the four years from 1979, by 3.7 per cent. Unemployment rapidly rose to 2.5 million and peaked at 3.1 million in the summer of 1985. There was a deep fall in industrial investment. The capacity of the industrial base declined by 17 per cent. The mainstream economists had to ask: was this really capitalism's creative destruction? Social analysts pointed out that it also created an impetus towards a two-tier society, with a low-skilled base level, which was compounded by the introduction of VAT at 15 per cent, a sales tax bearing hardest on lower-income groups; leading only too visibly to riots in Toxteth and Southall which were not racial (perhaps not even Brixton was racial), but revolts of the dispossessed. There were, of course, real concessions, the most important of which was Lord Scarman's Inquiry into Brixton, and the sending of Michael Heseltine as Minister for Merseyside. These were not simply palliatives; they were a real response to what, it had become admitted, were intolerable consequences.

Summing up from today's standpoint (in 2007), the anti-inflation aim had become apparently irreversible. For 25 years since then we have lived in an anti-inflationary world. Employment has in fact been restored, but mainly at a skilled level. The same thing that happened in Britain happened in the Netherlands in 1982, in Ireland in 1987 and in Finland in 1990. The exceptions are those countries that are often called the Rhineland capitalist states: Germany, France and Italy. In this sense, what happened to the British economy during the 1980s made it definitively part of a globalising process, in a northern European, Anglo-Saxon mode, a judgement which is to distance it a long way from Mrs Thatcher herself.

In private, she was always restless, searching for the tangible example, preferably a human one, yet refreshing, often stimulating: how, why, when, the questions came. In public she was a driving force, who established a public language – often highly populist – to endorse her beliefs. She gave these

---

[14] Interviews, Sir Ian Gilmour, Sir Leo Pliatzky, Sir Alfred Sherman, mid-1980s.

certainty, allied to a certain flexibility, so long as the core was held. She was never impersonal, and assumed that argument was the way to find out; and this regime did begin to work after 1983. The unfortunate thing was that recovery came not primarily via organic growth on the supply side, but through the benefits of North Sea oil, and through accrual from a swelling consumer boom, not essentially a different result from Ronald Reagan's deficit budgeting; all this was followed in Britain by an import surge, a huge trade deficit and the decline of sterling virtually to one dollar; a truly mordant outcome.

Three other paradoxes follow. Privatisation had never been an oven-ready Conservative policy, and it had no real history before 1980.[15] Its immediate cause, in the mid-1980s, was the need for more revenue (as today in France) and a way to revitalise management of those near-bankrupt industries, riddled with trades unions' restrictive practices. But one has to point out that British Airways, British Steel and British Gas were all made profitable by determined new management *before* privatisation, while the question of natural monopolies, such as water, was barely posed. British railways, a prime candidate, were not modernised at all.

The second paradox was the management of sterling. There was no future for UK trade with the pound at one dollar and MLR at 14 per cent. Industry could not export in those circumstances; the climate was simply too severe. So Nigel Lawson, Chancellor from 1983 to 1989, searched for an exchange rate management instrument. Margaret Thatcher would not then even contemplate entering the ERM, and so Lawson tried for three years – she claimed without her knowledge – to shadow the Deutschmark. When the DM was actually the centre of the ERM and at 2.90 DM to sterling, this worked, though not later.

But it did not curb the boom, neither did it affect the trade deficit much, before the bubble burst; and manufacturing activity did not recover its 1973 level until 1988. That was little reward for Keith Joseph's very sensible, far-sighted supply-side deregulation plans and the patient work of the National Economic Development Council (NEDC), which both Lawson and Thatcher despised.

The third paradox was that, by the 1980s, her personal position had changed so that she was no longer quite at the centre. In Lawson's day as Chancellor, she became more distanced, preoccupied with external affairs, and she could only stop the final move into the ERM by recalling Alan Walters, to Lawson's dismay, and then in effect sacking the Chancellor himself.[16] Even so, she was finally compelled to concede ERM entry, under John Major as the new Chancellor, but at the wrong time, in the wrong way, and at the wrong exchange rate. By then,

---

[15] Minutes of the CBI, *passim*, discussion papers, 1974–1980, and NEDC Council Minutes 1981–1985. Interview with Lord Kearton, 1982.
[16] Interview, Nigel Lawson, 1988.

she was older, more isolated and less flexible. As Beowulf found, in the great saga, the last dragon always wins.

Finally, there is the dissociated conclusion: 'Thatcher defeated the trade unions,' which is what many people now most easily remember. Of course the unions were not a peripheral problem; after all, they had been central to policymaking in the 1970s. But they also experienced a much more general, European-wide decline in their membership and in their levels of action during the 1980s. From Margaret Thatcher's own point of view, although her aim became simply the defeat of trades unions, it was initially only to defeat wrongful use of union power. Against this, Len Murray, TUC General Secretary, tried to evolve a more modern unionism, which had little to do with the political left-wing in the car industry, or among steelworkers and miners, whose lasting defeat was aided by the folly and arrogance of several of the union leaders themselves.[17] There had never been a master plan, whatever retrospective wisdom suggested. But the unions' apparent defeat and real decline contributed to the new configuration of the state, freed, as Thatcher had always sought, from its corporatist entanglements. The 'post-war settlement era' of brokering the interests of the nation, under different triangular labels, ceased.

Margaret Thatcher was, in fact, opposed to all closed corporations, all monopolies, however highly qualified. Whether or not she understood it as part of the long political legacy of Scottish Enlightenment thinking, it was their political/economic status that was her target, not simply their wages claims. Use of the Public Sector Borrowing Requirement and cash limits imposed on government departments were weapons enough to pick off some elements, such as local government. Her government abolished both the Greater London Council and the metropolitan County Councils, and worked later to reduce the teachers' unions, the universities and the BBC, at least to some degree – but, significantly, not the lawyers and doctors, then or later; that was a little too difficult.

All these institutions became the 'Other', obstacles if not the enemy. But this sequence had another less welcome consequence. The use of financial instruments, as if they were political ones, by bringing the Treasury into the forefront, centralised state power in one department, even if the state's actual geographical scope was being diminished, to the detriment not only of the spending departments but of the state's other functions in society at large. Cash limits shrank not only the Department of Trade and Industry, but also the Departments of Employment, Education and Health. One of her ministers was heard to refer to what he called 'the former welfare state', perhaps in the belief that a new law had been discovered: the fewer functions the state has, the more power.

---

[17] Interview, Sir Len Murray, 1986 TUC General Council Minutes, *passim*.

And society at large? There is no need to quote her much misinterpreted 1987 phrase, that there is no such thing as society; that is a distraction, even if it were ever said. Margaret Thatcher certainly did think things through. She once replied to a question at a private gathering on the difference between public service and public spirit. A slightly suspicious look followed, but she gave what very few prime ministers would have done in the post-war period, an honest and careful answer: 'Public service leads to the overblown state; public spirit is the key to the good society.'[18]

This distinction was enhanced by her rancorous contrast with Heath, his strong state, his European vision, his one-nation post-war settlement, based on consensus. She was not consensus-minded. She was also, and always, a successful, largely self-made woman, in tune with the Puritan creed. That may have been old-fashioned, certainly unfashionable, but it did not imply an aversion to society in the modern sense; rather, a reliance on the 'just society', one of England's post-Reformation historical staples.

It was not exactly Michael Oakeshott's compassionate civil society, and, in that sense, she was not a precursor of the present leadership of the Tory Party, and certainly not of Tony Blair, even if he aspired to association with it. She was much tougher than either Oakeshott or Blair about the role and responsibility of individuals, and not afraid of the religious connotations, as her address to the General Assembly of the Church of Scotland demonstrated when she put a novel interpretation on the story of the Good Samaritan. She never denied that civil society has to be underpinned by the state – but only as one priority among a list of others, among which upholding the law, national defence, wise regulation, and determination of the national interest were at least of equal importance.

The result now seems pre-ordained: in 1980–1982 the pains of transition were assumed to be a sort of purgatory, a preliminary to the virtuous circle, while the unfortunate effects at the lower end of an increasingly two-tiered society (which New Labour was later to call social exclusion) – the decaying city centres, the pockets of rural poverty, the decline in options for the unskilled worker – were inevitable accompaniments of the cure. To demonise her personally, as if she had sought all this, is unreasonable; it is more accurate to talk about the unintended consequences of plans to recover Britain from a serious sustained emergency at the start of a decade in which she never really accepted that politics was limited to the art of the possible. It is sad that her genuine concern about the loss of anchorage in the family and the creation of social outsiders tends now to be ignored, and that her values of work, diligence and deferred gratification are remembered only as facets of the worship of mere accumulation. Not only sad, but unjust.

---

[18] Encounter with the author at a CPC AGM, 1986.

Less noticed at the time, but perhaps more serious in the end for what she once referred to at a Conservative Political Centre meeting as 'this new Thatcherite democracy', was the almost irreversible decline of a mixed twentieth-century polity's system of checks and balances, which had been developed and enhanced ever since the First World War crisis of 1916–1917 and re-employed successfully in World War II. The 1980s endangered not just the subtle balances between the roles of local government, Whitehall, and the industrial and financial institutions, but the whole range of voluntarism left over from the nineteenth century. Instead, there grew up a polarisation within political society, an entrenching of a highly centralised governing process, and the installation and evolution of a managing governing elite, increasingly cut off from what has become the mass public in the last 25 years, whose own cultural evolution, in turn, has not exactly exhibited nostalgia for her Puritan values.

The second test case, foreign affairs, or, better, 'Margaret Thatcher and the outside world', should be split in two, because, while all prime ministers end up here, not all focus on the same geography. It goes almost without saying that it was an English-speaking world where she was most at home, as was the case with Ronald Reagan, whom she thought of as her friend. Their fundamental accord on the evils of the overmighty state and of Communism, their coincidence at the turning point of the Cold War, underpinned their relationship. It may be easy, from a British point of view, to poke fun at Reagan, to see him as laid-back, congenial and rather superficial. This ignores his acute perception of American long-term interests, his understanding that to win two-thirds of the battle is success, to get three-quarters is exceptional, as well as his tolerance of her argumentativeness, and his generosity in letting Britain take more of the front-line role and credit than its weight probably justified.

She, in turn, understood from her early Oxford studies and memories of the Second World War not to choose decisively in defining Britain's interests between America and Europe, in that long pendulum swing whose oscillations have affected what Britain has done ever since the 1890s. So long as Western Europe was held together in the shadow of the superpowers, so long as the Cold War continued, the British commitment to the European Community came second in her estimation. But that no longer applied by the late 1980s. With the collapse of the Soviet Union and the fall of the Berlin Wall, Western Europe was emancipated from fear, and former Eastern Europe from its prison. That was a hard point for her to come to terms with, and the evidence suggests that she never wholly did.

So the first part of the story consists of standing up to the Soviet Union, hand in hand with Reagan's United States, and her realisation that, much as she might have understood and liked Gorbachev, the system that he represented, and finally chose to defend, had to be destroyed. It was less easy, because of American ambiguity, for Britain to stand up to the Argentine generals in the Falklands War, which, in Wellington's famous words, turned out to be 'a damned fine-run thing'. Both endeavours utterly absorbed her, brought out the best in her, and are the most easily defined attributes of her leadership.

Other instances may have been more nuanced: the Commonwealth was not her scene, and she did not share the Queen's views about it, but at least she did not follow her own right wing in backing Ian Smith in Rhodesia; neither did she sympathise with South Africa's apartheid leaders. Instead, she supported Robert Mugabe, who was a very different man then from the dictator he later became, and Samora Machel of Mozambique. Indeed, though it may not be generally known, it was she who decided that the SAS should be sent to train the Mozambican Army against that repellent Renamo force in the civil war inspired by Rhodesia's and South Africa's white governments.[19]

She did not have any sentimental illusions about British influence. She disliked and despised corrupt Third World leaders wherever they were, but in most cases it was not in Britain's interests to do anything about it, and she eschewed the easy applause that came from merely denouncing them. She believed influence depended on arms, which is why Trident was never in question; and that it depended on firm allies, which is why the United States was never in question. She was bold enough to criticise Reagan for the invasion of Grenada, even if, perhaps, the island lay in the American sphere, but she was uncritical when what she saw as basic principles were involved. Thus the Russian invasion of Afghanistan offered a chance to undermine the 'evil empire', which in turn meant support for the guerrillas, the Mujahedin, the Jihadists, and supply arms via Pakistan (not forgetting, of course, arms for Iraq in its struggle with Iran from as early as 1981). There, in close association with the United States, lie two long roots of our present discontents.

She really did believe that British experience had something to teach the world, and saw her faith vindicated, certainly, in Eastern Europe once the Wall came down, and perhaps in the years since. Certainly, this is a view still widely shared among the new adherents to the European Union. She knew that Britain was not a world power, but it was a power in the world. So it was agony for her at the last meeting at Camp David with the new President, George H.W. Bush, when he made it only too clear that German unification in 1990 was a primary interest of the United States and more important than Britain's own response to that epochal event. After such long affinity with Reagan, that was devastating.

All this leads, of course, to Europe. It is perhaps unfortunate that Thatcher's perceptions of Europe were obscured from the first by economic crisis in 1980–1982, by her subsequent concentration on the British EU budget

---

[19] Encounter with the author at CPC AGM, 1985.

payment contribution, and by what she categorised as the unpleasant and frequently corrupt generation of European leaders with whom she had to deal. Nevertheless, the waste of the British presidency in 1981 was largely her fault – a symptom of both a deep misunderstanding of European perspectives and a lack of necessary affinity with the leaders of other member states. On the other hand, she did fully understand, as these leaders also did, the vast threats to European industry and to its financial survival from American and Japanese industries and banks and their higher levels of global competitiveness; above all in electronics, electrical goods, cars, steel, chemicals, and of course financial practice. In that awareness lay the multiple sources of the Single Market.

Her problem was that there was no one like Ronald Reagan with whom to collaborate, no ideological partner. Instead, her outlook was prejudiced by a profound suspicion of European socialism, which was doubled, if anything, when François Mitterrand set off on his 'socialism in one country' project with widespread nationalisation in 1981. She had an equally deep suspicion of Christian Democracy in Italy, and perhaps also Germany. All this made the first two years a rebarbative period. There was a futile attempt at bilateral relations with both France and Germany, but such a strategy proved to be long out of date. After all, the Franco-German understanding was still the European engine house. Geoffrey Howe was signally defeated in May 1982, in the EU Council, trying as a lone foreign minister to amend the Common Agricultural Policy and reform the EU budget.

At that stage, there were only a few individual leaders in British industry, and perhaps the Bank of England, who were pushing for what became the Single Market. It took two years to get anywhere, and the drivers did not emanate from London. Even the limited preparations came mostly from outside Mrs Thatcher's ambit – the work of the Commission, the work of EU committees, of many trade associations and pressure groups – all striving to demonstrate the virtues of a single market as the evidence of superior American and Japanese competitiveness built up. Then, as the recession of the early 1980s lifted, accompanied by Mitterrand's massive policy reversal, with the help of Jacques Delors, to a more market-oriented France in 1983, the fundamentals came together.[20]

At the EU summit meeting in June 1984, three key preliminaries were achieved: first, after arguments which had tried everybody's patience almost beyond endurance, a unique settlement was reached to give a rebate on the British budget; second, France at last agreed, after seven years' utterly unjustified obstruction, to admit Spain and Portugal as members; and third, Jacques Delors became the EU President, with Arthur Cockfield in charge of the Single

---

[20] Interviews, Commission officials and Directors General, 1984–1988.

Market. Mrs Thatcher only effected the latter. She voted for Delors, whose qualities she admired at that point, but she absolutely insisted on Cockfield. Thus, by 1984 she was thoroughly engaged in the single market project. Of course, in the nature of such things, Mitterrand got the glory, the Germans paid, while Spain began its remarkable post-Franco recovery.

One other event complemented that astonishing year: in March 1985, Gorbachev came to power. These were also, one should add, the best years of the ERM as a Deutschmark zone.

Thatcher's approach, even to the Single Market, was far more complex than her memoirs suggest. The insistence on Cockfield, who had once been her adviser, and her opposition to the other side of the reform coin, 'Social Europe' as defined by Delors, demonstrate the Manichean nature of her political philosophy.

Put simply, she saw Britain's role as instituting financial discipline and good economic practice in the pursuit of freer trade, and in opposition to protectionism laced with socialism. So she played her part in realigning the Conservative Party in favour of the Single European Act, helped by the fact that the City institutions woke up to what was in it for them, once financial services (in which Britain excelled, as it still does in Europe) became part of the Single Market policy complex. She wanted, of course, much more: a market-led assault on every barrier to trade, leading to a smaller political role for the member states themselves. Cockfield wisely advised her to settle for a narrower definition, knowing better what might actually be possible.[21] Even so, the Single European Act had 285 enactments by the time it was finished. Cockfield significantly excluded tax harmonisation – that was too difficult – and did not even discuss in print European monetary union.

Realistically, Thatcher came to accept that there were trade-offs that had to be made to achieve the Single Market, including qualified majority voting in Council, and that the process of creating it should be by Intergovernmental Conferences rather than by bargaining in the Council of Ministers itself. But even these concessions led her into direct competition with other member state leaders, whom she tended to dislike or even despise personally: and this fostered a sense of being enmeshed. She began to see herself, especially at the Milan meeting, as being outmanoeuvred; not exactly trapped by the French and Germans, but subjected to a more restricted margin of maneouvre precisely by what she wished to achieve.

Cockfield's empirical strategy was built from the bottom upwards. There had been three immediate barriers to bring down: frontier barriers, fiscal barriers and technical barriers. What we are today familiar with as competition law was largely implicit, kept for the future. But Margaret Thatcher had grasped the

---

[21] Interviews, Lord Cockfield, 1987.

long-term implications, and the main economic activities it would reinforce. So she chose to ignore the other side of the coin, what Delors was doing – social cohesion and monetary union – as contingent matters. In the practical sense, she may have been right – these latter are the questions which we still argue about 20 years later.

Of course the Single Act needed much more than that. It required the subtle diplomacy of Luxembourg leading towards the first Intergovernmental Conference. It needed the linkage of the Single European Act with the principle of monetary union, which drew together Cockfield and Delors, and eventually led to her thinking that Cockfield had 'gone native'.[22] These led on to Maastricht. But the genius of the Single European Act was that it offered something for all 12 member states, and for that reason Britain conceded a great deal – qualified majority voting, the European Central Bank, detailed stages to European Monetary Union – which was irreversible, as Thatcher ought to have known, and no doubt did know, but did not wish to know.

Meanwhile the extent of German leadership was shown very clearly at the Hanover summit in June 1988, without which resolution the nascent Single Market probably could not have been held together. Cockfield's 285 enactments were finally completed on 1 January 1993, after her fall. Afterwards she claimed to have been misinformed. In fact, after the decisive moment at Hanover in 1988, she seems to have been in slow retreat, rather like Napoleon's campaign of 1814 – winning tactical battles but, in her own retrospective view, losing the war.[23]

However, for a brief three-year period, she had had the vision, without which the greatest single achievement of the European Union, as it became, might have been missed or botched. Her assent, if not necessarily her consent, ensured that the Commission would acquire its full and proper role, realigned with the Council of Ministers, that the European Parliament would develop; and that the new EU entrants, first of all the Nordic countries and Austria, and then the countries of Eastern Europe, would become full members. Even if in a slightly negative way, by acceptance of compromise to gain a greater good, she contributed something massively important.

The negative side was a characteristic shift into reverse gear, as innate prejudice came to the surface, of which the high mark was undoubtedly her speech at Bruges in September 1988, when she declared that there was 'no substitute for the nation state'. What she never seems to have realised was that the other European leaders represented their countries too. Helmut Kohl, François Mitterrand, even Giulio Andreotti, defended their own national interests and had their own vision of the nation state, albeit in a different way, conditioned

---

[22] Interview, Lord Cockfield, 1987.
[23] See her memoirs, *passim*.

by their own very different histories since World War II. Her stereotypes, deployed at Bruges, were just that, stereotypes – they did not fit the facts, as facts were seen from 11 different capital cities. They did not even fit the facts in London.

As a result, Thatcher left several damaging legacies to her Conservative successors. The first was a failure to use existing European institutions and instruments to give British policy weight within the Commission. Even by 1994, the UK had only 3 per cent of top appointments in Brussels, as opposed to 5 per cent held by both France and Germany, theirs also being more senior than the British. This imbalance levelled in the end, but she was not the one who pressed for it. And, as most British prime ministers have done since, she regarded Members of the European Parliament as a somewhat inferior species – which in post-1990 conditions was a waste of a useful asset.

The second, equally far-reaching legacy concerned German unification. Her idiosyncratic world view imagined that the post-war four-power containment of Germany, based on bilateral relations, NATO, and the Common Foreign and Security Policy, would govern the reunification of Germany. But for that to have any chance required the support of the Americans and the French. Mitterrand would not play, and in due course he took the credit for claiming that German unity was a 'natural function' of European union. Worse, the United States undermined her, it being in American higher interests that German unity came about as it did.

The third legacy contributed to her own downfall. The other heads of member states had a lot of revenge stoked up by 1989/90. There was no specific conspiracy to do her down, but by the time of the EU Madrid summit in 1989, when she was coerced by Howe and Lawson into accepting that Britain would enter the Exchange Rate mechanism, it had become obvious to outsiders that she no longer controlled her Cabinet in the way she had done for nearly 10 years. She had tried, as Howe said later in his resignation speech, to be her own Foreign Secretary, and yet she remained isolated; and this weakened her in European circles.

She never got on with Mitterrand, and barely tried after German unification. When Helmut Kohl made an attempt to conciliate, in December 1988, she rebuffed him. In her last 18 months, she acquired a dangerous obsession about a Christian Democrat–Socialist conspiracy aiming at Brussels domination – hence one pungent criticism of her Bruges speech: 'not a policy but a spasm'. By the Dublin summit of 1989, she was in a minority of one to 11, and she may well have been manipulated at the final October 1990 Intergovernmental Conference meeting in Rome, by Andreotti and others, into commitment to monetary union. But if it were so, it is also true to say that she had isolated herself even from her own colleagues. Certainly, after she had gone, as one Conservative journalist remarked, 'a mood of *soulagement* spread across the

EU'.[24] John Major won Britain's opt-out from monetary union at Maastricht at least partly because he was not Margaret Thatcher.

The last long-festering element she bequeathed was the war inside her own party, which can perhaps be traced back beyond Joseph Chamberlain in the 1900s, but which had been contained for nearly 100 years. Now, as the Single Act blended with monetary union and 'social Europe', a deep clash developed between the pragmatists, including Lawson, Howe and Hurd, who accepted a confederal ideal but not a federal one, and those for whom the EU was already a dangerously federal state whose pretentions threatened the UK itself. Civil war was breaking out even before she went, and Major's embattled years, and retreat from the ERM, made it worse. It is still endemic, having blighted the careers of the three Tory leaders who followed Major. It has emasculated the party itself.

Yet did she think that the EU was a close conspiracy or a single market of consenting nation states? Did she ever ask the question: was not European Union what the Germans call a *Staatenverbund*, an association of nation states each for their own and for the greater good? The EU's inherent diversity can be gauged from the different answers to such questions one gets across the whole European subcontinent. Did she also ever reflect that those she always called 'they' rather than 'we', by which she meant Wales and Scotland, that the Scots and the Welsh did better from EU regional aid between 1975 and 1987 than any other region in the whole of Europe, except parts of Italy's south?

There is no simple conclusion to Thatcher's career, and maybe it is not possible even to achieve a synthesis, as the great Dutch historian Pieter Geyl demonstrated in his classic *Napoleon – For and Against*. What 'Thatcherism' meant back in 1981 is now so diversely interpreted, so stereotyped that it resembles Geoffrey Howe's definition of the Stuttgart Declaration: 'It was like hanging baubles on a moving Christmas tree.'[25] The simplest definition of Thatcherism is that it was what she believed. We do not require political leaders to be original thinkers. She drew eclectically on many sources – historical, even religious, as well as the economists, Hayek and Friedman and their interpreter–descendants, not all of whom coincided at any one time. We do expect political leaders to declare and implement what they believe with conviction, if elected, which is what she did.

It is doubtful if any other British twentieth-century prime minister has left a legacy so open to fiercely divergent interpretations: Churchill perhaps, Lloyd George certainly, possibly Baldwin. This has nothing to do with judgement about 'greatness' (however that is defined), only with the ratings on a historical and political scale. Argument is far from being over, as the current claims

---

[24] Conversation, Alexander Macmillan, 1993.
[25] Conversation, Sir Geoffrey Howe, 2000.

to her inheritance made by contestants from both Conservative and Labour parties indicate. What is certain, however, is that neither of the extremes can be accepted: Thatcher as Prime Minister was never as utterly single-minded as she is sometimes drawn, a legend to which she contributed in her own autobiography, nor as clear or original in her policies as is often maintained. Nor is what she said in public always the best guide to her private thoughts. Those who knew her well were often taken aback by her unashamed capacity to detach herself and reverse direction without pity or acknowledgement.[26] Like all prime ministers, she was subject to, and sometimes prisoner of, the complex interaction of personalities, colleagues, party hierarchy, Civil Service, business and financial leaders in Britain, and American, European, Russian, or African leaders, in that order. Historical analysis of her and her impact in the 1980s will continue as long as biography remains a fashionable key to historical appraisal. Nevertheless, a few things should be said, even if not in conclusion.

First, she contributed to an enduring change of outlook about the modern industrial state, and the limits of what government can do, and what its priorities and resources should be, in a middle-ranking nation. In terms of policy, this meant that counter-inflation should be a strategic aim of government, with an orientation towards financial discipline, across the whole of economic life and organisation, not just the political domain. What Denis Healey began in 1976, she took up and substantiated, leading to a fundamental and enduring cost/benefit approach to the state and its duties.

In foreign policy, already in accord with the United States, she helped to capture change as the Soviet Union fell apart, and in Eastern Europe as rebuilding began. A visitor to the countries of Eastern Europe today will find much praise for Margaret Thatcher. For a brief but vital point in the evolution of the European Union, as we now know it, she influenced events, above all in creating the Single Market; but things have evolved since 1989 in ways of which she did not later approve.

She herself was an executor of great determination, rather than an originator in the sense that Keith Joseph was one. That ought to have united her governments, even if at the price of the resignations of colleagues. But her convictions overrode her judgements, especially in the later years: she was almost reckless at the end. She divided – she did not unite her party or her last government.

Finally, she was driven from within. Rather lonely, except with her family, she lived for her work, she was argumentative, she led from the front. She was adrift after 1990. She would have laughed at the comment about Ledru-Rollin, French Minister in one of the revolutions of the nineteenth century, found at the back of the crowd in the streets, and his reply to the question: 'What are you doing there?' 'Je suis leur chef, il faut que je les suive.' Not her, she knew

---

[26] Interview, Sir Ian Gilmour, 1990.

her mind. She had no need for focus groups to tell her what to think. She exposed differences. She inflamed debate. She outstayed her time. But then so did Roosevelt and Nehru. She was not like Jefferson, minded to retire to Monticello, her political work done. But, to adapt a line from Stephen Spender, 'she left the vivid air signed with her brightness.'

10
John Major, 1990–1997

Vernon Bogdanor

There is a drawing by Max Beerbohm of Stanley Baldwin, Prime Minister for much of the interwar period, which shows the young Stanley looking up at his mature counterpart and saying, 'What. Prime Minister. You!' Like Baldwin, John Major was the unexpected prime minister. Until a short time before entering no. 10, he was little rated by insiders, and, even though he was Chancellor of the Exchequer, and had been, albeit for just three months, Foreign Secretary, he was barely known to the general public.

When John Major became Prime Minister in November 1990, he had been in the Cabinet for just three and a half years. Of twentieth-century prime ministers, only MacDonald and Tony Blair had less experience of government. When he was appointed Foreign Secretary in July 1989, just 18 months before becoming Prime Minister, only 2 per cent of the public had heard of him. In mid-November 1990, just after the first ballot for the Conservative leadership, when Margaret Thatcher had failed by only four votes to be confirmed as Prime Minister, the question was asked: 'Who would you like to see as leader of the Conservative Party and prime minister?' John Major was at the bottom of the list of eligible contenders.[1]

Margaret Thatcher	22%
Michael Heseltine	37%
Douglas Hurd	11%
Sir Geoffrey Howe	12%
John Major	3%
Don't Know	14%

---

[1] The present writer remembers his great surprise, having asked a special adviser to a Conservative Cabinet minister who might win on the second ballot, on being told that John Major would be a strong contender.

166

Major, nevertheless, succeeded in gaining the confidence of the majority of Conservative MPs. He said that he wanted to create a classless society. This wrong-footed his wealthy and patrician opponents, Michael Heseltine and Douglas Hurd. Heseltine was photographed by the press outside his palatial mansion near Banbury, while Hurd, seeking to rebut the accusation that his patrician background rendered him unfit to govern modern Britain, pointed to the fact that his father had been a tenant farmer with just 450 acres. Hurd had attended Eton on a scholarship and had spent his school holidays planting potatoes to earn pocket money. He was now reduced to just 10 acres. These confessions did not succeed in winning public sympathy. In a party that was ceasing to be deferential, John Major's very lack of grandeur and pomposity was a winning asset. But he was elected Conservative leader as much for who he wasn't as for who he was. In 1992, similarly, he was unexpectedly to win the general election because he wasn't Neil Kinnock. In 1995, he won another Conservative leadership election because he wasn't John Redwood. He was lucky in his opponents.

When he became Prime Minister, John Major was, at 47, the youngest prime minister since Lord Rosebery in 1894. But his background was rather different from that of the wealthy Whig peer. Rosebery had been born in Berkeley Square, and had grown up amidst great houses – Dalmeny House and Barnbougle castle. He was educated at Eton and Christ Church, where he had kept a stock of racehorses while an undergraduate. Major, by contrast, had spent his early years in the back streets of south London, and he had no higher education at all. He was the son of a trapeze artist, who, upon retiring from the circus, set up a business making garden ornaments, a business which failed, forcing him to move from Worcester Park to a tenement flat in Brixton. Major had won a scholarship to a grammar school, but had left school at 16, his talents unacknowledged. His educational qualifications, if any, were obscure. Rejected for the post of bus conductor because he was too tall, he drifted for a while, before beginning a modest career in banking. But he found himself when he joined the Brixton Young Conservatives, and began to speak regularly from a soapbox in the market every Saturday. When he became Prime Minister, the feature that struck most observers about him was his sheer ordinariness. A Conservative whip, Tristan Garel-Jones, characterised him as 'the sort of person I would expect to see with his car parked by the pavement on a Sunday, washing the car, eating some Polo mints and listening to the cricket match on the radio'.[2]

The election of John Major to the leadership was a remarkable symbol of the adaptability of the Conservative Party. Between 1951 and 1965, its leaders had been drawn from the patrician tendency. Churchill was the grandson of

---

[2] Penny Junor (1993) *The Major Enigma*, Michael Joseph, p. 112.

a duke, Eden the son of a baronet, Macmillan the son-in-law of a duke and Home a 14th earl. But they were to be succeeded by Edward Heath, the son of a builder and a lady's maid, Margaret Thatcher, the daughter of a provincial grocer, and John Major. The pattern continued after him with William Hague, the son of a soft drinks manufacturer, and Michael Howard, the son of a Jewish shopkeeper and the grandson of an illegal immigrant from Eastern Europe. Only with the election of David Cameron in 2005 did the patrician tendency come to be restored.

When Major became Prime Minister, it did not seem that he would last long. The Conservative government was now in its third term. No government had been returned for a fourth successive term since 1827. The Conservatives seemed to be on a withdrawing tide. Following the defenestration of Margaret Thatcher, they were around 10 per cent behind in the opinion polls. Most Conservatives felt, together with a sense of relief, some guilt at the way that their heroine had been toppled. She remained an icon for Conservative activists. They regarded the MPs who had brought her down as traitors to the cause. Any successor to Margaret Thatcher would have an almost impossible task; he would have to restore confidence while still, somehow, remaining true to her legacy.

Set against this background, Major's achievement in winning the 1992 general election was striking. Few expected him to succeed. For the election was held in the depths of the longest economic recession since the war, and one which, unlike the depression of the 1930s, affected the professional and managerial classes in the south of England who formed the backbone of the Tory vote. The Conservative victory in 1992, therefore, was a victory achieved against the odds. Even a week before the election, opinion polls showed the party 6 per cent behind Labour. The day after the election, the cover of *The Economist* showed a picture of Major wiping his brow with the caption 'Phew.' He had won a narrow victory with an overall majority of just 21 seats, barely sufficient for a full parliament, given the likelihood of by-election losses. And so it proved to be. By early 1997, the overall majority had been lost, and Major had to rely for the last few months of his premiership on the Ulster Unionists for his parliamentary majority. Admittedly, the Churchill government had been able to survive fairly comfortably, from 1951 to 1955, on a majority of just 17. But the Churchill government was broadly united on the main issues facing it, and the habit of back-bench rebellion had not yet taken hold. John Major's government, by contrast, was riven down the middle on the issue of European integration, which came to a head with the ratification of the Maastricht treaty in 1992–1993. So the overall majority of 21 was in a sense misleading. In later years, Major was ruefully to lament that he had a majority of just 21, half of whom were mad.

Lucky perhaps to win the election, Major was most decidedly unlucky in the smallness of his majority, a product of the electoral system rather than his own lack of popularity. For his victory was far greater than was indicated by the small overall majority. He had, in fact, achieved the highest vote ever gained by a British political party – over 14 million votes – half a million more votes than Tony Blair gained in his landslide victory in 1997, and more votes than Margaret Thatcher had ever achieved. Moreover, the Conservatives were 7.5 per cent ahead of Labour in the popular vote. That was the largest victory gained by the Conservative Party in the post-war era, with the exception of Margaret Thatcher's two landslides in 1983 and 1987. It was a larger victory than had been secured by Churchill in 1951, Eden in 1955, Macmillan in 1959 or Heath in 1970. It was larger indeed than Blair was able to secure in 2005, when he was just 3 per cent ahead of the Conservatives. Blair, however, would enjoy a comfortable working majority of 67 seats. The Conservatives were the victims of the first past the post system, of which they were such strong supporters; and many of John Major's troubles stemmed from the fact that he had only barely gained a working majority. It proved to be a frustrating victory. For it gave the small number of extreme Euro-sceptic MPs disproportionate leverage. With the majority of 100 that Margaret Thatcher had secured in 1987, dissidents could be ignored. But, with a majority of 21, any 11 Euro-sceptics, by voting with the opposition, could bring down the government. Thus, for much of the 1992–1997 parliament, Major's government was in effect a minority government, and he was forced on occasion to rely on Liberal Democrat or even Ulster Unionist votes to secure passage of the treaty ratifying Maastricht. This makes his parliamentary achievement even more remarkable.

Even so, Major's election victory in 1992 had fundamental long-term consequences. For it meant that the new settlement put in place by Margaret Thatcher could not be overturned by Labour. The public service reforms would continue. The internal market in the National Health Service and grant-maintained schools, later to be resurrected by Labour as city academies, were now safe from repeal; the industries privatised under Margaret Thatcher would not be renationalised. Most important of all, the fourth consecutive election defeat convinced Labour that it would have to abandon nationalisation as a principle entirely, which Tony Blair duly did, in 1995, when he succeeded, where Hugh Gaitskell had failed, in getting Clause Four, committing Labour to the nationalisation of the means of production, distribution and exchange, removed from the Party's constitution. The general election of 1997 was to be the first since Labour became a national party in which nationalisation was not an issue. Indeed, under Blair, the issue became not which industries will Labour nationalise, but which industries will Labour privatise. Socialism seemed dead, even to its most fervent supporters, one of the great ideological casualties of the twentieth century. This might never have happened had Labour won the 1992 general election. John Major is, then, together with Tony Blair, one of the founding fathers of New Labour; and the fourth Conservative victory had its main impact less on the Conservatives than on Labour, ensuring that it abandoned the last vestiges of its traditional doctrines. 'Above all,' Major insists in his autobiography, 'our victory in 1992 killed socialism in Britain. It also, I must conclude, made the world safe for Tony Blair. Our win meant that between 1992 and 1997 Labour had to change.'[3]

Major was to remain Prime Minister until 1997, when he led the Conservatives to their worst defeat in modern times at the hands of Tony Blair's New Labour. His period in office is sometimes seen as a mere interregnum, a premiership sandwiched between the rule of two giants – Margaret Thatcher and Tony Blair. He himself is sometimes seen as insignificant. I once asked the late Enoch Powell what he thought of Major. His reply was 'Does he really exist?' This perception seems to me radically mistaken.

John Major's premiership appears short only when measured against the long periods in office of Margaret Thatcher and Blair. He was, in fact, prime minister for over seven years, a longer continuous period in office than anyone else in the twentieth century, apart only from Asquith, Margaret Thatcher and Blair. He had the longest consecutive period in office of any Conservative, except for Margaret Thatcher, since the tenure of Lord Liverpool between 1812 and 1827.

John Major's premiership inaugurated a new period of consensus in British politics, during which the old political battles seemed to have been fought through to exhaustion. His years as Prime Minister were years of consolidation as well as reform. The Conservatives abandoned the idea of permanent revolution which had seemed the quintessence of Thatcherism and became, once again, a party of cautious and piecemeal change, as they had been in Stanley Baldwin's time. For the main enemies – overmighty trade unions, a bloated public sector and free-spending local authorities – seemed to have been slain, and the task now was to consolidate the gains and to ensure that the competitive individualism that Margaret Thatcher had unleashed did not destroy the very roots of social cohesion and community without which a market economy could not function. John Major sought to humanise the Thatcherite agenda, to achieve Thatcherism with a human face, while Labour, after Tony Blair was elected to the leadership in 1994, explicitly repudiated socialism. The sound and fury of the political debate obscured the fact that, on the big social and economic issues, the parties were now moving together, not further apart. By the end of Major's premiership a new consensus had arisen on the role of the state and on the priority to be given to combating inflation.

John Major had three great achievements to his credit. He kept Britain in Europe, he prevented the break up of the Conservative Party, and he reformed the public services. Against that, there was one great failure, the failure to

---

[3] John Major (1999) *The Autobiography*, HarperCollins, p. 311.

prevent ethnic cleansing in Bosnia. Some might think this failure so great as to nullify his achievements, considerable though they were.

Europe was the issue which dogged John Major's government from beginning to end. It had been the issue which had precipitated Margaret Thatcher's defenestration when, in the House of Commons, she had seemed to be undermining the patient diplomacy of her Foreign Secretary, Sir Geoffrey Howe, by ruling out the single currency, launching a frontal assault on the Community's institutions and rejecting German reunification. 'I was keen to rebuild shattered fences,' Major tells us in his autobiography, 'to prevent Britain from being seen for ever as the odd man out to be excluded from the private consultations that so often foreshadowed new policy in Europe.'[4] He seemed in a good position to achieve this aim. For he was, in a sense, the first post-war prime minister, the first prime minister for whom the war was not a defining moment. In particular, he had none of Margaret Thatcher's suspicions of the Germans. He told the German Christian Democrats in a speech in Berlin, at the beginning of his premiership, that: 'My aim for Britain in the Community can be simply stated. I want us to be where we belong. At the very heart of Europe. Working with our partners in building our future.'[5] But Major had to steer between, on the one hand, the desire on the part of the continental leaders of the Community to prepare a new Treaty on European Union, and, on the other hand, resistance from most of his party to any move towards further integration, or 'federalism' as they called it. At the Dutch town of Maastricht, in 1991, a new treaty was signed. Major, after hard negotiation in which he played a difficult hand with great subtlety and skill, secured two important opt-outs for Britain. The first was an opt-out on joining the euro as part of Economic and Monetary Union. The British government, instead of being committed to monetary union, would leave it to Parliament to decide whether Britain should join. Later Major promised, followed by Blair, that Britain would not enter the Eurozone without a referendum. The second opt-out left it to Parliament to decide whether to adopt the social chapter of the European Union, requiring certain minimum standards of employment law. This opt-out was perhaps primarily symbolic, since most large companies already observed these standards. It was, however, of considerable symbolic importance to the Conservative Party, and Conservative MPs would never have accepted a treaty which required adherence to the social chapter. Without the opt-outs, Major could never have succeeded in persuading the Conservative Party to ratify the treaty; even with the opt-outs, it was to prove difficult enough. Many Conservatives, and they included Margaret Thatcher, saw the treaty as a betrayal. Their opposition was for the moment muted since Parliament was nearing the end of its term, but it

---

[4] Major, *Autobiography*, p. 265.
[5] Ibid., p. 269.

would flare into open revolt after the general election of April 1992. From that time, Margaret Thatcher became, almost avowedly, an enemy of Major and of his consolidating brand of Conservatism. She still had much support within the Party, a support based partly on guilt at the way in which she had been ousted, and partly on memories, made somewhat hazy by time, of the supposed golden age of her rule.

That Maastricht became, despite his tenacity in negotiation, a problem for Major was due, in part at least, to bad luck. At first it seemed as if ratification would not prove a problem. When Major returned from Maastricht, and made a statement on the outcome to the House of Commons, he was, so he tells us in his autobiography, 'received with acclaim and the waving of order papers. – It was the modern equivalent of a Roman triumph'.[6] Just seven Conservatives voted against the principle of ratification. Had Major proceeded immediately with the necessary legislation, he would have had few difficulties, since he still enjoyed the large majority that Margaret Thatcher had bequeathed him from her election victory in 1987. But he made the tactical mistake of delaying ratification until after the 1992 general election. Twenty-two Conservatives then voted against the Second Reading of the legislation giving effect to Maastricht. In June 1992, the Danes rejected Maastricht in a referendum. As a result, 100 Conservatives signed a motion calling for a fresh start. Then, in September, Britain was forced out of the Exchange Rate Mechanism (ERM) of the European Monetary System (EMS).

Britain had joined the ERM in October 1990, during the last days of Margaret Thatcher's regime. She herself had always been hostile to it, but had allowed herself to be persuaded, much against her instincts, by her Foreign Secretary, Douglas Hurd, and her Chancellor, John Major. The ERM involved in practice pegging the pound to the German mark, and, when Britain entered, the pound was valued at 2.95 Deutschmarks. The purpose of entry was, by linking the pound to the Deutschmark, to strengthen anti-inflationary discipline in Britain. But, unfortunately, the pressures of German reunification after 1990 were to destabilise a number of European currencies. The pound, so it was thought in the international financial markets, was overvalued, and in 1992 massive pressure built up against it. After trying desperately to resist this pressure, and despite raising interest rates to 15 per cent, John Major's government was forced to 'suspend' membership of the ERM on 'Black Wednesday' in September 1992 – soon to be dubbed 'White Wednesday' by the Euro-sceptics. Britain was never to rejoin. Suspension of the ERM meant, in effect, a devaluation of the pound, which, by February 1993, was worth just 2.30 Deutschmarks. This did not have the catastrophic consequences that had been predicted by many. Inflation, far from rising, fell to 2.5 per cent in

---

[6] Ibid., p. 288.

1994, and remained low throughout the 1990s, while the fall in the value of the pound did much to assist Britain's export trade. So, although withdrawal from the ERM was widely regarded as a humiliation, the economy improved. Whether this was a consequence of withdrawal is still a matter for heated debate amongst economists. What cannot be disputed is that 1992 marked the end of a long period of fluctuations in the rate of economic growth and output, the end of a period of high unemployment, and the end of a period of high inflation. Inflation has remained low – between 2 and 3.5 per cent – and stable since 1992. Euro-sceptics argued that these good things occurred precisely because we were out of the ERM. Their opponents suggested that the ERM had in fact squeezed inflation out of the system, and locked low inflation into the economy, thereby paving the way for a long period of economic stability. Inflation had been 9.5 per cent in 1990 when Britain joined, but had fallen to 4 per cent when Britain withdrew. Perhaps the argument was best summed up by Sir Alan Budd, Chief Economic Adviser to the Treasury from 1991 to 1997, when he said that 'The period of membership of the ERM was not a very worthy episode. A slightly cruel summary of it would be to say that we went into the ERM in despair and left in disgrace. Nevertheless, we are still enjoying the benefits of it.'[7]

But, whatever the economic effects of ERM membership, there can be no doubt that withdrawal was a political catastrophe for the Major government, ruining the reputation for good economic management that Conservative governments had, on the whole, enjoyed since 1951. It was largely for this reason that the Party remained in opposition for so long after 1997. It could recover only when Labour, in turn, was to lose its reputation for good economic management before the 2010 general election. In the aftermath of withdrawal, taxation had to be raised, and this prevented the Conservatives from tagging Labour in the 1997 general election, as they had done in 1992, as the party of high taxation. The Conservatives were now tagged as the party of devaluation. Labour, for the first time since the 1970s, were being seen by the voters as more competent in economic affairs than their main opponents.

The 1992 general election had, in fact, been a good election for Labour to lose. For Labour had been at least as committed as the Conservatives to the ERM. A Labour government would have been forced to devalue, just as the Conservatives were, and that would have confirmed the popular belief that Labour was the party of devaluation. It would have confirmed the reputation of Labour as the party which mismanaged the economy, a reputation that had been gained in 1931 and 1951, and confirmed during the Winter of Discontent of 1978–1979.

---

[7] Alan Budd (2005) *Black Wednesday: A Re-Examination of Britain's Experience in the Exchange Rate Mechanism*, Wincott Lecture 2004, Institute of Economic Affairs, p. 33.

For the Conservatives, withdrawal from the ERM proved traumatic, confirming many MPs in their view that they were right to be suspicious of the European Union and all its works. Dissident MPs found a powerful ally in Margaret Thatcher, who became even more hostile to Europe after her premiership than she had been while occupying No. 10. By 2002, indeed, in her book *Statecraft*, she was advocating outright withdrawal from the European Union. She now expended much of her political capital in undermining her successor. During the parliamentary debates on Maastricht, she told wavering back-benchers that they would be regarded as traitors to their country if they voted for the treaty. Public opinion turned sharply against the Conservatives. John Major's standing, which had been high during 1991 and early 1992, became the lowest of any prime minister since polls began. The Conservatives were never to recover their lead in the opinion polls. In retrospect, it is clear that, from September 1992, John Major's government was doomed.

To have succeeded in ratifying the Maastricht treaty in such an atmosphere of parliamentary dissent and electoral unpopularity was a remarkable achievement of parliamentary skill. It is by no means clear that Margaret Thatcher would have had the delicacy or finesse to manage so small a majority. Major's European policy, though strongly criticised by Margaret Thatcher, was in fact in line with traditional British policy towards Europe since the time of Harold Macmillan, who had argued that Britain was part of Europe, but that her special needs should be recognised by the other member states. Had Maastricht not been ratified, Britain might well have found herself outside the European Union. She would certainly not have been at 'the heart of Europe'. The fact that Britain remains a member of the European Union, with the freedom of choice to decide whether or not to enter the Eurozone, is, for better or worse, due to John Major.

The ratification of Maastricht by no means ended Major's troubles over Europe. For he then had to face the question of whether Britain should remain open to entering the Eurozone, as pro-European ministers, such as Michael Heseltine and Kenneth Clarke, were urging; or whether, by contrast, he should promise that Britain should never, under any circumstances, join, as the Euro-sceptics, such as Michael Portillo and John Redwood, were urging. Once again, Major finessed the issue, refusing to give any binding commitments, but committing the Conservatives in 1996 to a referendum before Britain entered, a commitment rapidly copied by New Labour. This was an unheroic stance, giving rise to Tony Blair's jibe 'I lead my party; he follows his,'[8] but it did succeed in avoiding the sort of split that had occurred over the Corn Laws in 1846 and tariff reform after 1903.

Major was continually urged to emulate Margaret Thatcher by coming off the fence and taking a strong line on Europe – aligning himself with one side

---

[8] House of Commons Debates, 6th series, vol. 258, cols. 655–6, 25 April 1995.

or the other and risking ministerial resignations. But to take such a course would have split the Conservative Party from top to bottom, as Peel had done during the crisis over repeal of the Corn Laws in 1846. It has been said that the most powerful person in the modern Conservative Party is the ghost of Sir Robert Peel. For one consequence of the split in 1846 was that there would not be another Conservative majority government for 28 years.

In 1963, on his sickbed, having announced his resignation as prime minister, Harold Macmillan told Selwyn Lloyd that the most important quality his successor needed was the ability to hold the Conservative Party together. 'Balfour,' he said, 'had been bitterly criticised for not having a view on Protection and Free Trade. Balfour had said the important thing was to preserve the unity of the Conservative Party. He had been abused for that. But who argues now about protection and free trade? When was the last time the conventional arguments were exchanged? 1923? Whereas the preservation of great national institutions had been the right policy. Lloyd George might have been clear-cut on policy, but he destroyed the Liberal Party.'

In his autobiography, John Major declares that 'The day may come when a similar judgment is made on the single currency.'[9]

In 1960, Labour leader, Hugh Gaitskell, had adopted the slogan 'Fight, fight and fight again' against the nuclear disarmers in his party. John Major in effect adopted a less heroic slogan, 'Fudge, fudge and fudge again,' in order to hold his party together. But he secured the outcome that he wanted, ratification of the Maastricht Treaty, with his government remaining in office, albeit gravely wounded, for its full five-year term, an achievement that looks easier in hindsight than it did at the time. If the Conservative Party lived to fight another day, that, in large part, was due to the parliamentary and political skills of John Major.

Major's first achievement, then, was ratification of Maastricht. His second was to ensure that the Conservative Party was not destroyed by the process. His third lay in the field of public service reform.

His achievement in this area stemmed from his own life experience. 'My own life history,' he declares in his autobiography, 'was different from that of most of my predecessors at Number 10. When I was young my family had depended on public services. I have never forgotten – and never will – what the National Health Service meant to my parents or the security it gave despite all the harsh blows that life dealt them. Nor have I forgotten the care I received at a critical time after my accident in Nigeria. These personal experiences left me with little tolerance for the lofty ideas of well-cosseted politicians, the metropolitan media or Whitehall bureaucrats who made little use of the public services in their lives and had no concept of their importance to others. They

---

[9] Major, *Autobiography*, pp. xxi–xxii.

may have looked down on the public sector and despised it as second rate but many of them knew nothing of the people who worked there or the manifold problems they faced.'[10]

In a lecture delivered to the Audit Commission in 1989, before becoming Prime Minister, Major 'warned against denigration of the valuable inheritance of the public sector'.[11] One cannot imagine Margaret Thatcher using such words. She tended to give the impression that the public services were inherently second-class, and that most people should aspire to opt out of them, by sending their children to private schools, and using private doctors in preference to the National Health Service. If consumers wanted efficiency, they could find it only in the private sector. Independent and self-reliant citizens should be encouraged to provide for their own health care and the education of their children, rather than have these services provided by the state. The public services seemed almost residual, to be used only by those who could not afford the more attractive, private options. Major, on the other hand, believed that the high standards that people took for granted in the private sector should also be present in the public sector. The Left, he was accustomed to say, should be grateful to him, since he sought to show that the public services could be efficient and effective, that they need not be second-rate.

The central theme of John Major's defence of the public services can be summed up in the phrase 'the privatisation of choice'. Old Labour's defence of the public services often tended to mean the defence of the rights of those who worked in them, the providers. Major, on the other hand, sought to defend the rights of those who used the public services, the consumers. By contrast with Labour, Major proposed not the extension of state intervention, but the extension of choice, a choice hitherto available only to the better-off. The extension of choice in the public services was to prove also a central theme of Tony Blair's New Labour government.

The Citizen's Charter was the symbol of Major's approach to the public services. It sought to apply to the public services the kinds of standards that consumers had long expected in the private sector. The public sector was required to publish explicit performance targets, and to tell consumers how successful they had been in meeting them. They had to establish proper complaints procedures and provide redress where their services fell below standard. Independent agencies were to be set up to monitor performance. The Charter proved to be the precursor of 42 national charters in areas such as health and education, and around 10,000 local charters applying the principles of the national charter to varying local conditions. The charters were widely derided when they first appeared by cynics 'on both the right and the left', as Major writes

---

[10] Ibid., pp. 246–7.
[11] Ibid., p. 248.

in his autobiography. These cynics claimed 'from the comfort of privilege and the cushion of an expense account that these were trivial issues or somehow evidence that I had a chip on my shoulder'.[12] It was assumed, even by those sympathetic to the aims of the charters, that they would be ineffective because they did not offer more money for the public services. In fact, however, they did lead to real improvements, and they have been copied in many other democracies. The improvements were unspectacular, and were in no sense exciting. But they were a concrete achievement, and the idea behind the charters will survive when many more glamorous initiatives have been forgotten.

During the time of John Major's government, hospital waiting lists were radically reduced. In 1990, over 200,000 patients had to wait for over 12 months for an operation. By 1997 the figure had been reduced to 15,000. League tables for the performance of health authorities were introduced. The Major government introduced testing in all state schools and, from 1992, tables of overall performance were published. Grant-maintained schools, later to be re-established by Labour and renamed 'city academies', were established. In both health and education, it was possible for those using the service to discover details of the performance of the service in their area, a vital step in making services accountable to users.

All the reforms were criticised by Labour in opposition. Nearly all of them were to be adopted by New Labour in office. New Labour had no alternative but to accept their fundamental principles. Major had insisted that the one size fits all model of the comprehensive school was no longer adequate. New Labour agreed. Major had insisted that the market disciplines of the public sector had to be adapted to the National Health Service. New Labour agreed. Indeed, much of the meaning of New Labour lay in acceptance of the public service reforms introduced by John Major. New Labour's public service reforms and privatisation proposals were no doubt new for Labour, but, in another sense, they were not new at all, for they had been pioneered by the Conservatives. John Major is, with Tony Blair, the father of New Labour.

John Major's successes in ratifying Maastricht and in public service reform did nothing to endear him to the Conservative Right, who continued an endless process of guerrilla warfare against him. In what seemed a desperate attempt to smoke out the dissidents, Major resigned the Conservative leadership in 1995 and challenged his critics to stand against him. John Redwood, the Euro-sceptic Welsh Secretary, took up the challenge, gaining 89 votes against Major's 219. A further eight Conservatives abstained, while 12 spoiled their ballot papers. Thus 109 Conservatives, nearly one-third of the parliamentary party, and around one-half of Conservative back-benchers had failed to support the Prime Minister. Major had won, as he said in his memoirs, 'less than

---

[12] Ibid., p. 247.

I had hoped for, but more than I had feared'. Had he won just three fewer votes, he would, he says, have resigned as Prime Minister.[13] Far from reuniting the party, the leadership election served only to show how divided it remained.

Sleaze added to Major's problems. From September 1992, when David Mellor, the National Heritage Secretary, resigned, having unwisely accepted hospitality from a leading supporter of the Palestine Liberation Organisation (only two months before, he had survived allegations in the tabloid press of an affair with actress Antonia de Sancha), there seemed an endless series of scandals, either personal or political, engulfing ministers. In October 1993, at the Conservative party conference, Major insisted that it was 'time to return to core values, time to get back to basics'. He denied that he was referring to sexual morality, but that is how his remarks were interpreted. The slogan 'back to basics' gave *carte blanche* to investigative journalists, who could now claim that their prying into the sexual misdemeanours of Conservative ministers and MPs was their contribution to the debate inaugurated by the Prime Minister. In December 1993, a junior minister resigned, having confessed to fathering a child out of wedlock. In January 1994, another junior minister resigned after his wife committed suicide following revelations of his affair, while a Conservative MP admitted to sharing a bed in a hotel with another man. Further misdemeanours, both heterosexual and homosexual, were to come to light as the parliament progressed.

Sleaze, however, was not confined to matters of personal morality. Much more serious issues seemed at stake. In 1992, it was alleged that ministers had broken government guidelines by encouraging a Midlands machine tool firm, Matrix Churchill, to sell defence-related materials to Iraq; and that ministers had been willing to allow the directors of the company to be sent to prison, even though the firm was acting in accordance with government policy. In November 1992, the government set up an inquiry under a High Court judge, Sir Richard Scott, to investigate these allegations.

Then, in 1994, it was revealed that two MPs had accepted money in exchange for asking Questions in the House of Commons, and that two junior ministers had, when they had been back-benchers, accepted money in exchange for tabling Questions on behalf of Mohammed al-Fayed, owner of Harrods. Further wild and unsubstantiated allegations were made against various MPs. 'We have now reached a stage,' declared Edward Heath, former Prime Minister but now Father of the House, 'when every man and woman in this House is an object of suspicion.'[14] Major's response was to set up a standing committee under another judge, Lord Nolan, to monitor standards in public life.

---

[13] Ibid., p. 645.
[14] House of Commons Debates, 6th series, vol. 260, col. 506, 18 May 1995.

Neither the Scott Report, published in 1996, nor the various reports of the Nolan Committee confirmed any of the sensational allegations that had been made against ministers or MPs. Scott found that Britain had been one of the few countries to have maintained an arms embargo against Iraq, and that there had been no question of ministers conspiring to send innocent men to prison. Nolan proposed new codes of conduct for MPs and civil servants, but concluded that most politicians and officials were people of integrity, and that standards in public life were high. The new codes, however, began the process of translating hitherto unspoken and unwritten 'understandings' into explicit rules. They struck a powerful blow against the idea of club government, the assumption, natural perhaps when political leadership was confined to a narrow elite drawn largely from the landowning and professional classes, that gentlemen could be trusted to ensure that proper standards were maintained. From this point of view, John Major's premiership is one of considerable constitutional importance. For, under Major, as the constitutional historian Peter Hennessy has argued, 'the British Constitution began to move from the back of an envelope to the back of a code'.[15] This was a prelude to the much wider constitutional reforms of the Blair years.

The nuances of the Scott and Nolan reports did not, in the minds of the public, serve to exonerate John Major's government. The popular impression remained that the government had illicitly encouraged the sale of arms to Iraq, that the Conservative party was awash with sleaze, and that John Major was too feeble to do anything about it. These impressions were given powerful impetus as a result of the attacks made on the government by the new and more confident Labour leadership of Tony Blair and Robin Cook, the latter, in particular, proving a master at parliamentary invective. They did much to convince the public that Major was no longer in charge of events, and the government was never able entirely to eradicate the association with sleaze. It all seemed to point to the need for change, for a fresh start.

John Major's parliamentary skills, his concern for the unity of his Party, his very ordinariness and decency, link him with that other unexpected prime minister, Stanley Baldwin. Like Baldwin, he found himself ill at ease in foreign policy. In his autobiography, he says, 'Of all the jobs in government, the Foreign Office was... the one for which I was least prepared',[16] and he saw himself as a novice in this area. He relied heavily on his Foreign Secretaries, Douglas Hurd, the Foreign Secretary he inherited from Margaret Thatcher, who remained at the Foreign Office until 1995, and Malcolm Rifkind, Foreign Secretary from 1995 to 1997.

---

[15] Peter Hennessy (1995) *The Hidden Wiring: Unearthing the British Constitution,* Gollancz, p. 207.

[16] Major, *Autobiography,* p. 111.

When Major became prime minister in 1990, the Cold War had come to an end with the collapse of the Soviet Union. The American president, George H.W. Bush, proclaimed the coming of a new world order. But Douglas Hurd seems to have held to the view that nothing fundamental had changed. 'We do not have a new world order,' Hurd declared in April 1994. 'We have a traditional set of world disorders and we are trying, case by case and institution by institution, to equip ourselves to deal more adequately with these disorders.'[17] The corollary of this view was that the traditional basis of Conservative foreign policy could remain unchanged even in radically changed diplomatic circumstances. Britain should act, therefore, only where her national interests were involved. She could not be expected to act as an international policeman in Bosnia, where ethnic cleansing against the indigenous Muslim population was being committed by the Serbs in order to create a greater Serbia on the ruins of the former Yugoslavia. The Major government faced what Malcolm Rifkind was later to acknowledge as the worst crime in Europe since the Holocaust. Its response was to impose an arms embargo, which prevented Bosnia from exercising her inherent right of self-defence against massacre and rape. This had echoes of the policy of non-intervention adopted by the Baldwin and Chamberlain governments in the 1930s towards the civil war in Spain, a policy which denied arms to the legitimate government of Spain in the civil war raging there. The hope in the Balkans was that the arms embargo, by denying arms to the Muslims, would end the war rapidly. It was the classic motif of appeasement. If pressure is put on the weaker side, the fighting will quickly end. Indeed, war can always be avoided if the weaker side gives way to the aggressor. Both President George H.W. Bush, towards the end of his administration, and President Clinton sought to intervene on the side of Bosnia. Douglas Hurd ensured that they did not, so causing the greatest rift between Britain and the United States since Suez. Tadeusz Mazowiecki, the first democratically elected prime minister of Poland and the United Nations rapporteur on human rights, said that 'Any time there was a likelihood of effective action, a particular western statesman [Hurd] intervened to prevent it.'[18] Lifting the arms embargo, Hurd declared in April 1993, would serve merely to create a 'level killing field'. But, as Margaret Thatcher pointed out, there already was 'a killing field the like of which I thought we would never see in Europe again... It is in Europe's sphere of influence. It should be in Europe's sphere of conscience'.[19] One hundred and twenty-five thousand corpses, mainly, though not exclusively, Muslim, were later to be found in open graves in Bosnia, the victims of

---

[17] House of Commons Debates, 6th series, vol. 242, col. 26, 25 April 1994.
[18] Brendan Simms (2001) *Unfinest Hour: Britain and the Destruction of Bosnia*, Allen Lane, p. 5.
[19] Ibid., p. 50.

Serb ethnic cleansing. 'Who said Britain no longer has influence?' asked the liberal commentator, Hugo Young. 'Britain, in all her ancestral wisdom, was more influential than any other country, in guaranteeing the washing of the hands.'[20]

The Major government believed that the essence of the Balkan problem was not ethnic cleansing but a civil war based on ancient hatreds. There was, on this view, little to choose between the two sides, and Britain was wise, therefore, not to get involved. Douglas Hurd championed the doctrine of Tory realism in foreign policy. Conservatives were in politics to make things work, undistracted by fanciful ideas or utopian sentiments. 'By the test of the narrow national interest,' Hurd says in his book, *In Search of Peace*, 'Bosnia could not rate high for the British ... The instinct of the realist was to stay out.'[21] The United Nations began by sharing this view. But, by 1999, the United Nations Secretary-General, Kofi Annan, accepted that it had been mistaken. In November of that year, he issued a report on the Bosnian crisis in which he apologised on behalf of the international community for the policy of 'amoral equivalency' in the Balkans, which had equated victims and aggressors.[22] Unlike Kofi Annan, Hurd never apologised, offering the feeble and inaccurate excuse that there was no popular movement against the arms embargo. Yet, in April 1993, over two-thirds, in a MORI poll, supported the dispatch of British troops, while, in February 1994, over half wanted air strikes against the Bosnian Serbs.

'More than any country,' Hurd minuted to his Prime Minister during the Bosnian crisis, 'at some cost to our reputation, we have been the realists in this.'[23] The trouble was that the old geopolitical doctrine of Tory realism had as little to offer in the world of Slobodan Milosevic and ethnic cleansing as it had done in the appeasement years of the 1930s. It put Britain in the position of the man, in the parable of the Good Samaritan, who, in the face of suffering, walked on the other side.

John Major sought to create a Britain at ease with itself after the radical upheavals of the Thatcher years. His greatest success was in reducing both inflation and unemployment. When he became Prime Minister in 1990, inflation was approaching double figures and interest rates were around 14 per cent. Britain was also in the first phase of recession, with unemployment rising by 50,000 a month and house prices falling. Economic growth was a miserable 0.5 per cent per annum. By the time Major left office, interest rates were at 6 per cent and unemployment had fallen by 150,000. Inflation was negligible and the rate of economic growth was 3.5 per cent per annum. 'The Conservatives

---

[20] Ibid., p. 90.
[21] Douglas Hurd (1997) *In Search of Peace*, Little Brown, p. 97.
[22] Simms, *Unfinest Hour*, p. 1.
[23] Douglas Hurd (2003) *Memoirs*, Little Brown, p. 467.

could legitimately claim,' according to the Nuffield study of the 1997 general election, 'that Britain was setting an example to Europe and the world as a model of prudent and sustained economic growth.'[24] For the first time, perhaps, since the 1950s, a government could face the voters with an economic success story to tell. It is a paradox that Major was able to win a general election in the midst of a recession, only to lose one during a period of economic expansion, handing over to Tony Blair a strong economy, the basis for much of New Labour's success.

The outcome of the general election of 1997 seems at first sight, like the general elections of 1906, 1945 and 1979, to have presaged a radical upsurge. In fact, the election of New Labour served, except in the area of constitutional reform, to consolidate reforms that had already been achieved, rather than to yield a change of direction. There was less change, with the important exception of the constitution, than in any other post-war change of government since 1951. The 1997 general election confirmed the status quo. It did not repudiate it. 'The Conservatives,' Douglas Hurd insisted, 'lost the 1997 election, having won the fundamental arguments.'[25] The task for Churchill in 1951 had been to accommodate his party to the Attlee settlement. The task of Blair was to accommodate New Labour to the Thatcher/Major settlement. The real divide in British politics was less between the Conservatives and New Labour than between the Conservative Right, led by Michael Portillo and John Redwood, and their opponents. The real challenge to John Major was offered not by Tony Blair but by the Tory Right, which offered a policy of radical nationalism, based on Euro-scepticism, which meant repudiating Maastricht and perhaps putting Britain entirely outside the European Union; radical experiments in the public services such as, perhaps, vouchers in education and health insurance in place of the National Health Service, further privatisation of the public services, and drastic cuts in taxation and in public expenditure. The Right wanted a continuation of the permanent revolution of Thatcherism. Had John Redwood defeated Major in the Conservative leadership election in 1995, the country would have seen much more radical change than it was to see in 1997. But the Conservative Right never won the chance to put its radical agenda into action, largely, perhaps, because most Conservative MPs realised that it would never win acceptance in the country. By the 1990s, the British people seemed to have lost any appetite they might once have had for an ideological crusade.

There is, in the last resort, a paradox in the premiership of John Major. He had sought, like Stanley Baldwin, to achieve appeasement, in the best sense of that much maligned term. He sought to create a Britain more at ease with itself,

---

[24] David Butler and Dennis Kavanagh (1997) *The British General Election of 1997*, Macmillan, p. 3.

[25] Douglas Hurd, 'His Major Achievements', *The Daily Telegraph*, 30 June 1997.

a Britain in which people liked each other more. He wanted to tone down the acerbity of party warfare, to create a gentler society in which class and social divisions were less acute. In Europe, he sought conciliation, a more constructive engagement than had been possible in the last years of Margaret Thatcher's rule. In Bosnia, he sought to persuade warring tribes, whose motives he did not understand, to come to terms with each other.

Yet Major, who, like Stanley Baldwin, sought nothing more than to conciliate everyone, ended by conciliating no one. He found himself massively repudiated by the British people when, in 1997, Labour won its largest majority ever, while the Conservatives secured fewer seats than at any general election since 1906 and a smaller percentage of the vote than at any time since the Great Reform Act of 1832. He came to be rejected by Europhiles and Euro-sceptics alike, condemned on the Continent as insufficiently *communautaire*, and widely condemned for appeasement in Bosnia. Baldwin, too, had been repudiated by the British people once the fruits of appeasement had become apparent. His easy-going approach to foreign affairs seemed to have left his country in mortal danger in 1940. Indeed, he was advised, in that year, not to leave his Worcestershire home for London. 'They hate me so.'[26] Yet Baldwin's reputation has recovered, as historians have been able, with the benefit of hindsight, to appreciate that perhaps there was more to be said for his foreign policy in the 1930s than once seemed to be the case. The same will surely happen to John Major, except with regard to Bosnia, a terrible blemish on an otherwise fine record. Like Baldwin, John Major was not a prime minister for troubled times. Fortunately, Milosevic was not as serious a threat to the peace of Europe as Hitler had been. But if Britain today remains a tolerant, easy-going society, capable of absorbing major social and economic change without damage to her institutions, the credit lies, in large part, with John Major.

---

[26] G.M. Young (1952) *Stanley Baldwin*, Hart-Davis, p. 250.

11
Tony Blair, 1997–2007

Anthony Giddens

On 4 May 1997, together with a small group of friends I hosted a street party to celebrate the Labour victory in the election. Gordon Brown and many other prospective members of the new government were there. Tony Blair didn't come, pleading exhaustion after the tension of the preceding few days. It wasn't like the flag-waving episode that was to happen later when the Blairs moved into No. 10. The mode was one of quiet satisfaction, at a job well done; most were already starting to think about the problems that would have to be confronted over the next weeks and months.

Tony Blair was to remain Prime Minister for 10 years, easily the longest period served by any Labour prime minister in the history of the party. It was a time when left of centre parties or coalitions were in government, or about to become so, in a range of European Union countries – together with Bill Clinton in the United States. Blair outlasted all of them – not only Clinton, who came to power before Blair, and could in any case only serve a maximum of two terms – but also Lionel Jospin in France, Gerhard Schroeder in Germany and Romano Prodi in Italy. No other left of centre government on the Continent, was in power for three terms. Jospin left few lasting achievements behind him; Schroeder failed to follow through his programme of reform until much too late; he too bequeathed rather few achievements; in Italy, Prodi's Olive Tree coalition engineered Italy's entry to the euro, but did not achieve the structural reforms that Italy so badly needed; and even the Scandinavian social democrats fell upon hard times.

Tony Blair and New Labour

Tony Blair is irrevocably associated with New Labour – sometimes seen as a series of empty formulae, an invention of the spin doctors. In my view such a perception is quite wrong. New Labour won power and held it for three terms precisely because it was based upon an informed analysis of the state of the

184

world and derived a concrete policy programme from it. Three sets of changes were involved.

The first was the impact of globalisation. I believe that I was one of the first to make extensive use of the concept, in the early 1980s. Even some 15 years later, when the notion had become established in the academic literature, it was very difficult to get politicians to take the idea seriously, as I can attest from personal experience of trying. Blair was one who did, and who also came quickly to see the complex nature of the phenomenon. Globalisation means increasing world economic interdependence, but stretches well beyond this, having profound social, cultural and geopolitical consequences. On an economic level it meant that traditional Labour – old Labour – could no longer be effective. Old Labour was based on Keynesian demand management and control of the national economy. Even revisionist thinkers such as Anthony Crosland, in his classic text *The Future of Socialism*, published in 1956, had assumed that 'social democrats could pursue policies of their choice largely untrammeled by foreign opinion'. Perhaps this made sense in the 1950s when the British economy was sheltered by tariffs and exchange controls. It made little sense in the 1990s, by which time 'it had become clear that social democracy in one country was no longer a feasible option'.[1] There cannot, as François Mitterrand found out in 1982, be Keynesian demand management in a globalised economy. As Tony Blair pointed out in his Mais lecture in 1995:

> We must recognise that the UK is situated in the middle of a global market for capital, a market which is less subject to regulation today than for several decades. An expansionary fiscal or monetary policy that is at odds with other economies in Europe will not be sustained for very long. To that extent the room for manouevre of any government in Britain is already heavily circumscribed.[2]

Globalisation meant that Labour would need new strategies if it were to pursue left of centre policies in an effective way.

The second major transformation which New Labour had to confront was the move to a knowledge-based service economy. Thirty years ago, the British economy was still dominated by manufacturing, blue-collar labour and agriculture. Over 40 per cent of the population worked in manufacturing or in agriculture. Today, in Britain, only around 14 per cent do. This means that the class – the working class – which most socialists, including Karl Marx, thought would transform

---

[1] Vernon Bogdanor (2007) 'Social Democracy', in Anthony Seldon, ed., *Blair's Britain 1997–2007*, Cambridge University Press, pp. 172–3.
[2] Cited in Edmund Dell (2000) *A Strange Eventful History: Democratic Socialism in Britain*, HarperCollins, p. 568.

the world has been shrinking away. The working-class communities that were once so important no longer play such a crucial role in modern societies. Over 80 per cent of the population now has to earn its living through knowledge-based occupations – creative, technical or service occupations. A service economy is quite different in some ways from the traditional manufacturing economy. Blair appreciated this point at a very early stage, and understood that, in a knowledge economy, educational policy would come to be of crucial importance. If a country does not invest heavily in education, including higher education, it will fall behind in the global knowledge-based economy, particularly when countries such as China and India have been making huge investments, so threatening to overtake the countries of the West. Of course, the improvement of educational standards has many other potentially positive implications too, including fostering a responsible and creative citizenry, promoting a cosmopolitan and tolerant cultural outlook and helping to reduce inequalities.

The third factor was the rise of new forms of individualism – which should not be indentified simply with consumerism, a narrower notion. The new individualism concerns the retreat of tradition, custom and fixed habit from people's lives, producing greater freedom for most people in core areas of their daily activity. One example among many concerns pre-existing gender roles. Today, most women can escape the 'fate' of domesticity. Indeed, there are now slightly more women than men in the labour force in Britain. Growing individualism brings in its train a decline of deference, of tradition, together with an evaporating of traditional attitudes of respect for authority. This is a major transformation in our society, and any political party which seeks to be successful has to come to terms with it.

Tony Blair's political philosophy, the Third Way, refers to policies developed to respond to these far-reaching transformations. The post-war settlement, strongly supported by the Left, had been based on Keynesian demand management, a traditionalist, top-down welfare state and a relatively fixed division of labour between men and women. Policies based on this settlement, Blair argued forcefully, no longer worked. James Callaghan, the last Labour Prime Minister before Blair, had spoken at the Labour Party Conference in 1976 of:

> The cosy world we were told would go on for ever, where full employment would be guaranteed by a stroke of the Chancellor's pen ... We used to think that you could just spend your way out of a recession ... I tell you in all candour that that option no longer exists, and that in so far as it ever did exist, it only worked ... by injecting a bigger dose of inflation into the economy, followed by a higher level of unemployment ... That is the history of the last twenty years.[3]

---

[3] Cited in Kenneth O. Morgan (1997) *Callaghan: A Life*, Oxford University Press, p. 535.

But, until Blair, the Left was unable to produce an alternative to the traditional view. Margaret Thatcher certainly appreciated that the post-war economic settlement was breaking down, and her government sought to replace it with a free-market philosophy, emphasising the primacy of competitive rather than cooperative relationships. But that had, at best, mixed consequences. It produced a society with deficient public services and steeply rising levels of inequality. Therefore, Blair reasoned, the Left had to seek a third alternative. The Third Way was intended to be a new programme for the Centre Left, serving to distinguish it both from the old Left and from the Thatcherite New Right.

In my view, nothing much hangs on the actual term 'Third Way', which can easily be dispensed with. We are talking about Social Democratic revisionism – updating Social Democracy in the light of the consequences of the changes just mentioned. I personally never saw the Third Way as a 'middle way', as a compromise between left and right – I always conceived of it as an attempt to get beyond the two lapsed political philosophies of traditional socialism and Thatcherite market fundamentalism. I think Blair shared such a view, although he may have sometimes struggled to make it count in practice.

Blair's qualities

Apart from Margaret Thatcher, Tony Blair is the only British prime minister since Churchill to have become a global figure. Part of the reason was that Blair was a leader with great personal charm – articulate, witty and quick on his feet. It was these qualities that made him an obvious choice for Labour leader in 1994. Blair's friend and rival, Gordon Brown, agreed to withdraw his candidature, apparently on the basis of an agreement that Blair would stand down as Prime Minister in his favour at some point. It did eventually happen, but not before several years of wrangling between the two. Blair stayed on beyond the point that Brown believed had been agreed, although what actually transpired between the two men in their famous meeting in the Granita Restaurant in Islington has never been made public.

It was perhaps his ability to charm that led Blair self-confessedly to start off in government wanting to please everyone, and for several years he did indeed sustain a high level of personal popularity amongst the electorate. Towards the end of his tenure of the premiership, however, his level of support in the polls began to plummet. In his last few years as Prime Minister, he scorned the popularity he had once courted, and made a virtue of not caring a great deal what people thought about him.

When Blair first became Labour leader, he was sometimes referred to in the press as Bambi, meaning that he was soft, that he lacked willpower and drive. Because of his fondness for focus groups, he was accused of taking too much notice of public opinion. Later on, he was criticised for not listening enough. But he was a man of bold decisions. When he became Labour leader, Clause 4 – committing the party to 'the nationalisation of the means of production, distribution and exchange' – seemed like a fixed and irrevocable part of the Labour firmament. In 1960, Hugh Gaitskell had tried to remove it, but had failed. Many thought that it was a great mistake to repeat the attempt. But Blair ignored them. 'I did it because it was the right thing to do' – that is a phrase that crops up in speeches and interviews from the beginning to the end of Blair's political career. He used it in domestic contexts and in international settings when asked to justify his policies, from Bosnia and Kosovo through to Iraq. On a more intellectual level, it was encapsulated in a now famous speech he gave in Chicago in 1999, entitled 'The doctrine of the international community'. In his speech, Blair detailed the responsibility of the international community to override sovereignty and to intervene – by force where necessary – when human tragedies were occurring, such as genocide or ethnic cleansing: the doctrine he applied in Kosovo.

Blair brought an informality to the office of Prime Minister well beyond any previous incumbent. 'Call me Tony' was his instruction to his Cabinet; his easy smile and personal charm were his trademarks. He was never in the remotest sense hip, but he was fond of informality, in both his style of dress and his mannerisms. Although an outstanding speaker and debater, he was not by nature a parliamentarian. He had no particular fondness for the arcane details of parliamentary procedure, and as Prime Minister avoided the Commons whenever he could. Blair became Prime Minister as Britain entered a new era, in which politics became reshaped through the emergence of 24-hour news media. He believed that responding to the media was decisively important, and devoted a lot of energy to this end. Alastair Campbell, his communications adviser, became one of the most powerful and one of the most well-known men in the country.

Blair's mode of government was termed 'Presidential' by critics – with his inner cadre of advisers, he took decisions of key importance well away from public scrutiny. Debate in Parliament was assessed mostly in terms of how far he could get a majority for what he had already decided. His dominance in Cabinet was such that little of note was actively discussed in Cabinet meetings. Top civil servants found the Blair style of government challenging, and many felt they had been sidelined. Were these criticisms justified? In some part they were. Political leaders in current times have to be quick on their feet and must often respond to media stories in a direct way. Yet the Cabinet should be more than a cipher, while Parliament should remain at the core of the democratic process.

'Call me Tony' – was that a sensible approach to leadership? The media might, in fact, have decided to call Blair by his first name regardless of what he did. After all, Mrs Thatcher, who was quite a forbidding and aloof figure as Prime Minister, was widely referred to as 'Maggie', even by those who protested vociferously against her policies. However, Blair decided to adopt a much more personalised style than she had. Personal appeal works when things are going well, but can prove a handicap when they start to sour. The emotional tie on which it is based can go into reverse, in a version of what happens in relationships when love turns to hate.

I came to know Blair on a personal level mainly as a result of being involved in a series of dialogues held between the Clinton Administration and the Labour government. These were informal encounters, with limited numbers from both sides. The first was held at Chequers late in 1997. It was initiated by Hillary Clinton, who came with some leading members of the American Cabinet. The British participants included Tony and Cherie Booth, Gordon Brown, several ministers, plus a number of advisers, including David Miliband, at that time the head of the Policy Unit in No. 10. The only academic there besides myself was Joe Nye, from the Kennedy School at Harvard. Following this encounter, there were meetings at the White House in Washington, in New York and several cities in Continental Europe, as well as others in the US across the years. Bill Clinton came to virtually all of these subsequent meetings.

Blair could not be described as an intellectual – he did not have Clinton's fondness for wide reading, his mastery of policy detail, or his love of late-night debate about the state of the world. Yet he was open to new ideas and participated eagerly.

Focus groups

The ties between the New Democrats in the US and New Labour were close, having been initiated well before 1997. They involved the exchange of ideas – but Blair and his advisers also made a study of the techniques of persuasion and media management that the New Democrats had been developing in the US. These were eventually to rebound on their founders in the US, and tended to produce public distaste. In the UK, the rebound factor was even stronger.

Joe Klein, the American political commentator, in 2006, published an interesting book on American politics, called *Politics Lost*.[4] It carried the title: 'How American Democracy was Trivialised by People who Think You're Stupid.' Who were the trivialisers? They were the pollsters and political consultants, geared to branding and image-making. Their history stretches a long way, but they became more and more prominent in the 1980s and early 1990s. Bill Clinton's campaign in 1992 to become President started poorly. There was the Gennifer Flowers issue, draft evasion, and smoking marijuana at Oxford. To

---

[4] Joe Klein (2006) *Politics Lost*. New York: Doubleday.

counter the bad publicity, Clinton's consultants initiated what they labelled, tongue in cheek, the 'Manhattan Project' to repair the damage. Rather than the Rhodes Scholar from Oxford, he was reintroduced to the American public as the folksy Man from Hope (Hope was where Clinton was born, in Arkansas). He played the saxophone on a TV programme and did a whole round of non-political talk shows. A film was produced showing him, as a young delegate to Boys' Nation, shaking hands with John F. Kennedy in the Rose Garden at the White House. James Carville was the forerunner of Alastair Campbell. He was there wherever Clinton was, a 'walking sound-bite', as Klein puts it, and a favourite of the press. A new language was invented via testing slogans out on focus groups, much as film-makers do before they release a film. In the 1980s the Democrats used to talk about the needs of 'working families'; instead, Clinton spoke of the 'forgotten middle class'. This approach was not really needed with Clinton himself, whose political sense, Klein says, 'was better than any poll' – he frequently disregarded what his consultants advised. Focus groups were actually invented by a sociologist – a very famous one within the profession – Robert K. Merton of Columbia University.[5] He designed what he called the 'focussed group interview' as a tool of social research. It was intended to get behind the answers people give in opinion polls and explore their attitudes in greater depth. In the hands of PR consultants it became almost the opposite of what was intended.

Rather than focus groups as such, however, it was the whole PR paraphernalia that eventually rebounded on New Labour. Before 1997, few people in Britain spoke of spin, spin doctors, sound bites or control freaks – all American terms that entered the language around this time. The origins of the words 'spin' and 'spin doctor' are uncertain, but the terms probably came from baseball. A spin doctor is someone who coaches a pitcher in the art of deceiving the player on strike with the degree of rotation put on the ball.

Spin is not new if it simply means trying to put a good face on things. All organisations try to do that, as do all governments – as well as individuals in everyday life. It is different if this goes along with a whole technology of manipulation, staging and deliberate image-building, as well as control of information. Without putting too fine a point on it, New Labour was deeply into such a technology. It was not a good start for a government whose leader wanted to be 'whiter than white' – although this phrase itself was actually taken from an advertising jingle for a well-known washing powder. I do not mean to be too critical of this, as so many have been in a rather facile way. There were very good reasons why those involved with New Labour wanted

---

[5] Robert K. Merton (1949) *Social Theory and Social Structure*, New York: Free Press. Quite apart from focused group interviews, this is one of the great works of sociology in the twentieth century, on which as young sociologists we all cut our teeth.

to have their say about stories appearing in the press. The *Sun* newspaper, rightly or wrongly, claimed to have a determining effect on the 1992 election, after running an extremely critical – and highly personalised – series of articles about the then Labour leader, Neil Kinnock. 'Rapid rebuttal' was introduced as a way of countering false stories about Labour in the media in the run-up to the election. Newspapers like to excoriate spin, but much of what appears in them is exactly that, in the sense that considerable resources might be spent to promote a particular line on events. The media, printed and electronic, may deploy these resources to run campaigns in relation to individuals or issues. It was, and is, a thoroughly twisted circle. As far as the media are concerned, it has long been the case, as the saying has it, that bad news is good news. The reverse applies just as strongly – it is very difficult to get any positive achievements reported upon. However, studies show a large rise in negative reporting over the past two or three decades, as well as in personalised journalism, in which the journalist or presenter gets far more air time than the politician whose speech is being reported upon. Parliamentary debates are rarely described at any length, and then quite often simply to satirise them. There was a further factor after Labour won such a big majority in 1997. Some sections of the media took it upon themselves to represent the opposition, the Tories being too weak to do so effectively, or so they proclaimed.

Yet there is no doubt that some New Labour zealots took it all too far, and that the concentration on news management subverted itself. Jenny Kleeman, an investigative journalist, got a job in Labour's London press office which dealt with regional and local affairs. She was part of an effort made to influence the content of the letters pages in local newspapers. Party members were asked to put their name to pre-scripted letters defending Labour's policies. The sample of published letters the reporter traced all contained the same phrases.[6] Early on New Labour also tended to produce statistics which under scrutiny, did not show what was claimed for them. Thus 'new' money would be announced for projects of various kinds which included funds that had already been publicised earlier, as if the total sum were fresh investment. Whatever effect that might or might not have had, surveys show that official statistics are widely mistrusted. A survey by the Office of National Statistics showed that 68 per cent of a national sample of respondents believed that official figures were constructed to support the government's policies.[7]

Labour responded to the moral climate which, at least in some part, it had helped create by rejigging its approach. The monitoring of statistics

---

[6] William Dinan 'Undercover in New Labour', *Spinwatch*, 24 May 2005.

[7] Quoted in Polly Toynbee: 'It is New Labour, as Much as the Public, that Lacks Trust', *The Guardian*, 22 November 2005.

by independent agencies, setting up league tables and audited targets, was designed to provide more reliable benchmarks. Yet these also have led to problems, since targets themselves can lead to games-playing and even downright deception in the way that public bodies present themselves. As Chancellor, Gordon Brown introduced legislation to implement the conclusions of the Statistics Commission in a report published in 2004. The Commission was charged with advising on the integrity and quality of UK official statistics. A Statistics Board was set up, replacing the Office for National Statistics, operating at arm's length from government. However, New Labour under Blair was never able completely to shed the image of being addicted to spin-doctoring and the manipulation of information to its own advantage.

Blair and his critics

The Labour Party would probably have won the general election of 1997 under the leadership of John Smith had it not been for his untimely death. However, without the ideological changes Blair pioneered it is unlikely that there would have been the landslide that actually occurred; and equally improbable that Labour would have won three elections in a row for the first time in the party's history. Blair was never 'tribal Labour' – this was the source of his capability to think anew. For the majority of Labour supporters, especially the party activists, he was never 'one of us' in the way that, for example, Neil Kinnock so clearly was. It was Kinnock who began the modernising of Labour, but it was Blair who took the process by the scruff of the neck.

The fact that Blair had so little empathy with Labour traditions gave rise to many problems. He was widely suspected of wilfully abandoning basic Labour values, instead of – as he sought to do – adapting them to a new age. It is the fate of all left of centre parties to disillusion many of their erstwhile supporters once in power. Every such party is accused of not going fast enough, and not being radical enough. Blair was, in fact, very radical in some of his policies, but not in the sense that Labour traditionalists attached to that term. For them, it meant above all limiting the role of markets and protecting established welfare systems. At a rather later date, Blair was seen also as betraying Labour's liberal traditions by insisting upon taking a strong stance towards the control of immigration, by measures taken to reduce antisocial behaviour, and by legislation introduced to counter international terrorism.

Many critics in the press felt the same way. One would expect attacks from the political right, those who found it very hard no longer to be the 'natural' party of government. More difficult to cope with, for Blair, was the constant barrage of attacks from the left, including those led by *The Guardian*, *The Observer*, *The New Statesman* and other representatives of the liberal press. These seemed to him to rest upon an almost wilful misinterpretation of what New Labour's policies were aimed at achieving – and explains much of the hostility he came to feel for the media in general.

Blair was variously accused, from the left, of: control freakery – and its contrary too, presiding over a divided party, especially being unable to handle his Chancellor; lacking an overall agenda or vision for the country; favouring markets at the expense of the public sphere, or otherwise acting as a Thatcherite; failing to produce economic redistribution; cosying up to the rich; dissimulation or outright lying in the lead-up to Iraq; sticking by colleagues he should have fired – but also dismissing others he should have supported; privatising education and the health service; failing to promote the cause of the European Union; taking insufficient interest in the environment, at least until quite late in his premiership; undermining liberty by favouring the introduction of identity cards and by his policies on crime and terrorism; and probably numerous other failings or betrayals too.

Most of these accusations, though not all, seem to me misleading or false. When Blair first came to power, he declared: 'We were elected as New Labour and we shall govern as New Labour.' He made a similar assertion during the election campaigns of 2001 and 2005. He was right to do so. Far from being a series of sound bites without coherent policy, New Labour, from the mid-1990s onwards, developed a policy-rich agenda, worked out in part in the meetings mentioned above. This agenda can be summed up in terms of a few basic principles.

New Labour reversed the traditional Labour outlook, and insisted on placing first emphasis on a strong economy. A robust economy must be the precondition of effective social policy rather than the other way around. Employment – having a substantial proportion of people in work above a decent minimum wage – is at least as important as unemployment as a measure of economic success. An active labour market policy – the New Deal – was essential as a means of helping workers move between jobs. As a result, in 2007, Britain had around 75 per cent of the labour force in work – far higher than the European Union average of 64 per cent. Macroeconomic policy, New Labour believed, should concentrate upon creating stable economic growth, again an outcome that was, for many years, achieved. Revenue for the state should be generated primarily through job creation and economic success, not through higher tax rates. The Blair government consistently outranked the Conservatives in terms of public perceptions of its ability to run the economy. As a result, the government was able to make massive increases in spending in health and education in the years after 2000.

Electoral success means holding the political centre. Blair recognised that we no longer live in a society where support from a single class or social group can deliver political success. The working class is, as we have seen, shrinking, and the knowledge-based economy is a fundamental reality. Therefore, the Labour

Party had to widen its electoral appeal, to achieve the support of new groups. But keeping a grip of the centre did not mean relapsing into conservatism: the aim was to shift the centre of political opinion to the left. This aim seems to have been achieved. Britain became, under Blair, more of a social democratic society. To achieve electoral success, the Conservatives have had to accept much of New Labour's new dispensation.

In pursuing social justice, New Labour chose to concentrate upon the poor rather than the rich. The rich make up only a tiny proportion of the population – 1 per cent or less. Many of those who make money do so by creating wealth also for the wider community: a modern economy could not do without its entrepreneurs. They should act responsibly, pay their taxes, be encouraged to engage in philanthropic activities, and be good corporate citizens. But even a very substantial redistribution of their wealth, supposing it were economically neutral in other ways, would make little impact upon poverty. To reduce poverty, therefore, government should concentrate upon a redistribution of life-chances. It should focus particularly on reducing child poverty, since that is the most pernicious form of poverty of all.

The issues here are worth discussing at some length, since New Labour has so often been criticised from the left for having done nothing to counter inequality. Labour's classic mission – to create a socially just society – has, it is said, been largely abandoned. Instead, New Labour has opted for an essentially Thatcherite mix of increasing privatisation and flexible labour markets, with a few nods in the direction of social justice. How valid are these assertions?

The 1997 government did take a different line from its Labour predecessors in many policy areas. These included its approach to poverty and inequality. Gordon Brown, rather than Tony Blair, was the intellectual leader here. Brown argued that economic stability and consistent growth are the keys to social policy. It follows that programmes concerned with social justice must be connected to issues of economic dynamism and job creation – an outlook reflected in the Chancellor's extensive use of tax credits. Brown placed a strong emphasis upon what he called the realisation of 'human potential'. A healthy economy can go along with increasing equality where individuals are free to make the most of their capabilities and aptitudes.

Contrary to the critics, social justice did and does loom large in the New Labour lexicon. Indeed, the central leitmotif of New Labour could be said to be the idea that social justice and economic dynamism can go hand in hand. In 1997 the UK stood out from most of its EU counterparts in terms of its high levels of relative poverty, especially of child poverty, and the poor condition of its public services. Most of New Labour's energies were directed at tackling these problems at source – and in a manner consistent with the economic imperatives just mentioned. It is difficult to think of a single area of government intervention since 1997 where there has not been policy action related to inequality. The Child Tax Credit, Working Tax Credit, Pension Credit, plus cold winter payments; the minimum wage and the New Deal; the Child Trust Fund and child benefit increases; Sure Start and the Child Care tax credit; a veritable maze of programmes directed at deprived areas; Education Action Zones, Literacy and Numeracy hours; large-scale investment in public services, and so forth. The emphasis upon keeping labour markets flexible, above the floor of a minimum wage, far from betraying ideals of social justice, has directly contributed to furthering them. Full employment is a key aspect of social justice – on this point there is continuity between Old and New Labour. The government's emphasis upon work has been widely attacked, and is not without its problems, but has largely proven its worth. It is a key part of the drive to integrate economic prosperity and social justice. Getting a job, with appropriate safeguards, is the best way of moving out of poverty. That this stance is not a betrayal of left values is shown by the fact that the government's labour market policies closely follow those of the Scandinavian countries – by common agreement the societies with the lowest levels of inequality.

Since 1997 significant reductions have been made in overall levels of poverty, child poverty and poverty among the over-65s, all major aims the government set itself. By 2006, the numbers of those living below 60 per cent of median income – now the standard European Union measure of poverty – had fallen by about one and a half million. Using an absolute standard of poverty, the numbers are higher. From ranking 14th out of 15 among European Union countries in terms of child poverty, the UK in 2006 had moved up to 8. As measured after housing costs, poverty among older people fell by over a million between 2001–2002 and 2003–2004. 'Pensioner poverty' could in principle be eliminated more or less completely through the combination of pension floor and pension credits that has been instituted.

There has been redistribution, even if not from the very top to the very bottom. The lowest 10 per cent of income earners were 8 per cent better off in relative terms in 2005 as compared with 1997. Following a sustained period of increase, income inequality appears to have levelled off from the late 1990s up to 2008. According to the Institute for Fiscal Studies, the government's tax and benefit policy was the prime reason why rising inequality has been halted. This may, in fact, be the first Labour government to actually effect redistribution – albeit of a relatively modest nature – rather than just talk about it. The critics hark back to a golden age when Labour leaders really believed in equality. The fact that they did all too little about it could be safely ignored.

Blair believed that there should be investment in the public services, above all education and health care – but, unlike previous Labour governments, only on condition that they were reformed, and reformed root and branch. In this area, Margaret Thatcher had secured innovations which Blair in some part accepted. She had, for example, succeeded in reducing the power of the more aggressive trade unions, while the introduction of strike ballots ensured that the unions were no longer dominated by small and unrepresentative cliques. Blair did not, however, accept the whole of the Thatcherite legacy in this area. For example, he gave trade union rights to some workers who had been denied them under Margaret Thatcher. She had failed to invest in the public services. By 2007, however, Britain was the only member state in the European Union 15 which was investing more in the public services than it had 10 years earlier, the only state where investment in the public services was rising. Blair's insistence that investment be accompanied by reform took various forms over the years, but there were some consistent themes. Efficiency in the public services, but also increased choice and voice, were, for him, of crucial importance. He believed that centralised delivery by the state was by no means always the best means of delivering the objective of improved public services. Those working in the 'public' – i.e. state-dominated – sector do not necessarily represent the public interest. Public institutions are often unresponsive to citizens' needs, bureaucratic and dominated by the concerns of producers. Delivery by third sector groups or commercial organisations, if properly regulated, can sometimes provide better results than direct control by the state. We have to decide in each case which combination most effectively creates public goods. It is gratuitous and wrong to counterpoise, as so many critics do, 'public' (state-based) services and 'private' (not-for-profit or commercial) ones. The real test is which serves the public interest best in any specific context.

A core part of New Labour's approach was the idea that no issues should be ceded to the right – left of centre solutions to them should be developed. In the past, the left typically tried to explain away, rather than directly confront, questions to do with crime, social disorder, migration and cultural identity, as if the concerns that ordinary citizens felt about these issues were somehow misplaced or irrelevant. Hence crime was assumed to be an expression of inequality. When inequality is reduced, then, so many on the left suggested, crime levels will fall too. Whether or not this view is correct, crime and antisocial behaviour are problems for citizens in the here and now, and have to be dealt with as such. Tony Blair's famous aphorism – 'tough on crime, tough on the causes of crime' – was not just a sound bite but, if elaborated properly, an appropriate policy formula. Blair has been widely criticised for undermining civil liberties in his approach to these questions. But it is important to distinguish formal from substantive freedoms. Is a person free if he or she is afraid to walk in the local park, or go out at night, or if life becomes a misery because of rowdy neighbours? Sometimes the formal freedoms of the few must be constrained in order to increase the substantive freedoms of the many. It is, of course, difficult to get the balance right, but, unless a Labour government took concrete steps to deal with popular concerns on immigration and crime, it would always be in danger of being outflanked by the populist right, as indeed happened to social democratic parties in a number of countries in Continental Europe.

Blair accepted that the threat of the 'new terrorism' – networked, global in its spread, and involving groups prepared to use extreme violence to further their ends – was real. Some critics argued that we understand perfectly well the dangers of terrorism, having confronted the threat from the IRA for so many years: no new laws were needed to combat it, so they suggested, and any such new laws would pose a threat to civil liberties. But Al Qaeda and similar organisations offer a quite different threat from traditional terrorism. Groups like the IRA and ETA in the Basque country have quite concrete aims – to achieve the unity of Ireland and to establish a new nation where previously no nation had existed. New-style terrorism is quite different. It is a product of the communications revolution and of other aspects of globalisation. Organisations like Al Qaeda are not concerned just with establishing a nation; Al Qaeda seeks to re-establish Islamic rule over a wide swathe of the world, stretching in some versions from Pakistan to southern Spain. It seeks to shift the whole spectrum of global power. Al Qaeda has or had many cells in different countries. Everyone remembers the pictures of the planes flying into the Twin Towers at the World Trade Centre in New York, and of a further one hitting the Pentagon. The fourth plane was almost certainly aimed either at the White House or the Capitol building; the aims of those who had hijacked it were only aborted by the bravery of the passengers on board, who brought the plane down short of its target and lost their lives in the process. The terrorists were attacking the three symbolic centres of American power – financial power in the Twin Towers; military power in the Pentagon; and political power in the White House or Capitol. Three thousand people lost their lives, but the death toll could easily have been very much larger.

Blair accepted that, in the global era, the distinction between domestic and foreign policy has virtually disappeared. What happens in the wider world impinges upon our society in a more direct and profound way than was ever the case in the past. Development issues, for instance, become of importance to everyone, not just to countries struggling to move out of poverty. Blair's attempts to place development in Africa at the head of the concerns of the international community should be seen in this light. It also helps to explain his interventionism.

A (very) brief evaluation

Blair's period in power was marked by many significant achievements. Scotland and Wales now have their own devolved bodies, there is a more or less settled peace in Northern Ireland, crime rates fell for most categories of offences, there are human rights and freedom of information acts and gay relationships have been legalised. In spite of public perceptions to the contrary, there is no doubt at all that the large sums of money that have gone into the public services, as well as the various reform efforts, have borne fruit. Some of the most contentious policies, such as charging university students part of the cost of their education, have become widely accepted. The Blair government laid down the target of 50 per cent of the relevant age group going on to higher education. But such a massive expansion of higher education cannot be paid for wholly by the state. It is also fair that students themselves should contribute, since getting a degree confers major financial and career advantages on them.

Of course, Blair, like every other prime minister, also made mistakes. He left office a diminished figure from the one who entered Downing Street with such confident flourish 10 years before. Every government tries to present its aims and accomplishments in the most favourable light, but to try to market the party as though it were a commercial brand was a major error. In spite of its successes in Scotland, Wales and Northern Ireland, Labour made a mess of regional devolution, through not having a solid enough vision of what kind of country it wanted the United Kingdom to become, and failing to follow through on a radical policy of decentralisation – hence the importance that the 'English problem' has now assumed. In spite of a certain level of redistribution, inequality in Britain remains far too high; and alerting the country to the dangers of climate change ranked much too low on the agenda, certainly during Blair's early years. There was a failure significantly to raise productivity, and when Blair left office Britain lagged almost as far behind competitor countries, such as the United States, France and Germany, as it had in 1997. The prawn cocktail offensive that Blair and Brown launched to woo over the City to Labour's cause eventually degenerated into a fawning dependence, coupled with lax regulation. Blair was no more successful than his Tory forerunner John Major had been in seeking to move Britain closer to the heart of the EU; he made no significant dent in British Euro-scepticism.

Looming over all else, of course, there was the invasion of Iraq. It is this issue that, more than any other, turned many people against Blair. 'Blair-Bliar': is the accusation true? Did Blair deliberately mislead the British public in setting out the reasons why war against Iraq to unseat Saddam Hussein was necessary? After all, the stated reason for the war was the dangers posed by Saddam's possession of weapons of mass destruction – which he turned out not to have. I am sure that Blair did not lie. Along with almost all Western intelligence agencies, including those of countries whose leaders opposed the war (such as France), he believed that there were weapons of mass destruction in Iraq. Nevertheless, there are features of it all that are disconcerting. The 'dodgy dossier' the government produced to support its case for armed intervention was a shoddy piece of work. More importantly, many (including myself) assumed Blair had far more information about covert weapons programmes in Iraq than he was able to disclose publicly in the run-up to the war, for fear of compromising intelligence sources in Iraq. Yet there was nothing. Blair gave further reasons which persuaded him to go along with the Americans. United Nations sanctions were not working, serving only to impoverish the country and creating widespread starvation. Saddam may have had no immediate connection with Al Qaeda, but the two might very well have developed common cause. Blair was a strong believer in the transatlantic relationship. On 9/11 the United States was attacked without warning and Britain could not stand idly by. Blair believed that not just Britain, but Europe as a whole, owed the United States a long-term debt because of the security umbrella America had provided over some half a century. He argued that you cannot just be an ally when you want something; you have to be an ally in times of need as well.

But why did Blair choose to stay so close to George W. Bush, in such an uncritical way, for so long? Blair's declared view of international relations was quite different from that of the Bush administration. One has only to compare the speech on humanitarian intervention that Blair gave in Chicago with the views expressed by President Bush from the earliest months of his period of government. Blair argued for the primacy of multilateralism, of international law and of global governance. Force should be contemplated only when these clearly failed. Bush, by contrast, stressed the primacy of American power, which no other country should be allowed to rival. International agreements were for him a sign of weakness, not of strength, and the US began pulling out of some of them before 9/11. Condoleeza Rice spoke derisively of the 'illusory international community'. In the dying days of his leadership, Blair went to Washington to stand side by side with George Bush. 'The forces we are fighting in Iraq,' Blair asserted, 'are the same forces we are fighting everywhere...an enemy that is aiming its destruction at our way of life.' In response to a reporter's question, he confirmed that, if he had known in 2003 what he knew in 2007, he would still have made the same decision with regard to Iraq. 'It was the right thing to do,' he said once more.

Much has been made of Blair's religious beliefs, which clearly had an influence on his career as Prime Minister. But it was not religion as such that tied him so closely to Bush. Blair has said on several occasions that his beliefs have been highly important to him on a personal level. He even once said, on the Michael Parkinson show, that God would be his judge over the war in Iraq. However, he has also often made it clear that in his view religion should not intrude too far into political life. Answering questions after a speech to a Christian group in 2005, for example, he said: 'I don't want to end up with an American-style type of politics with us all going out there and beating our chests about our faith.'

A charitable explanation of Blair's closeness to Bush would be that, when he contemplated committing British troops to Iraq, he sought to apply the 'doctrine of the international community' that he had formulated. He tried very hard to get United Nations backing for the venture and believed until very late on that he would succeed in doing so. But, when it was not forthcoming, he decided that Britain should go along with the Americans nevertheless, on the grounds that the United States should not have to act alone, calculating also that there was no way other than force to confront the threat that Saddam presented.

For Blair, the war in Iraq had an important moral component – it was driven by much the same considerations that had led him previously to engage British troops in Kosovo, Sierra Leone and Afghanistan. He believed that he had persuaded President Bush to make a serious commitment to a road map to make progress in the Israel–Palestine conflict, and that international agencies would have a key role in post-war reconstruction. Neither was forthcoming, but by then Blair was locked in. He could not publicly criticise the Bush administration, since it would have shown the allies to be divided. Privately he must have agonised about the awful toll of death and disruption that the invasion had brought. His continuing belief in the essential justness of the war perhaps helped him stave off such thoughts. A public break with the Americans would not help the future of Iraq; hence he determined to show solidarity with the United States to the end.

Should further progress be made towards reducing tensions in the Middle East, and should, against the odds, stability return to Iraq, the judgment of history will be more favourable than perhaps looks likely at the moment. Blair's place in the pantheon of British prime ministers more generally will be decided by the historians. Ten years is a long time for someone to be prime minister: the second longest continuous period in office for a prime minister since the Napoleonic wars, exceeded only by the long reign of Margaret Thatcher. Even so, a decade is not long enough to produce profound and lasting changes in a society.

Conclusion

At the time of writing, Gordon Brown has been in power for around two and half years. The financial crisis of 2008 swept across the world and brought recession in its wake to many countries, including Britain. At first sight, it would seem that these events have thoroughly undermined much of both the analysis that drove Tony Blair's thinking and the policy framework built around it – New Labour is no more. Governments have decided all over again that it is possible to spend one's way out of an economic downturn – most, including the British government, have put in place large stimulus packages to do just that. Keynes is back in fashion.

Prime Minister Brown abandoned his previous advocacy of a light-touch approach to financial markets in favour of greater regulation, and pressed for a similar response on an international level. The government effectively nation-alised two of the leading financial institutions, Royal Bank of Scotland and Northern Rock Building Society. Taxes have been increased for the rich. 'No more boom and bust!' – one of New Labour's slogans during the Blairite period, albeit coined and propagated by Brown as Chancellor – sounds a sorry boast now. Because of the money spent to shore up the banks, an enormous debt has been built up. The main economic theorem of Blair's period of government – create a strong economy to generate a surplus to spend on refurbishing public institutions – is off the agenda for the foreseeable future.

So can we write off Tony Blair and New Labour as a temporary ideological aberration, a brief interim between Thatcherism and whatever will emerge on the other side of recession? Absolutely not. A great deal of rethinking and policy innovation is needed from the centre-left, but much of the analysis that produced New Labour remains intact. Globalisation has not gone away, but will probably become further intensified, at least along some dimensions – the global nature of the financial crisis shows how interdependent national econ-omies now are.

People may be reading Keynes again, but he was an altogether more subtle thinker than were some of those who sought to apply his doctrines. There will be no return to Keynesian demand management as anything other than a stimulus to recovery. The state is not going to be any better at directly running economic enterprises than it was in the past. We have to create a regulatory framework that will preserve the advantages that markets can confer – flexibility, creativity, competitiveness – while turning those qualities more towards long-term social purposes. That will not be an easy task.

It will still be necessary for left of centre parties to attract mainstream voters to have any chance of electoral success, against the backdrop of the changing political field where electronic communication and the internet will have a growing role. There is talk of the need for more active industrial policy, but manufacture will not return in a big way to the Western economies. We will continue to live and work in a post-industrial economy. The centre-left must continue to wrestle with problems of how to sustain voter appeal while forging progressive policies for dealing with immigration and multiculturalism, as well as coping with citizens' anxieties about crime. On an international level, there could, and should, be a return to multilateralism following the demise of the Bush administration; but the problem of how and when armed intervention can be justified in international affairs will return, and remains as problematic as ever.

Index